SOURCEBOOK
of Marriage and Family Evaluation

SOURCEBOOK
of Marriage and Family Evaluation

Luciano L'Abate, Ph.D.
Dennis A. Bagarozzi, Ph.D.

BRUNNER/MAZEL, *Publishers* • New York

Library of Congress Cataloging-in-Publication Data
L'Abate, Luciano
    Sourcebook of marriage and family evaluation / Luciano L'Abate,
Dennis A. Bagarozzi.
        p.   cm.
    Includes bibliographical references and indexes.
    ISBN 0-87630-676-8
    1. Family assessment.   I. Bagarozzi, Dennis A.   II. Title.
    RC488.53.L33   1992
616.89'156—dc20   92-22541
                                                                        CIP

Published by
BRUNNER/MAZEL, INC.
19 Union Square West
New York, New York 10003

Manufactured in the United States of America

10 9 8 7 6 5 4 3 2 1

CONTENTS

Section III.   Families

Section IV. Conclusion

INTRODUCTION

The soaring costs of medical care and mental health services have created two broad classes of citizens in the United States: those individuals and families who can afford to pay for private health insurance and those who cannot. The second group can also be subdivided into two segments: those whose health care insurance is paid for by the taxpayer and those who have no insurance coverage whatsoever. This latter faction is estimated to number around 30 million people. When one considers the federal budget deficit, the number of state and local municipalities that are on the verge of bankruptcy, and the growing number of third-party providers and health maintenance organizations that are unable to reimburse their policyholders or promptly pay their own health (and mental health) providers, the picture becomes bleak indeed. Socialized medicine has been proposed as a panacea, but when one looks closely at those countries that have moved toward this type of health-care solution, one finds exorbitantly high personal income taxes, massive bureaucracies, and mediocre health care across the board.

We do not claim to have a solution to these very real and complex problems, but we believe that eventually more and more pressure will be exerted from the federal and state levels of government, as well as from third-party providers, for health practitioners and mental health specialists to demonstrate their accountability. *It is our sincere belief that in the future practitioners who are able to evaluate their interventive endeavors by using reliable and valid measures of change and established research procedures will be more likely to receive third-party payments (from whatever source) than practitioners who cannot demonstrate their therapeutic effectiveness.* It is with this belief in mind that we have written this text.

Our philosophy about the practice of marital and family intervention is quite simple: We believe that the practice of marital and family therapy must be rooted in a broader theory of human behavior and developmental psychology. Theoretical statements are needed to explain how unwanted, deviant, and dysfunctional interaction patterns develop in marital and family systems. These theoretical statements must also describe and explain how and why such undesirable patterns persist and are maintained. A theory of marital and/or family therapy that is logically consistent with this view of human/systems behavior and deviance should specifically delineate dependable and valid intervention procedures designed to correct or modify those marital and familial patterns identified as dysfunctional. Increased knowledge of marital and family systems' functioning as well as better understanding about the dynamics of intervention and the therapeutic relationship can be gained most reliably through systematic evaluation and scientific inquiry.

Another goal of this book is to present a critical review of some of the most common assessment instruments and observational procedures used by marital/family specialists. We hope that by cataloging these materials and discussing their appropriateness for use by clinical practitioner, we will make the process of instrument selection less difficult, the practice of measuring one's therapeutic effectiveness more likely, and the demonstration of accountability easier. In structuring our material, we have tried to keep in mind two foci: the usefulness and helpfulness of the instruments or procedures to *both* practitioners and clients. We then suggest which instruments and procedures we believe to be the best available for the clinical task at hand.

Realistic limitations of space had to be taken into account in putting the volume together. Original attempts to treat assessment procedures in terms of insider-outsider perspectives, as described in the first chapter, proved to be impractical. Therefore, a different classification system had to be devised. The current table of contents represents the revised classification system. After the introductory first chapter, we begin with the simplest assessment procedure; that is, the interview and progress then through various levels of complexity. Interviews and social histories (Chapter 2) represent the most common methods of gaining information about couples and families. This information usually cannot be obtained in any other way. Direct observations of marital and family interaction provide valuable data about systems functioning. Ways to gather this information are reviewed in Chapter 3. Without this initial basis of knowledge, it would be difficult to understand how couples or families actually behave. The fact that observations become less inferential when specific behaviors take on the central focus forms the core of the discussion in Chapter 4. One the most behaviorally focused assessments probably is the one practiced by sex therapists, which is considered in Chapter 5. Most measures of marital and family quality are self-reports. These are reviewed in Chapters 6, 7, and 8.

An overview of instruments and procedures that are not grounded in any recognizable theory of marital and family functioning is presented in Chapter 9. Self-reports are always suspect because they are subject to social desirability sets. To avoid this pitfall, projective techniques have been used in an otherwise objectively oriented discipline, a topic that comes to the fore in Chapter 10. Chapter 11 deals with professional, ethical, and practical issues that still plague the field.

In addition to the seasoned practitioner who would like to be more involved in assessment and evaluation, we hope that this text will also serve as a resource for graduate students who are struggling with the task of selecting appropriate instruments to assess marital and family systems as part of their master theses or doctoral investigations. Teachers in family therapy programs or in family science who need to keep abreast of developments in the evaluation of couples and families may profit by what we have written here. Finally, we hope that researchers who need critical summaries of the literature in this field will find our work useful. We are sure that they will be most critical of our criticisms!

—L.L

—D.A.B.

SECTION I
Evaluation

1

The Evaluation of Couples and Families

The purpose of this volume is to provide the practicing family therapist and the clinical researcher with a critical review of diagnostic instruments, assessment tools, and testing procedures currently being used to evaluate the functioning of marital and family systems. We focus our attention on the instruments, tools, and procedures that have been developed specifically for use with couples and families. Time, space, and practical considerations prohibit us from reviewing measurement techniques that were developed to assess individual functioning, personality traits and characteristics, intrapsychic dynamics, personal predispositions, attitudes, and values, even though such assessment tools may be used to evaluate individual changes within the context of the family.

Our intention is not to duplicate the work done by Straus and Brown (1978) or by Touliatos, Perlmutter, & Straus (1990), who abstracted and briefly described over 1400 instruments used in marital/family studies research. Our goal is to review and critically evaluate instruments, techniques, and procedures that can be used by clinical practitioners to gather meaningful information for designing interventions, monitoring treatments, and evaluating outcomes.

A number of clinicians and researchers (Cromwell, Olson, & Fournier, 1976; Gurman & Kniskern, 1981; Kniskern & Gurman, 1983) have stressed the importance of gaining the perspectives of both "insiders" (spouse, family members) and "outsiders" (therapists, researchers) when evaluating the effects of marital and family therapy. We believe that both vantage points are of equal importance for developing treatment plans and for devising intervention strategies. Originally, we chose to review instruments and procedures according to insider and outsider perspectives. However, as we worked on the materials, we found this approach limiting and abandoned it as an exclusive framework for the book.

In addition to taking into account the insider-outsider dimensions of family

3

evaluation, Gurman and Kniskern (1981) noted the importance of considering the degree of inference involved in making judgments about family processes. The degree of inference required for a given judgment increases as one moves away from reporting simple behavior counts and attempts to assess marriage or family systems properties. However, as the degree of inference required to make evaluations increases, the more one must rely upon the judgments of experts. In our review of each instrument, we attempt to note the degree of inference required for its use. We also discuss the type of expertise that one should possess to make the best use of a given tool or procedure. Otherwise, we assume that most of the instruments presented here can be administered with a modicum of training, although they must be interpreted with a great deal of professional experience.

In our discussions of instruments devoted solely to the evaluation of marriage and marital quality, the same insider-outsider distinction was attempted. However, some additional and more implicit dimensions have influenced the sequence of the material. First, the degree of inference seems to increase in the first two sections of this book. For instance, inferences from a live interview (Chapter 2) are different from the inferences one can make from video- or audiotapes of marital interaction, especially when those inferences are made from scoring schemes rather than the actual behavior of the couple (Chapter 3). In Chapter 4, one might think that behavioral self-report measures would require a lesser degree of inference than would non-behavioral self-report measures. Actually, one paper-and-pencil test yields about as many inferences as any other paper-and-pencil test, regardless of whether or not it is behavioral!

One needs to consider extremes in an impressionistic-experimental (manipulative) dimension, which in some way still implies some of the value judgments inherent in various techniques. One might easily assume that an experimentally controlled method, such as the talk box Gottman (1979) used to measure marital interaction, is better (more valid) than a simple paper-and-pencil test. Actually, these procedures yield completely different types of information. No longer can we state with confidence that one source of information is any better (that is, more valid) than another. However, we can say that because they are different, they may complement or supplement each other. They may be relevant to each other in terms of how much they diverge or converge. The outsider's viewpoint is represented in observations of marital interaction (Chapter 3). The other chapters deal with self-report measures, including behaviorally designed measures (Chapter 4), sex and sexuality (Chapter 5), and traditional self-directed measures used to extract inferences about the marital relationship (Chapter 6).

The other chapters (8, 9, and 10) fall within the outsider's perspective. However, these last three chapters raise some serious questions about the validity of the insider-outsider distinction. The reader will have to decide whether the distinction seems a valid one.

Chapter 11 treats a number of professional and ethical issues that arise when one uses tests and instruments with clients.

Cromwell et al. (1976) described observational techniques as having been designed "to elicit specific sequences of interaction characteristic of typical behavior" (p. 37). They divided stimulus tasks used to generate family interaction into four broad categories: decision making, problem solving, conflict resolution, and naturalistic tasks. However, they emphasized that the behavior patterns observed under such conditions should not be considered typical of family behavior. Observations are only "clinical approximations" of behavior. These observations are thought to be limited by the same factors that affect therapeutic interviews conducted outside the natural environment. Behaviors, feelings, and interactional patterns observed under such conditions are no less representative of family behavior than are other behaviors exhibited in the presence of the therapist.

Most of us are aware that the expectations of experimenters (Rosenthal, 1966), the expectations of the subjects (Rosenthal, 1974), the context of the experimental setting (Bowers, 1974; Mischel, 1973), and the tendency of research subjects to give socially desirable responses (Edwards, 1957) affect both the internal and the external validity of research findings. Therefore, it would be naive to assume that the behavior of family members in treatment is not similarly affected by the presence of the therapist, the expectations of family members, the therapeutic context, the beliefs of family members concerning how people who come to therapy ought to behave, and the family members implicitly held models of personality and human behavior (Cronbach, 1955, 1958).

Cromwell et al. (1976) outlined several criteria that can be used to evaluate the clinical relevance and diagnostic utility of various assessment instruments. The criteria that are relevant to observational techniques are as follows:

(1) The method should operationalize some theoretical concepts or dimensions of family behavior that are relevant to the treatment process. Such measures should facilitate linkage among theory, research, and practice.
(2) The sample of stimuli should not only relate to the overall theoretical concepts or dimensions under consideration but should also be considered relevant, important, and representative for the group being evaluated.
(3) The procedures should include a multimethod approach in order to provide more than one perspective on the dimension being considered.
(4) The instruments and procedures should be evaluated for both reliability and validity.
(5) The procedure should be designed so that the participating family members do not feel tricked or deceived during test administration.

(6) The instruments and procedures should require minimal equipment, facilities, costs, and time to administer and score.

(7) The procedures should be appropriate for a wide variety of age groups, ethnic groups, and social classes.

In addition to these seven criteria, we propose the following:

(8) The stimulus tasks and the test administration procedures should be explained and described in sufficient detail to make reliable replications possible.

(9) The observational methods and the coding and rating procedures should be explained and described in sufficient detail to make reliable replication possible.

(10) The mathematical and statistical procedures used for data analysis should be appropriate.

Although we cite the key person or persons responsible for the development of each instrument or technique, we concentrate on the publications concerning subsequent methodological developments, standardization procedures, modifications, revisions, and refinements. Because our purpose is not to catalog or chronicle all studies in which an instrument was used, only the material germane to instrument construction is indexed.

We assume that any evaluation procedure represents the experimenter's attempt to operationalize and measure one or more important theoretical concepts or constructs derived from a recognized and clearly articulated theory of family development, family process, and family functioning. In our discussions, we evaluate the extent to which the experimenters used theory as a conceptual guide in their work. We also judge the degree of success the experimenters have achieved in their attempts to operationalize central concepts and constructs.

The second part of our analysis deals with more substantive methodological issues: sampling (e.g., the adequacy of sampling procedures and survey methods, the appropriateness of test items selected for inclusion, the comprehensiveness of domains sampled); the procedures used to establish validity (e.g., face, construct, content, concurrent, convergent, criterion-related, discriminant); and reliability (internal consistency, test-retest, alternate forms, split-half).

In the final part of this analysis, we attempted, not always successfully, to focus on issues of critical importance to clinicians. These include discussions concerning practical utility. For example, we report the approximate length of time required for test administration and scoring, the number of persons needed to carry out the testing, the type of clinical orientation and training required, the degree of expertise one must possess in order to use a given tool, and the cost of using each instrument.

Time and space considerations make it impossible for us to conduct a thorough assessment of each instrument and procedure reviewed in this volume.

However, we have devised the following rating scale to assess outsiders' and insiders' perspectives. These scales can be used by the reader who wishes to conduct a thorough analysis of a given instrument or procedure for use in research or clinical practice.

OUTSIDER'S RATING SCALE

(1) Extent to which theory was used as a conceptual guide for designing or selecting interactional tasks assigned to family.

Task highly tied to theory		Task loosely tied to theory		Task not related to theory
5————————4————————3————————2————————1				

(2) Theoretical and clinical relevance of the concepts or constructs being measured.

Very important (central)	Important (but not central)	Moderately important	Peripherally important (tangential)	Not at all important
5————————4————————3————————2————————1				

(3) Adequacy of sampling procedures used (for purposes of generalization of findings).

Highly adequate		Moderately adequate		Inadequate
5————————4————————3————————2————————1				

(4) Adequacy of assignment procedures used.

Highly adequate	Adequate	Moderately adequate	Poor	Inadequate
5————————4————————3————————2————————1				

(5) Validity of operationalization of concepts being measured.

Excellent (highly valid)	Good	Moderate	Poor	Very poor (invalid)
5————————4————————3————————2————————1				

(6) Quality of procedures used to establish reliability.

Excellent	Good	Moderate	Poor	Very poor
5————————4————————3————————2————————1				

Continued on next page

(7) Overall costs involved in using this procedure (e.g., financial, time, equipment, personnel).

Very costly	Costly	Moderately costly	Minimal cost	No cost at all
5	4	3	2	1

(8) Degree of deception and psychological/physical risk to which family members are exposed.

High risk, high deception	High risk, moderate deception	Moderate risk, moderate deception	Moderate risk, low deception	Low risk, low deception
5	4	3	2	1

(9) Applicability to various age groups, ethnic groups, social classes.

Applicable to a wide variety of families	Applicable to most families	Applicable to some families but not others	Applicable to a few families	Not applicable to many families (highly restricted)
5	4	3	2	1

(10) Clearly specified procedures for instrument use and test administration.

Very clear and precise	Clear	Somewhat unclear	Unclear	Not reported
5	4	3	2	1

(11) Clearly specified procedures for observation, recording, coding, rating.

Very clear and precise	Clear	Somewhat unclear	Unclear	Not reported
5	4	3	2	1

(12) Appropriateness of mathematical and statistical procedures used to assess family interaction.

Excellent	Good	Adequate	Poor	Not reported
5	4	3	2	1

(13) Clinical experience, specialized training, or expertise required for test administration, scoring, interpretation.

Very high level	High level	Moderate level	Low level	None
5	4	3	2	1

INSIDER'S RATING SCALE

(1) Extent to which theory was used as a conceptual guide for instrument construction.

Very high reliance on theory	High reliance on theory	Moderately high reliance on theory	Little reliance on theory	No reliance on theory

5————————4————————3————————2————————1

(2) Theoretical and clinical importance of the concepts or constructs being measured.

Very important (central)	Important (but not central)	Moderately important	Peripherally important (tangential)	Not at all important

5————————4————————3————————2————————1

(3) Adequacy of sampling procedures and survey methods used.

Highly adequate	Adequate	Moderately adequate	Poor	Inadequate

5————————4————————3————————2————————1

(4) Relevance of items selected for inclusion.

Highly relevant	Relevant	Moderately relevant	Peripherally relevant	Not at all relevant

5————————4————————3————————2————————1

(5) Comprehensiveness of domains sampled.

Very comprehensive	Adequate	Moderately comprehensive	Poor	Not at all comprehensive

5————————4————————3————————2————————1

(6) Quality of procedures used to establish validity (including statistical procedures).

Excellent	Good	Moderate	Poor	Very poor

5————————4————————3————————2————————1

(7) Quality of procedures used to establish reliability (including statistical procedures).

Excellent	Good	Moderate	Poor	Very poor

5————————4————————3————————2————————1

Continued on next page

(8) Overall costs involved in using this instrument (e.g., financial, time, equipment, personnel).

Very costly	Costly	Moderately costly	Little cost	No cost at all
5—————————	4—————————————	3—————————	2———————————	1

(9) Clearly specified procedures for instrument use and test administration.

Very clear and precise	Clear	Somewhat unclear	Unclear	Not reported
5—————————	4—————————————	3—————————	2———————————	1

(10) Clinical experience, specialized training or expertise required for test administration, scoring, interpretation.

Very high level	High level	Moderate level	Low level	None
5—————————	4—————————————	3—————————	2———————————	1

REFERENCES

Bowers, K. S. (1974). Situationism in psychology: An analysis and critique. *Psychological Review, 80,* 307–336.

Cromwell, R. E., Olson, D. H. L., & Fournier, D. G. (1976). Tools and techniques for diagnosis in marital and family therapy. *Family Process, 15,* 1–49.

Cronbach, L. J. (1955). Processes affecting scores on "understanding of others" and "assumed similarity." *Psychological Bulletin, 52,* 177–193.

Cronbach, L. J. (1958). Proposals leading to analytic treatment of social perception scores. In R. Tagiuri & L. Petrullo (Eds.), *Person perception and interpersonal behavior* (pp. 353–379). Stanford, CA: Stanford University Press.

Edwards, A. L. (1957). *The social desirability variable in personality assessment and research.* New York: Dryden.

Gottman, J. M. (1979). *Marital interaction: Experimental investigations.* New York: Academic Press.

Gurman, A. S., & Kniskern, D. P. (Eds.). (1981). *Handbook of family therapy (Vol. 1).* New York: Brunner/Mazel.

Kniskern, D., & Gurman, A. (1983). Future directions for family therapy research. In D. A. Bagarozzi, A. P. Jurich, & R. W. Jackson (Eds.), *Marital and family therapy: New perspectives in theory, research and practice* (pp.209–235). New York: Human Sciences.

Mischel, W. (1973). Toward a cognitive social learning reconceptualization of personality. *Psychological Review, 80,* 252–283.

Rosenthal, R. (1966). *Experimenter effects in behavioral research.* New York: Appleton-Century-Crofts.

Rosenthal, R. (1974). *The volunteer subject.* New York: Wiley.

Straus, M. A., & Brown, B. W. (1978). *Family measurement techniques: Abstracts of published instruments, 1935–1974*. Minneapolis: University of Minnesota Press.

Touliatos, J., Perlmutter, B.F., & Straus, M.E. (Eds.). (1990). *Handbook of family measurement techniques*. Newbury Park, CA: Sage.

2

The Interview and History Taking

THE INTERVIEW

A commonly used procedure in marital/family evaluation is the diagnostic interview. Historically, the clinical interview developed as an outgrowth of the medical interview. Medical interviews generally emphasize medical history for the purpose of establishing a correct diagnosis and selecting appropriate treatment. The medical interview is primarily centered on the current illness and its historical antecedents. Information about the emotional and interactional aspects of the patient's life is considered important only if it may have a bearing on the patient's illness.

The psychiatric interview differs from the medical interview in that many patients do not come voluntarily for psychiatric interviews. Also, psychiatric symptoms are not usually as readily volunteered by the patient as are medical symptoms.

Initially, the primary use of the interview was either to gain knowledge of how to better treat the individual patient or to obtain information relevant to family study. The pioneering work of Bowen (1961) and Ackerman (1958b) illustrated the development of the family interview as integral to diagnosis and treatment. Halleck (1978) further delineated how diagnosis and treatment can be formulated from an initial family interview. Various researchers, such as Herbst (1952) and Blood and Hamblin (1958), pioneered the use of the family interview. In particular, family sociologists have frequently used the interview as a vehicle for family study.

Both clinical and experimental assessments continue to be the primary arenas for the family interview. However, in recent years the family interview has come under closer study and is finally being used for experimental/clinical assessment, as in the work of Watzlawick (1966) and of Selvini-Palazzoli, Boscolo, Cecchin, and Prata (1980).

Types of Interviews

An artificial distinction between diagnostic and therapeutic interviews is frequently made (L'Abate & Goodrich, 1980). This distinction is based on the premise that some interviews are oriented only toward obtaining diagnostic information and that others are primarily concerned with therapeutic intervention. However, all family interviews can be considered therapeutic intervention. Frequently, the very act of getting the couple or the whole family together to encourage interaction may be a major source of change for the family. Not only are "diagnostic" interviews inevitably therapeutic interviews, but "therapeutic" interviews are also diagnostic. A therapeutic intervention presupposes the origin of a diagnostic hypothesis upon which the treatment of choice is based.

A more practical and relevant categorization of family interviews is as *structured* and *unstructured*. Structured interviews are organized sessions in which the interviewer actively leads the session and may ask direct questions. Topics for the interview are determined primarily by the interviewer rather than by the family. In contrast, in unstructured interviews the interviewer's stance is relatively passive, the topics discussed are presented by the family, and the interviews are less organized and planned. A review of the literature indicates that relatively unstructured interviews are much more common than structured ones.

As L'Abate and Goodrich (1980) pointed out, two additional types of interviews are often considered separate entities: the *semistructured* and the *focused*. The semistructured interview is structured but has the additional advantage of giving the interviewer freedom to pursue material initially elicited in response to the structured questions. Thus, the interviewer is allowed to clarify and expand his or her understanding beyond that provided by the structured question and response. The focused interview centers on a family event or a particular experience. The interviewer seeks to elicit the feelings, reactions, and interactions associated with the experience from the informants' frame of reference. Although these interviews are different from the structured and unstructured approaches, they seem to fall within the structured-unstructured continuum rather than being distinctly separate entities.

One method of classifying interviews on the structured-unstructured continuum could be based on the number of foci in the interview. *Foci* in this sense are defined as the planned questions or tasks asked of the family in the interview. In other words, an interview in which the only planned question is "What seems to be the problem in this family?" would be very unstructured. However, an interview that includes various planned questions and interactional tasks would be relatively highly structured. In this proposed type of classification system, all interviews could be objectively classified somewhere on the structured-unstructured continuum. The foci themselves would serve as the units of structure.

This classification system would also enable researchers to compare the effectiveness of structured versus unstructured approaches in family interviews. Furthermore, specific areas of interest, such as household tasks or communication between spouses, could be systematically assessed. It could very well be that through such testing we may discover that structured questions and tasks in one area of interest are very effective, while in another dimension of family functioning a more unstructured approach may be most beneficial.

The Structured Interview

Perhaps the best example of a highly structured interview can be found in Watzlawick's (1966) work. In addition to creating a useful clinical tool, Watzlawick created a research tool for assessing family interaction. Basically, his structured interview has five parts. First, each family member is asked individually what he or she believes the family's problem to be. Each member is assured that responses are confidential and will not be shared with the family. The family members are then reassembled and informed that their responses are discrepant and that they should reach a common conclusion about their problem (much like the revealed-difference technique). The interviewer leaves and observes the family from another room. Second, the family is asked to plan (together) something that can be done as a family. In the third segment of the interview, the parents are seen separately and asked to describe how they met. The fourth step requires that the parents decide upon the meaning of the proverb "A rolling stone gathers no moss." Then, the parents are asked to teach their children their agreed-upon meaning of the proverb. Finally, in the fifth segment, the whole family is asked to participate in a "blaming" exercise (Satir, 1972).

Other types of structured interviews have been used, but Watzlawick's structured interview remains the most popular and widely used. Specific structured analysis techniques have been and continue to be used within a more unstructured format. Usually, in these approaches a particular structured task is administered within the framework of an otherwise relatively unstructured interview. Examples of specific structured tasks and approaches include Bodin's (1968) use of tasks and decision making, the use of sculpting, Blechman and Olson's (1976) Family Contract Game, Straus and Tallman's (1971) use of SIMFAM (Simulated Family Activity Measurement), and Tallman and Wilson's (1974) simulation games.

Bodin (1968) described a structured family interview based on the administration of the Wiltwyck Family Tasks, which is composed of eight tasks. The interviewer observes all family interaction through a one-way mirror. The eight tasks are (1) agreeing on a meal; (2) talking about who is the bossiest, who gets away with the most, who is the biggest troublemaker, and who is the biggest crybaby; (3) discussing a remembered argument that occurred at home; (4) agreeing on a way to spend a hypothetical $10 gift; (5) having each family member tell what other family members do that pleases and that upsets the speaker; (6) asking the family to build something together; (7) choosing among three gifts; and (8) sharing refreshments consisting of one fewer soft drink and one more cupcake than necessary for the whole family.

The advantages of these types of structured approach are many. First, family process and interaction can be observed in a controlled and structured manner allowing for replication and comparison with other families. Second, time-consuming transactions and complicated scoring procedures are not necessary. Third, time required to identify the family's basic interactional patterns is reduced. Fourth, the procedure can be used by virtually anyone (very little specialized training is required). Finally, the structured interview has been found to be a simple, inexpensive, and effective teaching and training device.

Analysis: Early Investigations

Various studies have analyzed the usefulness of the family and/or couple interview as a method of examining interactions and transactions among family members. Several of these early studies are reviewed, and a systematic approach for future analysis and conceptualization is then proposed.

Jackson, Riskin, and Satir (1961) developed a method for analyzing segments of a family interview that included two types of analyses. The first focused on the family's patterns of communication. The second dealt with inferences concerning the type of individual who would initiate such communication. These experimenters analyzed the first 5 minutes of a tape supplied by Lyman Wynne.

In these analyses, symmetrical, complementary, and qualifying statements were identified and described. Contradictory messages were labeled disqualifications. Discrepancies between affect-verbal and statement-content were also analyzed. The authors concluded that disturbed families communicated more affect-verbal, statement-content incongruent messages and disqualifications than did normal, healthy families. The authors also examined self- and other perceptions in regard to who communicated to whom. The family's interactions were seen in terms of each person's perception of self, the other, and the perception of the other in relation to the self.

The problem with this type of analysis is that specific guidelines for developing inferences are not specified. A general introduction to communications analysis is offered, but no standardized guidelines and procedures are available. This inadequacy makes replication impossible, and reliability and validity are seriously compromised. Such a subjective evaluation seems highly dependent upon the evaluator's clinical expertise.

Laslett and Rapoport (1975) presented another type of interview technique and analysis. Basically, interviews are repeated with several members of a family by more than one interviewer. Each interviewer's work is monitored and recorded. Account is taken of the psychodynamic aspects of the interview that are likely to affect the validity of the research results. Other features of the technique are: (1) a collaborative rather than an authoritative approach by the interviewer; (2) an interview guide that is constructed differently for different members of the family (as opposed to a standard questionnaire for all members); and (3) a supervisor's feedback on his or her analysis of transference and countertransference phenomena.

Several advantages were cited by the authors for their technique. First, if the interviewer is responsive to, rather than seeking to avoid, the family members' reactions to the interview, internal validity of the interview process is increased. Although an interesting one, this hypothesis remains untested. Second, more than one interview increase the amount of information obtained. Third, this approach seems particularly appropriate for research into the more private and intimate character of family life. Fourth, this procedure can be readily applied to other samples (e.g., work groups, ethnic groups, political groups, and leisure groups). Finally, the collaborative approach provides process feedback that may make the interview more therapeutically helpful.

While the assumed advantages are impressive, the drawbacks are considerable. Although the authors claimed that their approach is more valid than others, they offered no empirical support to substantiate their viewpoint. Perhaps the biggest drawback is the cost. This kind of methodology is expensive because it is time-consuming and thus entails high labor costs. The number of interviewers and the repeated interviews make this method impractical for most research and clinical settings.

Riskin and Faunce (1970a, 1970b) used the interview method, specifically a standardized, structured interview that was taped and transcribed. They also used live observations. During a marital interview, parents were asked about their hopes and expectations for their marriage, how they met, and how they resolved certain problems. The family was then asked to plan something they could do together as a family. These family interactions were observed and recorded. Riskin and Faunce's work culminated in the development of the Family Interaction Scales, detailed in the chapter on observational techniques. (See Chapter 9.)

Quinton, Rutter, and Rowlands (1976) tackled the marital interview. Their method uses a nonscheduled, standardized approach. Standard questions are not used, but detailed instructions concerning information to be obtained are given. The interviewer is expected to use detailed and flexible cross-questioning until enough data have been obtained to make required codings on a structured coding index that targets activities, feelings, and attitudes. Scales for coding include the following: frequency of quarrels, husband's participation in household tasks, joint leisure activities, frequency of sexual intercourse. Feelings and attitudes are treated differently from other behavioral items that focus only on frequencies. Feelings are rated in terms of general measures (e.g., warmth, vocal tone, facial expressions, gestures). Interviewers receive approximately 3 months of training, during which they view tapes and observe interviews. The marriage is rated on a 6-point Likert scale, from marriages characterized by mutual concern and attention to marriages characterized by constant disruption or by indifference or dislike. A rating of 2 is considered representative of a "good, average marriage" in which tensions are mild and problems minor.

The results from these analyses are solid. Interrater agreement was well within acceptable levels (i.e., .82) in the pilot study of 30 families. Interrater reliability was assessed by comparing independent ratings made by two investigators who were present at the same interview. Particularly important is the fact that the high levels of agreement were independent of the personal values and orientations of the individual interviewers. Also, predictive validity for future discord in the marriage was extremely high in follow-up evaluations. One area that requires additional exploration is the degree to which this procedure can predict discord in nondistressed marriages.

A Systematic Approach

Recently, L'Abate (1986) suggested a classification of family patterns to evaluate the two main dimensions of what he considers to be the two sets of skills necessary for living satisfactorily as individuals, dyads, and families: (1) the ability to love and (2) the ability to negotiate (L'Abate & Colondier, 1987). The ability to negotiate services and information (Doing) as well as money and possessions (Having) is based on the style, level of competence, and priorities of the individuals involved in the needed negotiation. Style is made up of three nonoverlapping patterns. From the most debilitating and dysfunctional to the most functional, these three patterns are (1) apathy-atrophy, (2) reactivity-repetitiveness, and (3) conductivity-creativity. Each of these patterns (the ARC model) has differentiating characteristics and correlates.

According to L'Abate, family competence is made up of five resources: emotionality (E), rationality (R), activity (A), awareness (Aw), and context (C). For successful negotiations, each of these five resources (the ERAAwC model) must be used, and the five must be balanced. Priorities relate to three different submodels: (1) familial (self, marriage, children, relatives, work, friends, and leisure); (2) interpersonal (attachments, beliefs, and commitments); and (3) resources for living (i.e., Doing, Having, and Being, the last of which, Being, cannot be negotiated; it can only be shared because Being consists of feelings, i.e., love and status). L'Abate (1986) provided questions to ascertain the nature of and the dysfunctionality in the ability to negotiate and the ability to love.

Problems with the Interview Method

Assessing interview studies presents various problems, some new to this method and some shared by other methodologies. Rabkin (1965), who summarized some of the problems inherent in this methodology, reported that one of the primary problems is the type of research method used in the interview. For instance, interview studies may involve varying degrees of structure and family participation, thus making adequate assessment very difficult. Because of this variation, control groups are characteristically omitted and generalizability is thus greatly reduced.

In part, the very strengths of the interview are also its weaknesses. For instance, the interview can focus on specific aspects of the family. Yet, if the interview does this, it can also be criticized for narrowing the scope of the information gathered. One must then be concerned with data not reported or, if reported, not clarified. In the end, the interviewer is left with many unanswered questions that had been assumed to be unimportant.

In the 1960s most family interviews were based on subjective impressions; and it is true that personal biases, personality factors, clinical orientations, and the interpretations and impressions of the interviewers definitely affect outcome (both positively and negatively). However, the relatively recent accent on more structured interviews will, we hope, minimize this problem in the future.

In general, the problems with interviews are very similar to those associated with case histories: blocking, selective recall, loss of needed information, denial, deliberate deception, social desirability. These same problems are likely to be operative in a marital and family interview because of the emotional atmosphere. Therefore, adequate controls must be developed.

Finally, in terms of limitations, Couch (1969) suggested that family interviews not be used when anxiety about exposure to other family members is excessive or when severe psychopathology is present. Nevertheless, family interviews are regularly called for in these situations. For instance, the family interview is often deemed essential in crisis intervention work and where extreme pathology is present. However, in terms of general assessment, these guidelines seem to apply.

Clinical Assessment

Pragmatic Considerations

To provide beginning family clinicians with some practical considerations in making clinical assessments about family functioning, structure, and process, a number of therapists have developed specific guidelines. These guidelines help the novice focus on crucial areas of family functioning.

Resnikoff (1981), for example, presented in question form some key issues that should be considered.

(1) What is the outward appearance of the family? How far apart do family members sit from each other? Who sits next to whom? Who stays closest to the therapist?

(2) What is the cognitive functioning in the family? Are two messages being communicated between family members when only one message is intended? Who gives and who receives various communications?

(3) What repetitive, nonproductive sequences do you notice?

(4) What is the basic feeling state in the family, and who carries it?

(5) What individual roles reinforce family resistances, and what are the most prevalent family defenses?

(6) What subsystems are operative in this family?

(7) Who carries the power in the family?

(8) How are family members differentiated from each other, and what are the subgroup boundaries?

(9) What part of the life cycle is the family experiencing, and are the problem-solving methods appropriate to that stage of the life cycle?

Following is a more detailed set of guidelines offered by Bagarozzi (1986).

Structural Considerations

(1) To what degree have spouses/parents been able to develop a spousal/parental coalition enabling them to set goals, solve problems, negotiate conflicts, handle crises, and complete individual and family developmental tasks?

(2) To what degree do intergenerational ties exist? To what degree do these ties constitute a problem for a successfully functioning married couple/family system?

(3) To what degree has each spouse/parent achieved separation-

individuation (autonomy) from his or her parents and significant others in his or her family of origin?

(4) To what degree have children achieved age-appropriate levels of separation-individuation (autonomy) in the family?

(5) To what degree have generational boundaries been developed in the family (e.g., between parental subsystems and children subsystems)?

(6) To what degree have the spouses/parents successfully developed clear and definite personal system (ego) boundaries?

(7) What types of communication-relational patterns exist between spouses and all combinations of dyads within the family (e.g., complementary, symmetrical, parallel, pseudocomplementary)?

(8) To what degree is the marital relationship or any other family dyad restricted by a predominant communication-relational pattern?

(9) To what degree do individual, conjugal, sibling, and other familial subsystems use positive feedback?

(10) To what degree do individual, conjugal, sibling, and other familial subsystems use negative feedback?

(11) To what degree is the spousal/family system open to input from outside the system?

(12) What type of authority or power structure exists between spouses and among family members? To what degree does this structure prevent constructive goal setting, problem solving, conflict negotiation, and crisis resolution?

(13) To what degree have the spouses and all family members been able to negotiate mutually acceptable patterns of separateness (distance) and connectedness (closeness)?

(14) Is there a recognizable hierarchy in the family? To what degree is this hierarchy flexible? To what degree does this hierarchy prevent the family from setting goals, solving problems, negotiating conflict, resolving crises, and meeting individual and family developmental tasks?

Process Considerations

(1) To what extent have spouses and family members been able to devise and agree upon rules for sharing, for exchange, and for distributive justice in the family?

(2) To what degree are spouses and children successfully resolving their individual developmental tasks at this time in their lives?

(3) To what degree is the couple/family successfully resolving current family developmental tasks?

(4) To what extent are spouses emotionally supportive of each other? To

what extent are parents supportive of their children? To what extent are children supportive of their parents and their siblings?

(5) To what extent are spouses capable of being intimate (physically, emotionally, intellectually, and psychologically)?

(6) To what extent are family members appropriately intimate with each other (physically, emotionally, intellectually, and psychologically)?

(7) To what degree have spouses and the family as a whole developed successful goal setting, problem solving, conflict negotiation, and crisis management strategies?

(8) To what extent are marital and family problem solving, goal setting, conflict negotiation, and crisis resolution impaired by unresolved issues of transference between spouses and among family members?

(9) To what extent are marital and family problem solving, goal setting, conflict negotiation, and crisis resolution impaired by unresolved issues of projective identification between spouses and among family members?

(10) To what degree are spouses and other family members involved in unconscious collusion that prevents them from successfully setting goals, solving problems, negotiating conflict, and overcoming crises?

(11) To what degree do spouses, family members, and the family unit as a whole use functional communication skills?

(12) To what degree is scapegoating used between spouses and among family members?

(13) To what extent do redundant, cyclical interactional patterns prevent spouses and the children from setting goals, solving problems, negotiating conflict, overcoming crises, and achieving family developmental tasks?

(14) To what extent do marital or family rituals stand in the way of successful goal setting, problem solving, conflict negotiation, and crisis resolution?

(15) What are the recurrent themes in the marriage and the family? To what extent do these themes symbolize or represent unresolved marital or family conflicts?

(16) To what degree do spouses/parents enact roles that are more appropriately filled by children?

(17) To what degree do children enact roles that are more appropriately filled by parents?

(18) To what degree do parents serve as appropriate sex role models?

(19) What are the socialization patterns in the family? Do these patterns differ substantially from this family's particular subcultural, ethnic, and religious group? Do these patterns differ substantially from the general patterns of society?

(20) What type of acculturation patterns exist? How does this family pass down traditions from one generation to the next? To what degree do

these acculturation patterns and traditions get in the way of goal setting, problem solving, conflict negotiation, crisis resolution, and the
successful resolution of individual and family developmental tasks?

(21) What is the couple/family defensive process?

(22) What are the predominant triangular patterns in the family?

(23) What are the personal, conjugal, and family myths that prevent the
family members from setting goals, solving problems, negotiating
conflicts, overcoming crises, and achieving individual and family
developmental tasks?

(24) What are the central rules in the marriage or the family that stand
in the way of successful goal setting, problem solving, conflict negotiation, crisis resolution, and achievement of individual and family
developmental tasks?

(25) To what degree are family goal setting, problem solving, conflict resolution, and crisis management curtailed by the presence of family
secrets or unresolved mourning?

THE FAMILY CASE HISTORY

Pioneering Efforts

In his classic book *The Psychodynamics of Family Life*, Ackerman (1958a)
outlined his guide for collecting data for "family diagnosis." This guide
remains a classic for completeness and detail. In the first section—family-
focused assessment—the main categories are the reason for seeking help,
the data identifying the family, the family as a group, current family functioning, current parental relationship, personality of each individual member, relationships with primary parental families, developmental history of
the primary patient, and summary interpretation of the mental health of the
family group. In the section focusing on the couple, or marital dyad, the
main considerations are past interaction, current interaction, achievement
(measured according to family expectations and to an ideal of healthy marital and parental interaction in our culture), interrelationships of individual
personality and of marital and parental roles, neurotic component of the relationship, the consequences of neurotic conflict, and the patterns of
restitution.

In the section devoted to the child, or the identified patient (IP), the first
considerations are intelligence and physical status (including general appearance and behavior) and symptoms. Other areas in which information is
sought are adaptation to external reality, interpersonal relations, quality of
affects, anxiety reactions, patterns of control, defense patterns, and central
conflicts. Additional considerations include the stages of childhood, such

as the intrauterine stage, the neonatal stage, the stage of primary identification, the stage of individuation, the stage of sexual differentiation (oedipal stage), the stage of extrafamilial development, the stage of adolescence, and the stage of entry into adulthood.

To devise these assessment guidelines, Ackerman drew upon material from a variety of sources (e.g., psychoanalytic and object relations approaches to individual personality development and family behavior, biology, psychiatry, psychology, social work, sociology, family sociology, and systems theory). The case-history approach characteristic of psychoanalysis and psychiatric social work is clearly evident in Ackerman's schema. This approach requires the therapist to have a solid conceptual understanding of the psychodynamic theories of child development, personality formation, and family dynamics.

Satir (1967) showed graphically how she blends initial assessments with hypotheses formulation, treatment planning, and interventions. Again, the importance of history taking is stressed. The Family Life Chronology, as Satir calls it, provides the therapist with a concrete vehicle for becoming actively involved with the family and for structuring the interview. It allows the therapist to gain some understanding of the meaning and etiology of psychiatric symptoms. It permits the interviewer to learn more about how parental models might have influenced mate selection, role expectations, parenting skills, and interpersonal styles.

Satir believes that the security experienced by family members when the therapist structures the interview in this fashion minimizes anxiety and reduces threat. Such directness and structure are thought to engender hope that a solution to the presenting problem can be found. The initial interviews center on a number of broad topic areas.

(1) The identities and relationships of all persons now living in the household, as well as the identities of persons and family members not currently living in the home but who received or contributed to the nurturance, financial support, direction, and guidance of any family members in the past, are described.
(2) The family's goals for therapeutic outcome and the therapist's own views about his or her role in the therapeutic process are explored.
(3) A history of the parents' dating and courtship is taken (children are actively encouraged to become involved in this discussion), including a discussion of their decision to marry. Specific questions are asked about the marriage ceremony, the wedding celebration, and the wedding guests. The couple is also asked to describe any obstacles to their getting married.
(4) Both spouses are asked to discuss their perceptions of how the mate responded to the decision to marry. Any discrepancies between spouses' reports are discussed in depth.

(5) Parental reactions to the couple's decision to marry are explored, followed by an in-depth look at the couple's relationships with parents and in-laws.

(6) A detailed history of each spouse's family of origin and family relationships is taken. Special consideration is given to descriptions of each spouse's parents and their marital relationships.

(7) Parental, familial, and spousal relationships are then discussed in terms of differences and similarities. The goal is to explore how differences are handled in the family and to identify dysfunctional patterns of resolving differences within the family.

(8) Spouses are then helped to realize the difference between their approaches to resolving differences and the approaches used by their families of origin. (Satir underscored how transference distortions may prevent couples from learning new ways to resolve differences.)

(9) Discussions are introduced that focus on disagreement between individuals, pain in family relationships, and joy in family life.

(10) Discrepancies between what parental models did and what they said to each other and other family members are explored.

(11) Spouses' plans, hopes, and desires for their lives together at the beginning of their marriage are reviewed and discussed in the light of what actually has taken place and the couple's current life situation.

(12) Spouses are then asked what they had expected from marriage and their spouse-to-be and to what degree these expectations had been openly communicated. In addition, spouses are asked to describe what they particularly liked about their partner during courtship. The changing perceptions of these traits are explored (e.g., what was once liked is now a source of irritation).

(13) Discrepancies between hopes and marital choices are highlighted to help couples take some responsibility for their marital choices. This also underscores the necessity for learning clear communication.

(14) The birth of each child, the circumstances surrounding each birth, and the different experiences the couple had with each birth are discussed to highlight the impact of childbirth on the couple's relationship. The need for separate time as a spousal system is underscored.

(15) Everyday routines for all family members are reviewed in detail to determine the amount of time family members have for face-to-face contact, sharing experiences, and communicating.

(16) Children are questioned (as the spouses were) about their perceptions of their parents' relationship.

Even though Ackerman and Satir have placed much emphasis upon history taking in their guidelines for family assessment, their focuses tend to be the here and now of each family. However, other therapists evaluate and intervene on the basis of their understanding of family history. Bowen's (1978) family systems theory and therapy probably represent the most clear link between family history and treatment. Framo's (1970) and Boszormenyi-Nagy & Ulrich's (1981) couple's-family-of-origin approach are examples of other therapies that depend upon a thorough understanding of family history. However, their conceptions and integrations of historical data differ considerably.

Framo (1970) attempted to elucidate the relationship between an individual's intrapsychic conflicts and the transactions that occurred within the family of origin. The conflicts are believed to be replicated or defended against in transferential relationships with current intimates.

For Framo, assessment of systems includes several history-gathering interviews pertaining to each spouse, his or her relationships (enmeshments of families of origin), and current contextual variables.

Boszormenyi-Nagy's approach transcends the history of the family's life cycle. He assumes that the family's relationship symptoms are the product of a three-generational transmission process that results from "the struggle of countless preceding generations" and that "survives in the structure of the nuclear family" (Boszormenyi-Nagy & Ulrich, 1981, p. 162). Intergenerational negotiations and exchanges (e.g., of affection, trust, and responsibility) are researched through inquiries about families of origin. According to Boszormenyi-Nagy, responsibility and the ability to reciprocate love, trust, and other payments should increase as parents provide opportunities for their children to become more autonomous. In evaluating the system, the clinician attempts to determine how the presenting problem relates to the negotiation of changing loyalty commitments; corruptive exchanges; old, invisible (unacknowledged) loyalty commitments; and new, untapped sources of loyalty development.

Bowen (1978) makes the most use of family histories to understand current family functioning. He has argued that family members constantly balance forces of intense emotionality and togetherness (fusion) against needs to be more autonomous (i.e., differentiated). Relationships that tend toward fusion are accompanied by a sense of imbalance, impaired rational functioning, and chronic anxiety, which is absorbed by a spouse (leading to internal discomfort and symptomology) or, more commonly, is detoured in relationship fusion with a third person (triangulation). According to Bowen, assessing the level of undifferentiation in the families of origin provides the clinician with the best estimate of the level of fusion in the current family. Similarly, the amount of "emotional cutoff," or imposed psychological or physical distancing, from extended family members may be related to the level of emotional pressure and fusion in the current system.

Thus, the intensity of system fusion depends upon the family's particular style of binding anxiety, the number and kind of anxiety-generating events that have impinged upon the system, the basic self-differentiation of each family member, and the extent of emotional cutoff in the system. The genogram (discussed later in this chapter) was developed by Bowen and his associates to aid in history taking.

Another pioneering effort to identify important family dimensions for the purpose of diagnosis and treatment was made by Hess and Handel (1959). These authors targeted five broad areas:

(1) patterns of separateness and connectedness;
(2) establishment of satisfactory congruences of images between spouses;
(3) evolving modes of interaction into central family themes or concerns;
(4) establishment of the boundaries of the family's world of experience;
(5) significant biosocial issues of family life (e.g., the family's disposition to evolve definitions of male and female, older and younger).

Although Hess and Handel did not present specific assessment guidelines for each of these five crucial areas of family life, three of the areas outlined by them have become central sources of diagnostic concern for the structural and the strategic schools of family therapy as typified by Minuchin and Haley. For example, the structural school emphasizes system and subsystem boundaries, their erection, maintenance, and permeability (Aponte & Van Deusen, 1981). These emphases reflect Hess and Handel's concern with patterns of separateness and connectedness and the establishment of boundaries in the family's world of experience. The strategic approach focuses on family developmental processes and life cycle stages (Stanton, 1981), underscoring the significance of biosocial issues and the family's disposition to evolve definitions of male and female. Finally, both structural and strategic orientations concentrate on family developmental stages and the evolution of dysfunctional hierarchical arrangements, cross-generational alignments, and coalitions. This emphasis can be seen as the logical extension of Hess and Handel's concerns with boundaries and the definition of older and younger, male and female.

Structural School

Minuchin (1974) and his coworkers developed an approach to family therapy that emphasizes the relationship between a presenting problem and the organization, or structure, of the family. The structural model was founded within the context of empirical investigations (Minuchin, Montalvo, Guerney, Rosman, & Schumer, 1967) conducted at the Wiltwyck School for Boys, an institution serving delinquents from lower-socioeconomic-status Black and Puerto Rican families.

The language of the structural model seems to be derived primarily from organizational and role theory, relying heavily on spatial metaphors. The cornerstone of this model is the concept *structure*. Aponte and Van Deusen (1981) defined structure as the regulating codes manifested in the operational patterns through which family members relate to one another in order to carry out various functions or jobs required within a family.

Three central concepts in the structural model are (1) boundaries, which define rules about who participates in the family and how one should participate; (2) alignments, which are concerned with relatedness between and among family members; and (3) power, which deals with the relative influence each member has on behavioral outcomes in family processes.

The initial assessment interview includes three overlapping stages: (1) joining the system, (2) obtaining a problem description, and (3) exploring the family structure by encouraging and observing transactions around the presenting problem. Six foci based upon the three central concepts of the structural approach are stressed: (1) family structure, (2) system flexibility, (3) sensitivity to individual members' actions, (4) family life context (5) family developmental stage, (6) the ways in which the IP's symptoms are used to maintain dysfunctional transactional patterns and family structures. The therapist is active and, after joining the system, induces stress in order to test the system's flexibility. A goal of assessment is to shift focus from the IP to the system as a whole.

Strategic School

The Mental Research Institute (MRI) group can be credited with the development of systemic diagnosis (Watzlawick, 1966; Watzlawick, Beavin, & Jackson 1967). Their pragmatic view of dysfunctional behavior is best summed up in the following four statements.

(1) The problems people bring to psychotherapists persist only if the problems are maintained by ongoing current behavior of the patient and others with whom he or she interacts.

(2) If such problem-maintaining behaviors are eliminated, the symptom will vanish.

(3) Assessment should focus on immediately observable behaviors. It is not necessary to think in terms of intrapsychic states or even in terms of fundamental levels of systemic organization.

(4) Most problems are maintained through either underemphasis (i.e., denying the existence of difficulties) or overemphasis (i.e., labeling behavior problematic because it does not fit some vague ideal expectation).

The information about the structures and processes responsible for maintaining the presenting symptom or problem is gained by direct questioning of family members. Observations are not considered necessary, and all family members need not be present for effective interventions to be carried out. In addition to gaining a behavioral description of the problem, the MRI group attempts to get a behavioral description of the family's attempted solutions, because it is the attempted solutions that are thought to maintain the presenting problem or symptom.

The Milan School

The theoretical formulations of the Milan school (Selvini-Palazzoli, Boscolo, Cecchin, & Prata, 1978) are similar to those of the MRI group. However, the Milan school sees intrapersonal and systemic organizational interpretations as unnecessary for change. Instead, the Milan school stresses the importance of understanding interpersonal relationships and viewing the family system as a whole. Therefore, the Milan group requires all family members to be present during clinical interviews.

In a paper entitled "Hypothesizing, Circularity, Neutrality: Three Guidelines for the Conductor of the Session," Selvini-Palazzoli, Boscolo, Cecchin, and Prata (1980) discussed their interviewing technique. Using videotapes of interviews conducted by members of the Milan school, Penn (1982) outlined their *circular questioning*. The main dimensions of circular questioning follow, accompanied by examples.

(1)   What is the problem in the family now?
(2)   What are the specific behaviors that are problematic?
(3)   What are the *cue* words used by family members that are embedded in the problem statement?
　　　Examples:
　　　　　Mother has a "drinking problem."
　　　　　She is an "alcoholic."
　　　　　We "can't understand" her behavior.
　　　　　He gives me "ulcers."
　　　　　We cannot "communicate."
　　　　　She "falls apart" in the face of trouble.
(4)   Translate these cue words or phrases into *relationship statements*. Ask questions that highlight coalition alignments.
　　　Examples:
　　　　　Who gets most upset when mother drinks?
　　　　　Who gets least upset when mother drinks?
　　　　　Who feels most responsible for helping mother with her alcoholism?

Who feels least responsible for helping mother with her alcoholism?

(5) Discover the *sequence of events* and the *behaviors surrounding the problem* to get a picture of the cycle. Important: The sequence can be used as a solution. Ask what each family member does when the problem occurs.

(6) Ask questions that *classify and rank family members' responses.*
> *Examples:*
>> Who finds out first that mother has been drinking?
>> Who finds out next?
>> How does each person learn of mother's drinking?

(7) Ask what each family member does next.
> *Examples:*
>> What does son do when he finds mother drunk?
>> What does oldest brother do when youngest brother calls him to say that their mom is drunk?

(8) Ask questions that *classify and compare.*
> *Examples:*
>> Is your parents' life together better or worse since John has been having trouble in school?
>> Who is closest to mother when she gets upset?
>> Who is next?
>> Who is least close?
>> Who is most able to calm father down so his ulcers don't act up?
>> Who is next able?
>> Who is least able?
>> Is your father more involved with you or less involved with you since you have been having trouble in school?
>> Have you been more like a father or a son since your father's death?

(9) Ask agreement questions that allow you to *rank coalitions and alignments* in terms of strength or priority.
> *Examples:*
>> Who in the family agrees with you that mother is an alcoholic?
>> Do you agree with your sister that mother is an alcoholic?
>> Do you agree that when mother drinks, your brother gets upset?
>> Do you agree that when brother and sister disagree, mother gets more upset?

(10) Gossiping in the presence of the other family members requires each family member to *comment on the relationship of two other family members.*

Examples:
> How do you see your mother and father behave when your brother steals something?

(11) Ask questions that elicit *comparisons between subsystems*.
Examples:
> Mom, you say you have difficulty understanding John's behavior. Which daughter do you have the least trouble understanding? Who, after John, do you have the most trouble understanding?

(12) Ask questions that elicit *comparisons within subsystems*.
Examples:
> How would your parents get along without you?
> Do any other children have a problem?
> Which one of you will always stay home with your parents?
> Which one of you will take care of your aging parents?

(13) Ask questions that elicit *comparisons both between and within subsystems*.
Examples:
> If John stopped stealing and got along better with your father, what would happen to your relationship with your father?

(14) Ask *explanation* questions.
Examples:
> What is your explanation for your father's closeness to John?
> What is your explanation for John's stealing?
> What is your explanation for John and mother's agreeing?

Information gathered from such interviews can be used to develop treatments designed to interrupt the behavioral sequences that are thought to maintain the particular symptom or problem behavior in a family system.

Jay Haley

Haley is considered a pioneer in the development and formulation of strategic marital and family therapy (Haley, 1963, 1971, 1976, 1980, 1984). The basic assumption underlying his approach is that problems or symptoms are maintained by a faulty hierarchical arrangement within the family. The goal of therapy is the alteration of this faulty hierarchy. For Haley and his associates, diagnostic interviewing and therapy are inextricably tied.

Haley believes that the best way to gather the information needed for accurate diagnosis is through the clinical interview. The initial interview with the family can be divided into four stages:

(1) social, or joining, stage, in which the family is made to feel comfortable;
(2) problem identification stage, in which the problem is behaviorally outlined;
(3) interaction stage, in which the family members are asked to discuss the problem as a group;
(4) goal-setting stage, in which behavioral outcomes are specified.

The Genogram

The genogram, which grew out of Bowenian theory, is one of the primary clinical aids for exploring intergenerational dynamics and influences on the nuclear family.

The focus of Bowen's approach is the individual (Guerin, 1976); his central concept is the degree of maturity and differentiation from one's family of origin. The more differentiated an individual, the more that individual will be able to master anxiety and the various stresses of daily living. Less differentiated individuals are said to be at the mercy of their emotions. As anxiety develops between two family members, one member will make an effort to diffuse it by including a third person. This process—triangulation—explains the multigenerational transmission of interactional patterns.

The genogram graphically illustrates a family's multigenerational history, not unlike a family tree. Recurrent patterns of interaction across generations (usually in terms of triads) and critical stressful or toxic events are emphasized. Outlining a genogram enables the therapist to gather information about transgenerational patterns.

Family members are asked to pay particular attention to dynamic events such as births and deaths of family members; birth orders; and spacing between siblings' births, stillbirths, and miscarriages.

Family moves and the reasons for these moves are also considered important. How the decision to move was made and by whom it was made are explored. The effects of these moves on family life and family members should be noted.

Job changes constitute another dynamic consideration. The reasons for job changes, the results of such changes on the family and its members, and the degree of stress engendered by these changes are all important.

Family separations are another source of stress. During which stages of the individual's development and during which stages of the family life cycle these separations occurred represent another important area to be investigated. The reasons for the separations and the impact upon family members, as well as the length and frequencies of separations, should be thoroughly analyzed.

Illnesses, hospitalizations, accidents, and suicides comprise another area of concern. For example, if parents were ill for extended periods of time, who was responsible for running the home and caring for the children?

Toxic issues and habits make up another source of inquiry. Alcohol use and abuse, chemical abuse, and eating habits that might result in health problems are important considerations. Physical or sexual abuse, criminal behavior, antisocial behavior, psychiatric symptoms, and habits and rituals should also be explored.

Environmental stressors should be noted. Some examples are parental separations, divorces, remarriages, and extramarital affairs; both parents being students or both parents being employed; the impact of subcultural, ethnic, racial, and religious influences on the family; and extremely high or unrealistic expectations for family members.

Obviously, the list of toxic issues, habits, and patterns can be extended to account for the problem behaviors manifested in the family system. When they are combined with specific diagnostic questions, intergenerational patterns are easily identified and the degree to which parents have been able to separate and individuate from their families of origin can be assessed. For a comprehensive discussion of the use of genograms in clinical practice, see McGoldrick and Gerson (1985).

John G. Howells

The model of family assessment developed by John G. Howells is an outgrowth of his work in family psychiatry (Howells, 1971). This approach was designed for use by consulting psychiatrists trained in medical models of psychopathology. In family psychiatry, the patient is the family; and presenting symptoms are indicators of more global problems that exist along several dimensions of family life. According to Howells, family psychiatry is a refinement of individual psychiatry and is the appropriate mode of treatment when an individual family member has symptoms.

This model can be considered eclectic. Five interrelated areas are targeted for assessment: (1) individuals, (2) internal communication, (3) general psychic properties, (4) external communication, and (5) physical properties.

The clinical interview is divided into five steps. Step I, the complaint, is an inquiry about the symptom from the patient's experience, expressed in the patient's language. Step II, formal questioning, includes questions about total body and emotional functioning, developmental history of the individual and the family, and onset of the symptom and premorbid state. Step III, formal examination, is a traditional psychiatric intake of the IP (psychometric testing may be considered). Step IV is the differential diagnosis. Finally, Step V is determination of the process of psychopathology, or what Howells (1975) termed the "psychic noci-vectors."

After completing assessment of the individual dimension, Howells turns to the second dimension, internal communication, which includes communication dysfunctions and relationships within the family. Marital stress indicators include incompatibility, sexual disharmony, and psychosomatic symptoms. Parent-child interaction should be assessed not only in terms of the effect of the parents on the child but also the child's effect on the parents. Howells noted that the importance of sibling interaction has been underestimated. Howells recommended that "the family diagnostic process must evaluate any signs of disruption in the dimension of internal communication" (Howells, 1975, p. 68). These include excessive arguing, withdrawal, lack of communication, and absence of sexual intercourse.

Assessment of the third dimension—group properties—entails description of the family along 15 dimensions (e.g., attitude, character, and conscience). Of particular note are issues of control (leadership and decision making), roles and tasks, arrangement-cohesiveness (alignments of members), and conflict.

The fourth dimension—family and society—includes relationships between family and other relatives, friends, neighbors, school, and work.

The fifth dimension—physical properties—includes demographic material, physical characteristics of individuals, physical illnesses, possessions, neighborhood, home, food, clothing, transportation, income, recreation, and education.

CONCLUSION

The interview remains the most important tool of evaluation. Unfortunately, this tool is only as good as the skills of the interviewer, making it a rather chancy and variable process. The more structured, or prestructured, the interview, the greater the probability that it will be valid and reliable. However, mechanizing the interview through structuring may decrease the relationship-building considerations, such as warmth, establishing rapport, and giving support. We suggest that freewheeling, open-ended interviews be kept in the hands of advanced professionals and that more routine and structured interviews be left to trainees and paraprofessionals. Someday, family therapists may learn to delegate responsibility and use a lattice-and-ladder of paraprofessional personnel who will be given the responsibility of gathering data, rather than the responsibility of establishing rapport.

In recent years the family interview has developed from a very ambiguous, unstructured entity into a valuable tool for family assessment. In particular, since the early 1960s there has been an increase in the use of this technique. Now there seems to be a trend toward more structured and empirically based interview formats that allow for replication, testing, and research.

The interview serves both as a vehicle for other assessment tools and as a tool itself. All too often, the family interview has been used strictly as a vehicle for other techniques, thus obscuring its advantages. What is indicated now is the careful and comprehensive planning of economical techniques to fulfill the potential of the family interview.

In the future, additional research could include (1) the clarification of the units of structure under consideration, such as foci; (2) studies assessing the usefulness of specific types of theory-based family interviews, particularly in comparison to other theory-based techniques; (3) experimental studies to determine the most effective degree of structure for obtaining different kinds of information for a given theoretical orientation; (4) further research on what constitutes an effective interview in regard to a particular theory of family process/therapy; and (5) studies relating the interview process to diagnosis, treatment, and outcome evaluation.

Finally, the basic need in this area seems to be the development of more systematic ways of conducting and assessing the interview itself. The family interview provides a wealth of information about the family and its interactions. Instead of discounting this technique, researchers must refine and develop the family interview so that its bountiful information can be properly harvested.

REFERENCES

Ackerman, N. W. (1958a). *The psychodynamics of family life.* New York: Basic Books.

Ackerman, N. W. (1958b). Toward all interpretive therapy of the family. *American Journal of Psychiatry, 114,* 727–733.

Aponte, H. J., & Van Deusen, J. M. (1981). Structural family therapy. In A. S. Gurman & D. P. Kniskern (Eds.), *Handbook of family therapy (Vol. 1,* pp. 310–360). New York: Brunner/Mazel.

Blechman, E. A., & Olson, D. H. L. (1976). Family contract game: Description and effectiveness. In D. H. L. Olson (Ed.), *Treating relationships* (pp. 133–149). Lake Mills, IA: Graphic Publishing.

Blood, R. O., Jr., & Hamblin, R. L. (1958). The effect of the wife's employment on the family power structure. *Social Forces, 36,* 347–352.

Bodin, A. (1968). Conjoint family assessment. In P. McReynolds (Ed.), *Advances in psychological assessment (Vol. 1,* pp. 223–243). Palo Alto, CA: Science and Behavior Books.

Boszormenyi-Nagy, I., & Ulrich, D. N. (1981). Contextual family therapy. In A. S. Gurman & D. P. Kniskern (Eds.), *Handbook of family therapy, Vol. I* (pp. 159–186). New York: Brunner/Mazel.

Bowen, M. (1961). Family psychotherapy. *American Journal of Orthopsychiatry, 31,* 40–60.

Bowen, M. (1978). *Family therapy in clinical practice.* Northvale, NJ: Jason Aronson.

Couch, E. H. (1969). *Joint and family interviews in the treatment of marital problems.* New York: Family Service Association of America.

Framo, J. L. (1970). Symptoms from a family transactional viewpoint. In N. W. Ackerman, J. J. Lieb, & J. K. Pearce (Eds.), *Family therapy in transition* (pp. 125–171). Boston: Little, Brown.

Guerin, P. (Ed.). (1976). *Family therapy: Theory and practice*. New York: Gardner.

Haley, J. (1963). *Strategies of psychotherapy*. New York: Grune & Stratton.

Haley, J. (1971). A review of the family therapy field. In J. Haley (Ed.), *Changing families: A family therapy reader* (pp. 1–12). New York: Grune & Stratton.

Haley, J. (1976). *Problem solving therapy: New strategies for effective family therapy*. San Francisco: Jossey-Bass.

Haley, J. (1980). *Leaving home: The therapy of disturbed young people*. New York: McGraw-Hill.

Haley, J. (1984). *Ordeal therapy*. San Francisco: Jossey-Bass.

Halleck, S. L. (1978). Family therapy and social change. *Social Casework, 57*, 483–493.

Herbst, P. G. (1952). The measurement of family relationships. *Human Relationships, 5*, 3–35.

Hess, R. D., & Handel, G. (1959). *Family worlds*. Chicago: University of Chicago Press.

Howells, J. G. (1971). *Theory and practice of family psychiatry*. New York: Brunner/Mazel.

Howells, J. G. (1975). *Principles of family psychiatry*. New York: Brunner/Mazel.

Jackson, D. D., Riskin, J., & Satir, V. (1961). A method of analysis of a family interview. *Archives of General Psychiatry, 5*, 321–339.

L'Abate, L. (1986). *Systematic family therapy*. New York: Brunner/Mazel.

L'Abate, L. & Colondier, G. (1987). The emperor has no clothes! Long live the emperor! A critique of family systems thinking and a reductionistic proposal. *American Journal of Family Therapy, 15*, 19–33. (Reprinted in L. L'Abate [Ed.] [1987], *Family psychology II: Theory, therapy, enrichment, and training* [pp. 3–17]. Washington, DC: University Press of America.)

L'Abate, L., & Goodrich, M. (1980). Marital adjustment. In R. Woody (Ed.), *Encyclopedia of clinical evaluation* (pp. 60–73). San Francisco: Jossey-Bass.

Laslett, B., & Rapoport, R. (1975). Collaborative interviewing and interactive research. *Journal of Marriage and the Family, 37*, 968–977.

McGoldrick, M. J., & Gerson, R. (1985). *Genograms in family assessment*. New York: Norton.

Minuchin, S. (1974). *Families and family therapy*. Cambridge, MA: Harvard University Press.

Minuchin, S., Montalvo, B., Guerney, B., Jr., Rosman, B., & Schumer, F. (1967). *Families of the slums: An exploration of their structure and treatment*. New York: Basic Books.

Penn, P. (1982). Circular questioning. *Family Process, 21*, 267–280.

Quinton, D., Rutter, M., & Rowlands, O. (1976). An evaluation of an interview assessment of marriage. *Psychological Medicine, 6*, 577–586.

Rabkin, L. Y. (1965). The patient's family: Research methods. *Family Process, 4*, 105–132.

Resnikoff, R. O. (1981). Teaching family therapy: Ten key questions for understanding the family as patient. *Journal of Marital and Family Therapy, 7*, 135–142.

Riskin, J., & Faunce, E. E. (1970a). Family interaction scales: 1. Theoretical framework and method. *Archives of General Psychiatry, 22*, 504–512.

Riskin, J., & Faunce, E. E. (1970b). Family interaction scales: 3. Discussion of methodology and substantive findings. *Archives of General Psychiatry, 22*, 526–537.

Riskin, J., & Faunce, E. E. (1972). Evaluative review of family interaction research. *Family Process, 11*, 365–455.

Satir, V. (1967). *Conjoint family therapy*. Palo Alto, CA: Science and Behavior Books.

Satir, V. (1972). *Peoplemaking*. Palo Alto, CA: Science and Behavior Books.

Selvini-Palazzoli, M., Boscolo, L., Cecchin, G., & Prata, G. (1978). *Paradox and counterparadox*. Northvale, NJ: Jason Aronson.

Selvini-Palazzoli, M., Boscolo, L., Cecchin, G., & Prata, G. (1980). Hypothesizing-circularity-neutrality: Three guidelines for the conductor of the session. *Family Process, 19*, 3–12.

Stanton, M. D. (1981). Strategic approaches to family therapy. In A. S. Gurman & D. P. Kniskern (Eds.), *Handbook of family therapy* (Vol. 1, pp. 361–402). New York: Brunner/Mazel.

Straus, M. A., & Brown, B. W. (1978). *Family measurement techniques: Abstracts of published instruments, 1935–1974*. Minneapolis: University of Minnesota Press.

Straus, M. A., & Tallman, I. (1969). Simulated family activity measurement (SIMFAM). In M. A. Straus (Ed.), *Family measurement techniques* (pp. 263–265). Minneapolis: University of Minnesota Press.

Straus, M.A., & Tallman, I. (1971). SIMFAM: A technique for observational measurement and experimental study of families. In J. Aldous, T. Condon, R. Hill, M. Straus, & I. Tallman (Eds.). *Family problem solving: A symposium of theoretical, methodological, and substantive concerns.* (pp. 381–438). Hinsdale, IL: Dryden.

Tallman, I., & Wilson, L. (1974). Simulating social structures: The use of a simulation game in cross-national research. *Simulation and Games, 5,* 147–167.

Watzlawick, P. (1966). A structured family interview. *Family Process,* 256–271.

Watzlawick, P., Beavin, J. H., & Jackson, D. D. (1967). *Pragmatics of human communication.* New York: Norton.

SECTION II
Marriages

3

Observations of Marital Interactions

Implications of Research Findings
for Marital Therapy

Until the past few decades, marital research has been the domain of sociologists and social psychologists. Sociologists have tended to rely on questionnaires and demographic data to investigate marital quality and interaction. In the late 1960s, social researchers began questioning the utility of such approaches.

Like much of the seminal research in child development (which relied upon mothers' reports about their children's growth and behavior), early work in the area of marital interaction was based upon wives' reports of husband-wife interaction. With the exception of quite a few pioneering studies (e.g., Bauman, Roman, Borello, & Meltzer, 1967; Carter & Thomas, 1973a, 1973b; Ferreira & Winter, 1974; Huntington, 1958; Kenkel, 1959; Kenkel & Hoffman, 1956; Komisar, 1949; Navran, 1967; Olson, 1969; Ravich, Deutsch, & Brown, 1966; Ryder, 1968; Ryder & Goodrich, 1966; Santa-Barbara & Epstein, 1974; Speer, 1972; Strodtbeck, 1951; Willi, 1969), before 1975, most research dealing with marital interaction was based upon self-reports of perceived or inferred marital behavior.

About the same time that research into the interactional dynamics of married couples was beginning to get under way, family researchers interested in the etiology of psychiatric illnesses such as schizophrenia began to devise methods of measuring interpersonal behavior. Haley (1959a, 1959b, 1962, 1964), Mishler and Waxler (1968), and Winter and Ferreira (1967, 1969a, 1969b, 1973) were among the first investigators to attempt to quantify the relationship between interpersonal behavior and symptomatology.

SUBSTANTIVE FINDINGS: NONVERBAL COMMUNICATION
AND MARITAL SATISFACTION

The hypothesis that marital distress results from dysfunctional or ineffective methods of communicating has been documented empirically (Lewis & Spanier, 1979; Raush, Greif, & Nugent, 1979) and is accepted as axiomatic by most marital/family therapists (L'Abate & McHenry, 1983).

Nonverbal behavior is a particularly important component of communication. Many researchers believe that the nonverbal part of a message carries more weight when the verbal and nonverbal components conflict (e.g., Argyle, 1975; Griffin & Patton, 1971; Mehrabian, 1972). It has also been found that a couple's nonverbal channels are better discriminators of distressed and nondistressed couples than are the verbal channels (Gottman, 1979; Gottman, Markman, & Notarius, 1977). Unlike the verbal channels, nonverbal channels are not under voluntary control (Vincent, Weiss, & Birchler, 1975).

In general, studies investigating nonverbal communication and marital satisfaction have focused on three main areas: (1) the decoding and encoding of nonverbal cues and the attempt to discover where deficits in distressed couples may lie; (2) the differences in the base rates of the display of nonverbal "affects" between distressed and nondistressed couples; and (3) the reciprocation of positive and negative "affects" between distressed and nondistressed couples.

In the first section, we present a brief historical overview of the field of nonverbal communication and interpersonal relationships and then review studies in each of the three areas already mentioned. A limitation of this review is its restriction to research studies that examined nonverbal behavior and its relationship to marital satisfaction. We do not review studies that did not consider levels of marital satisfaction or studies that have examined the nonverbal behavior of persons who are not part of a marital dyad (e.g., strangers, dating couples, or other family members).

Historical Background

The study of nonverbal communication is by no means a recent undertaking. In 1872 Darwin investigated the universal nature of facial expressions. However, nonverbal communication between individuals has been a target of investigation only within the past 35 years or so. Because much of this research has focused on nonverbal interaction among strangers, these studies have looked at nonverbal communication outside the context of an intimate interpersonal relationship (L'Abate, 1985; Noller, 1980a, 1980b).

Many of the findings have been extrapolated and used to explain the behavior of people in intimate dyads (Knapp, 1983). If nonverbal behavior were traitlike (consistent across all situations), these extrapolations would be valid. However, it has been found that nonverbal communication skills can vary according to the context of one's interpersonal relationship. For example, spouses in unhappy marriages have been found to be worse at decoding (interpreting) nonverbal cues from their mates than at decoding nonverbal cues from strangers. This result is produced even when no deficit has been found in the encoding (sending) spouse (Noller, 1984).

Most researchers seem to agree that nonverbal communication is a better discriminator than is verbal communication of distressed and nondistressed couples. Yet, because of contradictory findings, drawing general conclusions about the types of nonverbal cues that differentiate these two groups becomes difficult.

Even common notions about what constitutes positive behaviors between spouses have been called into question. For example, the amount of eye contact between spouses has been used as an indication of feelings of closeness or intimacy: the more eye contact between the partners, the closer they are thought to be (Mehrabian, 1976). However, Noller (1980a, 1980b) found marital adjustment and eye contact to be negatively associated.

Such findings bring home the importance of remembering that all behavioral exchanges between intimates have some symbolic meaning (Bagarozzi, 1981). No matter how objective they may seem to the outsider, behaviors exhibited between spouses carry symbolic messages concerning the sender's evaluations of the receiver. Behaviors exchanged between spouses convey much more meaning than the actual pleasurable or displeasurable value of the behaviors themselves. Clinicians believe that marital difficulties arise whenever the sender's rules and the receiver's rules for the same behavioral message do not correspond (Bagarozzi & Anderson, 1989).

One of the first researchers to find a positive relationship between nonverbal communication and marital satisfaction was Navran (1967), who compared the responses on the Primary Communication Inventory (PCI) of 24 happy couples with those of 24 unhappy couples. He found that well-adjusted couples reported significantly better communication (both verbal and nonverbal) than did their maladjusted counterparts.

The importance of nonverbal communication in marital satisfaction was further supported by Kahn (1970), who was interested in examining the differences in nonverbal communication among satisfied and dissatisfied couples. Kahn did not use self-report measures as did Navram (1967). Instead, he attempted to study the actual nonverbal communication process between spouses. To accomplish this task, Kahn devised the Marital Communication Scale (MCS).

The MCS consists of 16 standard verbal messages (8 for the husband; 8 for the wife) that require the spouse to communicate one of three possible attitudes or intentions (positive, negative, or neutral). For example, one of the hypothetical situations in which the husband must display the three types of nonverbal messages is the following: "You come to the dinner table as your wife begins to serve chicken, a main course that you recall having had for dinner four days ago." The verbal statement that the husband is to make is the following: "Didn't we have chicken for dinner a few nights ago?" The spouse (in this case, the husband) is instructed to express one of three intentions designated by the experimenter: (1) "You are irritated with her for preparing the same meal again and are warning her that in the future she had better not make the mistake of a closely repeated meal!"; (2) "You do not mind but want to see whether your memory for meals is accurate"; or (3) "You are elated because chicken is one of your favorites and you are not accustomed to her graciousness in serving it so often for you." The receiver's task is to pick the one alternative that he or she believes the spouse is sending. Because each item requires the contribution of both spouses (sender and receiver), the couple receives a combined score on the MCS.

In this study, 21 couples made up each of the two groups—dissatisfied and satisfied. Kahn found that the dissatisfied couples obtained significantly lower scores on the MCS than did the satisfied couples. He concluded that dissatisfied couples tended to attribute hurtful intent to their spouses more frequently than did the satisfied group. In effect, Kahn assumed that the source of conflict lay in the receiver's interpretation of the spouse's message.

In an attempt to determine whether the distress was a result of poor sender skills or poor receiver skills, Noller (1980a, 1980b) used a modified version of the MCS. In addition, Noller included a group of judges who independently rated each sender's (encoder's) message as either a "good" or a "bad" communication. Noller studied three groups of subjects: nondistressed couples, distressed couples, and moderately distressed couples. Each group consisted of 16 couples. Noller found that the distressed couples received significantly fewer ratings of "good communication" than did their nondistressed counterparts. The distressed group also had the most decoding (receiving) errors. Husbands made more decoding errors regardless of the couple's satisfaction status.

These findings were replicated by Gottman and Porterfield (1981), who used the Locke-Williamson Marital Relationship Inventory (MRI) (Burgess, Locke, & Thomas, 1971) as their measure of marital satisfaction. In this study, couples were not divided into separate groups based upon their satisfaction scores; instead, individual MRI scores and MCS scores were correlated. These researchers found a significant correlation between wives' dissatisfaction and husbands' MCS scores; the lower the wife's satisfaction, the lower the husband's MCS scores. These findings suggest a communication deficit in the husbands as receivers.

To test this hypothesis, Gottman and Porterfield (1981) analyzed data from the stranger dyads. From these analyses, they concluded that the communication deficit was due to the husbands' faulty decoding skills, because strangers, regardless of the wives' satisfaction, were able to decode the wives' nonverbal cues equally well. Using strangers' marital satisfaction scores, Gottman and Porterfield found no difference between the marital satisfaction scores of the males and their ability to decode nonverbal cues of females from the non-spouse group. These findings seem to suggest that the husbands' decoding deficit was specific only to their own wives. In other words, although husbands had difficulty interpreting their wives' nonverbal cues, they had no difficulty interpreting the cues of female strangers.

Further support for this finding comes from Noller's (1981) follow-up study, in which couples from the 1980 study were used again. However, this time each partner was asked to decode the spouse's nonverbal cues and those of an opposite-sex stranger. Noller found that subjects in poorly adjusted marriages were better able to discriminate (decode) an opposite-sex stranger's nonverbal cues than the nonverbal cues of their own spouses.

How one perceives one's mate; how one interprets the spouse's behavior; how one experiences the partner's intentions and the hidden, symbolic meanings that one attributes to the spouse's verbal statements, coupled with one's unspoken assumptions and expectations for the mate—all play a part in the degree to which the message received is consistent with the message sent. These factors can be considered noise in the communication channel. The more noise, the more distorted the message. Pioneering researchers (Birchler, Weiss, & Vincent, 1975; Gottman, Notarius, Markman, Bank, Yoppi, & Rubin, 1976) found that distressed spouses perceived, experienced, and recorded the behaviors of their mates as more negative and maliciously intended than did spouses whose relationships were not stressful. In addition, Noller (1980a, 1980b) found that spouses, regardless of their adjustment status, were better at sending (encoding) negative messages than they were at sending either neutral or positive messages.

It is fruitless (if not linear) to attempt to answer the chicken-or-egg question as to whether marital distress "causes" communication to break down or vice versa. This issue is more academic than pragmatic. What we do know is that there is a wealth of data showing positive correlation between couples' communication effectiveness and overall marital satisfaction (Lewis & Spanier, 1979).

Two of the coding systems most frequently used to assess affect in relationships are the Couple Interaction Scoring System (CISS) (Gottman, 1979; Gottman et al., 1977; Notarius, Markman, & Gottman, 1983) and the Marital Interaction Coding System (MICS) (Birchler et al., 1975; Weiss & Summers, 1983).

CISS codes are divided into two parts: content and affect. Both speaker and listener are rated. There are 28 content codes that have been grouped into 8 summary codes. The affect codes are used to assess nonverbal behaviors. Both the speaker and the listener are rated for positive, negative, or neutral affect. Face, body, and voice tones are rated separately in each of these dimensions. The basic coding unit of the CISS is the "thought unit," "speech act," or "utterance." Coders are required to code each thought unit, using both a written transcript and a videotape (Gottman et al., 1977).

The MICS, on the other hand, uses time units. Each speaker and each listener is coded in 30-second units. The most recent version of the MICS contains 32 codes (Weiss & Summers, 1983), 28 of which are called behavior codes. These codes are used for verbal and nonverbal affect and speaker-listener behavior.

The other 4 codes are modifiers, used to qualify the remaining 28 codes. Two of the modifier codes are used to define listener attention rather than behavior acts. The other two modifier codes are "state" codes used to identify questions and commands. To increase reliability, most researchers combine categories (Noller, 1984).

Although two studies (Gottman et al., 1977; Noller, 1982) found different results as to whether positive affect can discriminate distressed from non-distressed couples, both found that distressed couples expressed significantly more negative affect than did nondistressed couples. However, Margolin and Wampold (1981) found that the expression of negative affect did not discriminate between distressed and nondistressed groups.

To test the generality of Gottman et al.'s (1977) results across different types of tasks, Rubin (1977) studied the use of verbal and nonverbal behavior by distressed and nondistressed couples on a low-conflict nondecision-making task and six conflict-inducing improvised tasks. On both tasks, nondistressed couples were more positive and less negative. A significant difference between the two groups was also found for neutral affect, with the nondistressed couples displaying significantly more neutral affect.

Schaap (1984) also studied affect in distressed and nondistressed couples across different types of situations. Schaap found that distressed and conflicted couples were similar in their behavior. During the initial phase of the study, distressed couples displayed more negative affect than their nondistressed counterparts. In the second phase, distressed couples were found to exhibit more negative and significantly less positive affect than did nondistressed couples.

All studies discussed in this section have assessed couples' affect through observational methods. Thus, these findings are based upon outsiders' viewpoints. To compare these results with the couples' perceptions of their behavior during interaction, Gottman and his colleagues (Gottman, 1979; Gottman et al., 1976) used the *talk table*. This device was designed to compare the intentions and accompanying effects of messages sent by spouses. The talk table is described as a double sloping box with a toggle switch that lights a button on the side toward the spouse whose turn it is to speak. Each side of the box also has two rows of five buttons. One row of buttons is used by the speaker to code the intended message; the other row is used by the listener to code the impact of the message received. The five buttons are labeled *super negative, negative, neutral, positive,* and *super positive.* Although the partners can see each other across the table, a shield blocks the buttons, preventing either partner from seeing the responses given by the other.

Gottman et al. (1976) described two studies using the talk table device. In the first study, clinical and nonclinical couples were used. Couples interacted on the talk table on three low-conflict and two high-conflict tasks. The researchers found no significant differences in intent over all tasks. However, there was a significant difference between the two groups on impact. The impact of messages was more positive for nondistressed than distressed couples. In addition, although the difference was greater for negative affect, distressed couples were found to be significantly less positive and more negative than nondistressed couples.

To test the generalizability of results obtained in their first study, Gottman et al. (1976) conducted a second study. One high-conflict task and one low-conflict task were used in the second study. The results of the second study were generally consistent with the results of the first. The main difference was that in the second study it was easier to discriminate distressed from nondistressed couples on the high-conflict task.

Methodological Problems

The reasons for contradictory findings across studies are difficult to assess because the methodological procedures are not comparable: (1) criteria for assigning couples to distressed or nondistressed group, (2) the nature of the task being coded, (3) methods of coding data, and (4) noncompatibility of groups. These same methodological problems appear in studies designed to assess reciprocity in marital dyads. Like the studies dealing with affect in the marital dyad, empirical investigations into affective reciprocity among distressed and nondistressed couples offer contradictory results.

One of the first researchers to investigate sequential patterns in marital interaction was Gottman (1979, 1980; Gottman et al., 1977), who investigated reciprocity in clinical and nonclinical couples. Gottman et al. (1977) found that clinical couples were more likely to reciprocate negative affect than were nonclinical couples. However, the findings for positive reciprocity were less clear cut. Although clinical couples showed greater positive reciprocity than did nonclinical couples at early lags, nonclinical couples displayed more positive reciprocity at later lags.

Support for greater negative affective reciprocity among distressed couples was also found by Margolin and Wampold (1981). In addition, distressed couples were found to exchange negative affect in a more contingent fashion than did nondistressed couples.

Using sequential analysis, Revenstorf, Vogel, Wegener, Hahlweg, and Schindler (1980) also investigated differences in affective reciprocity between distressed and nondistressed couples. German adaptation of the MICS was used to code the videotapes in this study. These researchers found that even over long sequences, distressed couples tended to engage in significantly more negative and less positive reciprocity than did nondistressed couples.

Findings are affected by how reciprocity is measured. For example, using "simultaneity-based" reciprocity, which measures similarities in proportions of behaviors between partners, Schaap (1984) found that nondistressed couples displayed higher rates of positive reciprocity and lower levels of negative reciprocity than when sequential analyses were used. As a matter of fact, no significant differences were found between distressed and nondistressed couples in their reciprocation of negative affect. However, the two groups did differ significantly in their use of positive affect. Initially, all couples were likely to reciprocate positive affect; at later lags, the reciprocation of positive affect was greater for the nondistressed couples.

In an effort to determine the consistency of his findings across high- and low-conflict tasks, Gottman (1980) examined reciprocity of affect among 19 clinical and 19 nonclinical couples. In all tasks used in this research, clinical couples were found to reciprocate more negative affect than did the nonclinical group. However, the two groups did not differ in positive reciprocity. Surprisingly, at later lags, clinical couples exceeded nonclinical couples in their display of positive reciprocity.

In a reanalysis of Gottman et al. (1976), Gottman (1979) found similar results using the talk table paradigm. Over all tasks used, negative reciprocity discriminated between clinical and nonclinical groups. Griffin and Crane (1986) used behavioral base rates to assess nonverbal reciprocity in 40 nondistressed couples. The experimental group had a significant increase in touches compared to a control group, suggesting that reciprocity patterns within couples may be predictable.

Comparison of Studies

Once again, as is true of studies measuring base rates of affect, comparing results is complicated by the same methodological issues discussed above. These are assignment, nature of tasks used, noncomparability of coding systems, and differences among sample groups.

Summary

If any conclusions can be drawn from the literature on nonverbal communication and marital satisfaction, it is that conclusions are difficult to make. Nondistressed couples seem to be better nonverbal communicators than are distressed couples. However, where the deficit lies in distressed couples is still open to debate.

In general, most studies found greater positive and neutral affect among nondistressed groups and greater negative affect among distressed groups. Although the difference in positive reciprocity of affect between the two groups is unclear, most studies have shown that distressed couples reciprocate more negative affect.

The confusion over differences in the display of affect and the reciprocation of affect between distressed and nondistressed couples may be a result of the subjective labeling of affect. How does one decide whether an affect is positive, negative, or neutral? Not only do different researchers group different emotions under different categories (Knapp, 1983) but also how they determine which emotions are positive, negative, or neutral is unclear. No agreed-upon system of categorization exists. To categorize an emotion, the context within which the emotion is displayed must be considered (L'Abate & Frey, 1981). To label an emotion neutral or negative, as Gottman (1979) and other researchers have done, implies that the emotion has no context. Actually, the use of neutral emotion in the CISS really means that the coders failed to understand the context within which the emotion was expressed.

Crying is a good example of how an emotion can be mislabeled. According to Gottman (1979), crying is a negative emotion. To the contrary, however, depending upon how it is used, crying can be a positive emotion. Crying may be a vital part of getting in touch with one's feelings or hurts. L'Abate (1983) believes that "It is at this time of grieving that we are at our best, that we have finally reached our humanness and vulnerability" (p. 102). Thus, it is the context in which crying takes place that determines its meaning. Crying because one is sharing hurt feelings is very different from crying to manipulate one's partner or when one is angry. These are three very different phenomena.

Similarly, in clinical work one finds that the same affect may have different meanings for males and females. For example, many women are socialized not to express anger. When they are angry they may shed tears. Most men, on the other hand, are socialized not to display hurt feelings. They often show anger when hurt. Although the emotional experience itself cannot be labeled, one can label the outward expression and the interpersonal consequence.

As important as nonverbal communication may be, a full understanding of this process must also take into account its verbal components. By ignoring the verbal dimensions, one misses the context as well as the interpersonal influence component of affective displays. Even when taking context into account, assigning negative or positive valences to behaviors still creates a problem. Inherent in such labeling is a judgment factor about the merits of a particular action, that is, as "good" or "bad." Labeling specific behaviors without consideration of the interactional context is inappropriate.

Although distressed couples may display more "negative" reciprocity, one must also ask how much negative affect is harmful in an intimate relationship. Most studies seem to demonstrate that some degree of negative reciprocity is present in all couples. It may well be, then, that some expression of negative affect is essential to all intimate relationships. To be considered psychologically healthy, a person should be in touch with all his or her emotions, including negative ones.

It can be said that couples who display no negative affect at all are not communicating effectively and honestly. If, as I have suggested (L'Abate, 1986), emotions are viewed on a continuum whose polar opposites are abusive apathy and creative conductivity with repetitive reactivity in the middle, a couple who display too much emotion (a reactive couple) may actually be functioning at a higher level than a couple who display no emotion at all (an apathetic couple). Thus, a couple who exhibit negative affect may be functioning at a higher level than a couple who display no negative affect at all.

For clinical purposes, it is less important to determine whether a couple's exchange system is high or low on negative reciprocity. The crucial issue for treatment is whether the spouses are able to decrease punishing and aversive reciprocal exchanges while increasing positive reciprocity, and whether the spouses are able to learn more constructive alternatives to problem solving and conflict negotiation. Another important issue to consider is whether there are optimal lines of negative reciprocity that do not effect marriages adversely.

Determining optimal levels of these behaviors could be investigated by studying negative reciprocity in happily married couples or in well-adjusted couples. This type of data would also eliminate the need for artifical division of couples into discrete groups (e.g., distressed and nondistressed). A continuum ranging from minimal to optimal negative reciprocity could result from this study.

In summary, future research must dispense with labeling, considering instead optimal levels for types of nonverbal affect, affect reciprocity, and encoding and decoding skills. In the assessment of affect, the context in which it occurs must also be considered. Such an approach necessitates that the therapist assess both verbal and nonverbal behaviors.

CONJOINT MARITAL TESTING

Conjoint marital testing is an area of relatively recent clinical interest. *Conjoint* signifies that the test is administered to both spouses, who work together on a specific task. In short, conjoint means simultaneous work on the same task.

Historical Background

Conjoint marital testing can be traced to 1963 when two researchers, Goodrich and Boomer (1963), developed a task to investigate conflict in marital dyads. Instead of relying on the spouses' reports of how they handled conflict, Goodrich and Boomer induced and quantified the conflict in a controlled experimental study. This work stimulated a new approach to investigating marital conflict resolution.

Goodrich and Boomer (1963) developed the Color Matching Test (CMT): Individual spouses match a colored square on separate displays and reach a joint decision about the best match. The couple is deceived into believing that their respective color displays are similarly numbered. Through the design of the test, the couple is led to disagree on the best match. Their attempts to resolve their supposedly dissimilar perceptions are assumed to represent the couple's general style of coping with and resolving ambiguities associated with differing perceptions.

The couples studied constituted two main groups: couples who considered only the alternatives presented by the experimenter and couples who tended to seek answers other than the colors on the easel. Couples differed in their readiness to commit to a decision as well as in the kind of decision they reached. Couples also differed in the amount of mutual esteem displayed.

The CMT assumes that (1) spouses' interactional styles are determined by the situation and by the behavior of the other spouse; (2) couples' styles can be compared by analyzing recordings of the actual behavior from a common reference point; and (3) spouses' interactional styles during experiments reflect how the spouse ordinarily handle conflicts (Glick & Gross, 1975).

Shortly after Goodrich and Boomer's original attempt, Bauman and Roman (1964) effectively used the Wechsler-Bellevue to investigate marital dominance. Constructs like dominance, hierarchy, power, and control had been considered important in understanding the etiology of dysfunctional interactions in couples and families. Bauman and Roman pioneered the use of individual tests in studying couples' interactional patterns. Their work stimulated other researchers who then made use of projective techniques to study marital interactions (Gentile, 1981; Klopfer, 1968; Levy & Epstein, 1964; Loveland, 1967; Loveland, Wynne, & Singer, 1963; Silbergeld & Manderscheid, 1976; Willi, 1969).

Objective Tests

When Bauman and Roman (1964) first administered the Wechsler-Bellevue to subjects and their spouses four kinds of data were generated: (1) individual test protocols; (2) a family or dyadic protocol, which represents a conjoint or group effort; (3) comparison data, that is, individuals' answers compared with answers from the entire group; and (4) data based upon behavioral observations.

The results showed a reliability (split half of .54) that was significant. Dominance was characterized as high or low, husband or wife, with a reliability of .76 for the husbands and .84 for the wives. As predicted, husbands dominated more than wives, the more competent individual (higher individual scorer) dominated the less competent individual, the nonpatient dominated the inpatient, and the test recorder dominated the nonrecorder. All these relationships were significant. However, because no significant differences could be shown within these relationships, no conclusions could be reached about the importance of one factor in comparison with the others. These results, however, could not be replicated by Reddy (1972).

The clinical implications are as follows:

(1) The showing of negative dominance is a specific, objective, and reliable demonstration of inefficient and often dysfunctional marital interactions.

(2) The authors claimed that the administration of the test is a good forum in which to confront resistant couples and to provide them with substantiating data (about their inappropriate behaviors), allowing them to accurately assess their strong and weak points.

The second point is useful clinically: Spouses are resistant to interventions that will require them to change patterns of interactions that are well established, well practiced, and well reinforced. A clinician using this administration can objectively demonstrate the "maladaptiveness" of a couple's interaction. Even the most resistant person will not be able to argue that he or she should be allowed to dominate when faced with evidence that the domination forces the couple to sacrifice efficiency.

One cannot help wondering whether dominance is a global trait, similar to the trait that may underlie Bauman and Roman's assumptions. They assumed that the interaction resulting from an intelligence test question is the same kind of domination that occurs in daily living. The father/husband may decide whose answer is used on a test but may have no say in how the children are raised or where they spend Saturday nights. Dominance is more complex than the authors lead us to believe.

Olson and Ryder (1970) developed a procedure similar to the CMT, the Inventory of Marital Conflicts (IMC), which consists of 18 short vignettes depicting common marital conflicts. Unknown to the respondents, some of the vignettes are altered so that one spouse receives a biased view of the vignette, a view that would lead to a clear decision about "rightness" or "wrongness." This technique ensures disagreement. The couple is asked to discuss each situation fully and answer the following questions: (1) Who is primarily responsible for the problem? (2) Is there a way to resolve the conflict? (3) Have you had a similar problem? (4) Have you known couples who have had a similar problem?

Two kinds of data are derived from this test. The first concerns the clinical relevance of these situations: Do the vignettes portray real-life difficulties that couples have? The results confirmed that the issues examined are real-life issues. The second kind of data is the *win score*, or which spouse's solution is mutually acceptable.

The split-half reliability of this procedure has been shown to be acceptable but not extremely high. On a 2-point scale (2 means that the husband always wins; 0 means that the wife always wins), the average score for 200 couples was 1.08, with a standard deviation of 1.06 and a range of 0 to 1.88. Once again (unfortunately), because no data (other than those reported) were given, neither validity nor reliability can be discussed in any meaningful manner.

An innovative approach to conjoint testing was developed by Ravich (1969), who based his work on game theory. Ravich devised a simulated game in which partners earn points. The Ravich Interpersonal Game/Test (RIG/T), also known as the "Train Game," consists of a toy railroad set with one common area of straight track; two barriers for the common track; two alternate route sections three times longer than the common stretch; a screen preventing each partner's view of the other's track; and two control panels. The control panels have switches that affect the train's speed and direction and a switch that operates the barrier (which prevents one's partner from using the common track).

Ravich (1969) believed that a couple's performance reveals much about a couple's *in vivo* interactions. Ravich found four main patterns of interaction for the more than 350 couples tested: competitive, alternating, dominant-submissive, and mixed (in systems terms—symmetrical, complementary, and parallel).

The author went on to explain the clinical implications of his classification system (e.g., alternating couples should learn that inequality of rewards is an acceptable outcome). The positive qualities of the Train Game are (1) it is a purely interactional measure that does not address intrapsychic processes, (2) it tends to minimize anxiety because it is a game, and (3) it does not require deception.

Liebowitz and Black (1974) replicated and extended but then disparaged

Ravich's work. They claimed that the test is not discriminating because an easily attainable maximizing solution is available, one that was used quite often with the subjects in their study (i.e., an alternating "after-you" approach). They also were unable to find any evidence for external validity of this measure. Kennedy (1976) also found that the RIG/T could not discriminate alcoholic from nonalcoholic marriages.

Summary

Interaction testing is expensive and time-consuming (especially the scoring). However, it provides the evaluator with real-life samples of a couple's interactional patterns.

At least four methodological issues need to be considered in evaluating the usefulness of interaction testing:

(1) Outcome testing relates to process observations.
(2) Most studies lacked external criteria to evaluate and document the main issues of construct and predictive validity.
(3) None of these studies solved the problem of unique couple style, which may defy quantification at this time; yet this needs to be addressed if data from interaction testing are going to be of any use in evaluation and intervention.
(4) Marital interactional patterns are related to individual styles, personality traits, and characteristics. This is also a theory-related issue that many of these studies did not consider.

MARITAL OBSERVATION CODING SYSTEMS AND MARITAL INTERACTION

The main purposes of observational coding systems are to describe marital interaction, to test hypotheses about distressed and nondistressed relationships, and to develop reliable and valid procedures for intervention and outcome evaluation.

Historical Background

Since their collaboration with Jay Haley in the early 1960s, Winter and Ferreira have remained in the forefront of research in marital and family interaction. Expanding on their early work concerning decision making in families, they began to investigate similar processes in married and unrelated (stranger) dyads.

One study (Winter, Ferreira, & Bowers, 1973), with 20 married and unrelated couples, examined the subjects' responses to a game task in which couples were required to reach a conjoint decision. The authors concluded that married couples show greater spontaneous agreement, are less polite, interrupt more, and exchange less information than do unrelated couples. In later studies (Ferreira and Winter, 1974; Winter & Ferreira, 1967, 1969b), it was found that overall spontaneous agreement was higher for normal couples than for clinical couples and synthetically matched couples.

Markman, Notarius, Stephen, and Smith (1981) found that distressed couples exhibited more negative behaviors and exchanged fewer positive behaviors than did nondistressed couples (Birchler et al., 1975; Gottman, 1979). They noted also that distressed couples are more likely to respond to coercive behaviors with countercoercive responses, which lead to reciprocal coercive escalations (Billings, 1979; Gottman, 1979). In addition, distressed couples were found to use fewer problem-solving statements (Vincent et al., 1975) and were more likely to interpret a spouse's behavior as negative rather than positive than did their nondistressed counterparts (Gottman, 1979).

Validity and Reliability

Although technical and analytical advances have made observational research easier to carry out, there are still a number of problems. The validity and reliability of many of the systems used in these studies are questionable and most summary codes have not been shown to reflect adequately the content codes they are supposed to represent. Finally, the putative validity of most coding systems has yet to be demonstrated (Markman, 1979).

In general, the reliability of coding systems has not been overly impressive, and many researchers have used the less stringent percentage-agreement method to establish reliability. Only Gottman (1979) and Wieder and Weiss (1980) have begun to apply more rigorous statistical procedures to assess reliability and generalizability of coding procedures.

Numerous studies (Gottman, 1979; Jacobson, 1978a, 1978b; McCarrick, Manderscheid, Silbergeld, & McIntyre, 1982; Turkewitz, 1977) have used coding systems to assess the effects of behavioral marital therapy and communications training. In general the coding systems used have been sensitive to changes in couple interaction. However, in at least one study (Turkewitz, 1977), self-report measures were found to be more sensitive to changes than was the coding system employed (MICS). Consequently, we have some evidence that coding systems may miss significant dimensions of couple interaction and satisfaction. Most observational coding systems focus on discrete behaviors. They do not measure interactions per se (Landy,

1988). Consequently, behavioral measures may show discriminant validity but do not offer evidence of construct validity.

Some improvements have been made in the procedures used in observational coding. The hand-held Datamyte recorders and Allred's sophisticated physiological sensors are just two of the numerous electronic devices now being used. In fact, it is now possible to code interaction *in vivo* on a keyboard and then transfer the information directly to a computer for analysis. Such a procedure greatly speeds the coding process.

Unfortunately, along with the increase in technology has come a comparable increase in cost. It has often been argued that the coding system approach to marital assessment is simply too costly in equipment and in time. This is a pragmatic consideration that cannot be ignored. Nevertheless, we hope that marital observation coding will continue to be used because very useful and reliable information about couple interaction has been gathered that can be used in work with distressed marriages.

Perhaps an increase in technology and a decrease in cost will one day enable marital therapists to routinely use these methods. Of course, that day may be long in coming. At this time, the status of marital observation coding systems can be said to be much like the NASA space program: It is very expensive, very exciting, and we hope that someday it will really pay off.

MAJOR CODING SYSTEMS

Interaction Process Analysis (IPA)

One of the earliest observational coding systems is the IPA. This instrument, developed by Bales (1950a & b, 1970) and his colleagues in the late 1940s, was originally designed to study small group behavior. (Another observational method, the Hill Interaction Matrix [Hill, 1971], was also developed to code small group behavior.)

The purpose of the IPA was to "discover the pattern of the system . . . by looking at the social system and not simply at the individual roles . . . [;] each act is part of an interaction system" (Bales, 1950a, p. 58). The basic unit of analysis is the *act*—"the single item of thought or the single item of behavior" (p. 37), including overt, skeletal, verbal, gestural, and expressive behaviors (provided that they can be coded with one score). The IPA has 12 basic category codes. Because coding requires the "reading in of content" (p. 6), it has been criticized for being highly subjective (Gottman, 1979).

Comparing the marginal distribution of the 12 categories, Heinicke & Bales (1953) computed a .86 overall interrater reliability. However, Waxler and Mishler (1965) noted that the scoring procedure (typescript, or tape and typescript) affects the distribution of one third of the acts in the categories. The comparison of different procedures yielded only a 55% agreement by Cohen's kappa. In addition, an act-by-act comparison, by the tape and transcript procedure, resulted in only a 43% kappa agreement.

In spite of the criticism, a modified form of the IPA has been used by a number of marital and family researchers (e.g., Russell, Bagarozzi, Atelano, and Morris, 1984; Strodtbeck, 1951; Mishler and Waxler, 1968; Winter and Ferreira, 1967).

Marital Interaction Coding System (MICS)

An extensive and well-researched device, the MICS is an observational coding system used by highly trained raters. It consists of 30 behavioral categories that can be combined to form six summary categories: (1) problem solving, (2) verbal positive, (3) nonverbal positive, (4) verbal negative, (5) nonverbal negative, and (6) neutral.

The MICS began as an observational system for use in homes of families with problem children. Later the coding system was used to study marital interaction (Patterson & Reid, 1970).

Interrater reliability figures, reported in ratio of agreements to disagreements, have been reported in the 80% range for the MICS (Bagarozzi, Bagarozzi, Anderson and Pollone, 1984; Wieder & Weiss, 1980). Jacobson, Ellwood, and Dallas (1981) have discussed reliability of the MISC in great detail. Validity of the MISC has been questioned by Margolin (1978a, 1978b), although some evidence for discriminant validity has been offered (Vincent et al., 1975). In general, findings are inconsistent (Haynes, Follingstad, & Sullivan, 1979). Therefore, the validity of the MICS still remains an empirical question.

Couple Interaction Scoring System (CISS)

The CISS was designed to "describe couple interactions in a variety of situations" (Markman et al., 1981). Codes were based on the MICS and on Olson and Ryder's (1972) Marital and Family Interaction Coding System (MFICS). Social exchange and communication theory provide the basic theoretical framework for the CISS.

Gottman (1979) and colleagues developed this empirically derived system. Behavioral codes were compiled and operationalized in accordance with data collected from the research literature having to do with marital and family studies, marital and family therapy, social learning theory, and developmental psychology. Each response is coded for content and affect so that any CISS content code can be paired with any affect code.

Borrowed from Sackett, Holm, Crowley, and Henkins (1979), Gottman used lag analysis in his work with the CISS. He selected one behavior as the criterion behavior and statistically computed the probabilities that other coded behaviors would follow the criterion behavior. Eventually, by treating all behaviors as the criterion behavior, he discovered not only which behaviors typically precede and follow each other but also he could determine where sequences began and ended (Gottman, 1979).

Interrater reliability for CISS codes is high and is essentially the same as for the MICS when traditional percentages of agreement–disagreement are computed. CISS generalizability coefficients for both content and affect codes range from 0.78 to 1.00 (Gottman, 1979).

Several CISS content codes have been found consistently to discriminate between distressed and nondistressed couples (feeling expression, mind reading, disagreement). CISS nonverbal codes alone have also discriminated between clinical and nonclinical couples (Gottman, 1979).

Concurrent validity was assessed by comparing CISS coding of an interaction with the couple's perception of their interaction. Couples who tended to perceive each other's message as positive were differentiated by the CISS codes as less rigidly structured and less prone to engage in negative reciprocity.

The CISS is the only system we were able to find that has been shown to have some predictive validity. Using the degree of positive impact of statements, as reported by each spouse, Markman (1979) was able to predict the degree of marital satisfaction in a 2-½-year follow-up evaluation of married couples.

Marital and Family Interaction Coding System (MFICS)

Olson and Ryder (1972) developed the MFICS to code verbal interactional patterns based on data generated from the IMC (Olson & Ryder, 1970). The basic unit of analysis in this system is the statement. The instrument was developed to code verbal behavior; the only nonverbal code used was "tone of voice."

Initially, 29 code categories were devised. To increase reliability, these were later reduced to 13. Three dimensions of interaction were coded: task leadership, conflict, and affect. Interobserver reliability for the 13 codes was .94. The average split-half reliability was .73 (Olson, 1981).

Validity data on the MFICS have yet to be presented. The MFICS can be used to code the interactions of two to eight people. It also offers important information about the power dimension of interactions.

Coding Scheme for Interpersonal Conflict (CSIC)

The CSIC was designed to "encompass the range and refinements in the events produced by couples faced with conflict-producing issues" (Raush, Barry, Hertel, & Swain, 1974, p. 112). It offers perhaps the most complex and conceptually richest analysis of conflictual interaction between spouses.

Raush (1965), who produced some of the earliest theoretical analyses of mutually conditioned behaviors in interactional sequences, was particularly interested in the study of constraint—the extent to which the "antecedent act of one person exerts control on the actions of another" (p. 487). Like Gottman's CISS, the CSIC is particularly suited to studying the controlling aspects of marital interaction. In addition, Raush is one of the few researchers to use psychodynamic constructs in his analyses of couple interaction.

The unit of analysis is the *act* or *statement* (as in the MFICS). There are 36 individual codes and six summary codes. Despite the fact that the system requires a good deal of inference, interobserver levels of agreement as high as 95% have been reported (Billings, 1979).

Content validity of the CSIC seems to be adequate, but there is no evidence that summary codes necessarily reflect individual codes. Billings (1979), using the CSIC, differentiated communication interactions between distressed and nondistressed couples engaged in Raush et al.'s (1974) Improvisational Scenes task, providing some data for discriminant validity. Gottman (1979) also found high levels of negative reciprocity in distressed couples, thus offering some evidence for concurrent validity.

The CSIC has proved to be a reliable instrument, one that is able to discern the more subtle inferential aspects of marital interaction.

Dyadic Interaction Coding System (DICS)

A "machine-aided method of collecting observational data on the interaction between two people" (Filsinger, 1981, p. 149), the DICS is based on the MICS, the CISS, and the MFICS. The particular theoretical constructs that influenced the design are derived from social learning theory.

The interactional data are coded directly into a hand-held keyboard, the Datamyte 900. This procedure had been used by Conger and McLeod (1977) to code family interaction. The coding unit is the *statement* (as in the CSIC and the MFICS). There are 21 individual codes: 19 *content* codes and 2 *structure* codes. There is no double coding of a behavior, but specific behaviors can be separately coded when they occur within the same *statement*.

There are two summary codes: *dysfunctional* and *facilitative*. Here again, no evidence was offered to support the assumption that summary codes accurately reflect the individual codes. Filsinger (1981) noted that the facilitative and dysfunctional codes had been significantly related to self-report measures of marital quality, thus providing some evidence for discriminant validity. Average interobserver agreement was found to be .77.

The strength of the DICS lies in its convenience. It allows for the direct coding of interaction while it occurs. Since observers have little or no time to reflect upon the choice of codes, reliability may suffer. An important consideration is the cost of training and of the Datamyte unit.

Relational Communication Coding System (RCCS)

The RCCS (Ericson & Rogers, 1973) was designed to "measure the control dimension of ongoing messages through which interactors reciprocally define their positions relative to one another . . . [and]to index the structure or form of conversation more than the content" (Rogers & Bagarozzi, 1983, p. 57). The codes draw heavily upon systems constructs developed by such researchers as Bateson (1972) and Haley (1964). One of the main purposes of the RCCS is to adequately operationalize and code *symmetrical* and *complementary* patterns of marital interaction.

The basic coding unit is the "message . . . each verbal intervention of each member in a conversation" (Rogers & Bagarozzi, 1983, p. 57). Each message is given a *speaker code* (first or second person), a *grammatical code*, and a *response code*. There are 5 grammatical codes (e.g., assertion, question) and 10 response codes (e.g., support, nonsupport). The message, coded in these categories, is then assigned a *control* dimension, which is inferred from the grammatical and response forms of the message. The three control codes are represented by arrows: (1) one up ($\uparrow$)—asserting one's own definition of rights; (2) one down ($\downarrow$)—accepting the other's definition of the relation; and (3) leveling ($\rightarrow$)—minimizing the issues of power and control.

The coders "combine control directions of one message with that of a contiguous message, thereby operationalizing . . . concepts of symmetry, complementarity, and transition" (Rogers & Bagarozzi, 1983, p. 69). Thus a matrix of three control dimensions generates nine cells, which designate different classes of transaction between spouses.

Four codes attempt to summarize interactions. *Domineeringness,* is defined as the percentage of one-up codes in the total messages. *Dominance* is a complementary transaction in which a one-up message is followed by a one-down response. *Submissiveness* and *submission* are the reverse of the control dimensions listed above. Two additional summary codes describe rigidity of interaction (*transactional redundancy*) and the regulation of distance between the couple.

Interobserver percentage agreement for the grammatical codes is .93. The reliability for the response code is .91. The total level of interobserver reliability reported is .86 (Ericson & Rogers, 1973).

Evidence of the discriminant validity of the instrument has come from Rogers-Millar and Millar (1979) and Courtright, Millar, Rogers and Bagarozzi (1990), who found that greater domineeringness levels for the wife were associated with "role strain" and decreased levels of marital satisfaction. The reverse was true when the husband was more domineering.

McCarrick et al. (1982) used the RCCS to measure the effects of brief marital group therapy. They found that for four of five couples therapy seemed to "enhance the flexibility of control patterns" (p. 3) in the relationship. However, the study was flawed by the absence of a control group and by the lack of clear evidence that a change in "transactional patterns" necessarily leads to an increase in marital adjustment.

Bernal and his coworkers (Bernal & Baker, 1979; Bernal & Golann, 1980) devised the *metacommunicational framework*, which uses Bateson's (1972) hypothesis that interpersonal communication is based on different levels of response and that each level affects the meaning of the others.

Using couples' self-reports of their interactions, Bernal and Baker (1979) and Bernal and Golann (1980) attempted to determine the "level" of communication. In an attempt to establish reliability of his system, he employed judges to code transcripts of couple interaction on four levels of communication (objective, individual, interactional, and contextual). The interrater reliability among the judges was .83.

All ratings of communication levels were determined by couples' self-reports. The RCCS has never been used solely as an observational tool for measuring couple interaction. The RCCS is a promising systems-oriented marital observation coding instrument, but much more empirical work needs to be done before it can be adapted as a clinical assessment aid.

Allred Interactional Analysis Code (AIAC)

Developed to "research the interaction between human subjects" (Allred, Harper, Wadham, & Wooley, 1981, p. 168), the AIAC uses a computer to gather and analyze data. The coding system is based on Adlerian constructs that discriminate different forms of couple communication. Two main summary codes—*vertical* (competitive) and *horizontal* (cooperative)—refer to classes of interpersonal behavior (similar to the one up (↑) and one down (↓) of Ericson & Rogers (1973).

The system uses 12 individual verbal codes, including 6 horizontal (e.g., disclose thoughts, negotiate), 5 vertical (e.g., solicit attention, bossing), and 1 *confusion* (neither vertical nor horizontal) code. There are also codes for nonverbal behavior (face and body movements); physiological sensors, attached to the body, assess variables such as pulse and temperature. During testing, subjects have consoles on which they can express covert feelings (sadness, happiness). All data are collected and analyzed by computer. The interobserver reliability coefficient for the verbal codes was .82 to .96, with a mean of .90 (Allred et al., 1981). No reliability has been reported for the nonverbal codes.

Although concurrent and content validity are adequate, summary codes were determined a priori. The AIAC is among the most comprehensive of the observational coding systems we have seen. However, like many of the procedures discussed in this chapter, further research is necessary to demonstrate construct validity and the reliability of interactional patterns over time.

Miscellaneous Coding Schemes

There are a number of coding systems that have been developed that the reader may wish to consider using. Some of these systems—for example, the Self-Disclosure Coding System (Vosk, Chelune, Sultan, Ogden, & Waring, 1981), the Communication Skills Test (Floyd & Markman, 1984), the Verbal Response Modes approach of Premo and Stiles (1983), and the Kategorien system for Pastnerschatliche Interaktion (Hahlweg, Reisner, Kohli, Vollmer, Schindler, & Revenstorf, 1984)—focus on communication between interactants. However, none of these systems is based upon a clear theory of marital behavior or marital relationships. The control focus is the communication patterns between spouses; essentially they can be considered atheoretical measures of communication skills.

Benjamin (1977) and her coworkers developed the Structured Analysis of Social Behavior classification scheme, a sophisticated, fairly comprehensive system used to categorize marital and family interactional patterns. However, it is extremely time-consuming and costly; the average clinician would be hard pressed to incorporate such an expensive assessment procedure in clinical practice.

CONCLUSION

Many of the coding schemes reviewed in this chapter leave much to be desired. For instance, one of their most glaring weaknesses lies in how they evaluate, or actually fail to evaluate, verbal, abusive, profane, and scurrilous language that may be the order of the day or the major form of communication in chaotic or grossly deviant families. This failure raises a whole host of questions about the sample of behavior evaluated by these schemes. It is possible that when couples or families are under observation they are going to put their best feet forward and monitor, modulate, and modify their linguistic behaviors, omitting socially unacceptable forms of communication. The fact that most, if not all, of these schemes have few, if any references to abusive behavior, whether verbal, physical, or sexual, makes one wonder about their comprehensiveness and usefulness, let alone their validity.

Another common pattern of verbal behavior that does not seem to be accounted for by these coding schemes refers to speed of reaction, reaction time, or reactivity on the respondents' part. How fast does one partner or family member answer, rebut, or repeat what the other partner or family member has just said or done in an oppositional (right-wrong, black-white, yes-no) dichotomous fashion? Repetitive reactivity may encompass up to 50% of most intimate relationships. Yet, these coding schemes fail to capture the real core and lore of family living. By failing to include persistent and frequent patterns of apathy and abuse, as well as repetitive reactivity, they should be reevaluated in terms of their validity and comprehensiveness.

REFERENCES

Allred, G. H., Harper, J. M., Wadham, R. A., & Wooley, B. H. (1981). Expanding the frontiers of interaction research. In E. E. Filsinger & R. A. Lewis (Eds.), *Assessing marriage* (pp. 160–170). Beverly Hills, CA: Sage.

Allred, G. H., & Kersey, F. L. (1977). The AIAC, a design for systematically analyzing marriage and family counseling: A progress report. *Journal of Marriage and Family Couseling, 3*, 17–25.

Argyle, M. (1975). *Bodily communication*. London: Methuen.

Bagarozzi, D. A. (1981). The symbolic meaning of behavioral exchanges in marital therapy. In A. S. Gurman (Ed.), *Questions and answers in the practice of family therapy* (pp. 173–177). New York: Brunner/Mazel.

Bagarozzi, D. A. (1982, November). *That was no lady, that was my wife: The role of cognitive constructs in the development of marital conflict and marital therapy.* Paper presented at grand rounds, Department of Psychiatry, Medical College of Georgia, Augusta.

Bagarozzi, D.A., Bagarozzi, J.I., Anderson, S.A., & Pollane, L. (1984). Premarital education and training sequence (PETS): A three year follow up of an experimental study. *Journal of Counseling and Development, 63*, 91–100.

Bagarozzi, D. A., & Anderson, S. A. (1989). *Personal, marital and family myths: Theoretical formulations and clinical strategies.* New York: Norton.

Bales, R. F. (1950a). *Interaction process analysis: A method for the study of small groups.* Cambridge, MA: Addison-Wesley.

Bales, R. F. (1950b). A set of categories for the analysis of small group interaction. *American Sociological Review, 15*, 257–263.

Bales, R. F. (1970). *Personality and interpersonal behavior.* New York: Holt, Rinehart & Winston.

Bateson, G. (1972). *Steps to an ecology of mind.* New York: Ballantine.

Bateson, G., & Jackson, D. (1964). Some varieties of pathogenic organization. *Journal for Research in Nervous and Mental Diseases, 42*, 270–283.

Bauman, G., & Roman, M. (1964). Interaction testing in the study of marital dominance. *Family Process, 5*, 230–242.

Bauman, G., Roman, M., Borello, J., & Metltzer, B. (1967). Interaction testing in the measurement of marital intelligence. *Journal of Abnormal Psychology, 72*, 489–495.

Benjamin, L. S. (1977). Structural analysis of a family in therapy. *Journal of Consulting and Clinical Psychology, 45,* 391–406.

Bernal, G., & Baker, J. (1979). Toward a metacommunicational framework of couple interactions. *Family Process, 18,* 293–301.

Bernal, G., & Golann, S. (1980). Couple interaction: A study of the punctuation process. *International Journal of Family Therapy, 2,* 47–55.

Billings, A. (1979). Conflict resolution in distressed and nondistressed marital couples. *Journal of Consulting and Clinical Psychology, 47,* 368–376.

Birchler, G. R., Weiss, R. L., & Vincent, J. P. (1975). A multimethod analysis of social reinforcement exchange between maritally distressed and nondistressed spouse and stranger dyads. *Journal of Personality and Social Psychology, 31,* 349–360.

Burgess, E. W., & Locke, H. J. (1945). *The family institution of companionship.* New York: American Books.

Burgess, E. W., Locke, H. J., & Thomas, M. M. (1971). *The family.* New York: Van Nostrand Reinhold.

Burgess, E. W., & Wallin, P. (1953). *Engagement and marriage.* Philadelphia: Lippincott.

Carter, R. D., & Thomas, E. J. (1973a). A case application of a signaling system (SAM) to the assessment and modification of selected problems of marital communication. *Behavior Therapy, 4,* 629–645.

Carter, R. D., & Thomas, E. J. (1973b). Modification of problematic marital communication using corrective feedback and instruction. *Behavior Therapy, 4,* 100–109.

Conger, R. D., & McLeod, D. (1977). Describing behavior in small groups with the Datamyte event recorder. *Behavior Research Methods of Instrumentation, 9,* 418–424.

Courtright, L. A., Millar, F. E., Rogers, L. E., & Bagarozzi, D. A. (1990). *Western Journal of Speech and Communication, 54,* 429–453.

Ericson, P. M., & Rogers, E. L. (1973). New procedures for analyzing relational communication. *Family Process, 12,* 295–267.

Ferreira, A. J., & Winter, W. D. (1965). Family interaction and decision-making. *Archives of General Psychiatry, 13,* 214–223.

Ferreira, A. J., & Winter, W. D. (1974). On the nature of marital relationships: Measurable differences in spontaneous agreement. *Family Process, 13,* 355–369.

Filsinger, E. E. (1981). The dyadic interaction scoring code. In E. E. Filsinger & R. A. Lewis (Eds.), *Assessing marriage* (pp. 148–159). Beverly Hills: Sage.

Floyd, F. J., & Markman, H. J. (1984). An economical observational measure of couples' communication skill. *Journal of Consulting and Clinical Psychology, 52,* 97–103.

Friedman, H. S. (1979). The concept of skill in nonverbal communication: Implications for understanding social interaction. In R. Rosenthal (Ed.), *Skill in nonverbal communication: Individual differences* (pp. 2–27). Cambridge, MA: Oelgeschagler, Gunn & Hain.

Gentile, S. (1981). Valori normativi del Rorschach comune (Willi) calcolati su un campione di 50 coppie. *Rivista di Psichiatria, 16,* 493–502.

Glick, B. R., & Gross, S. J. (1975). Marital interaction and marital conflict: Critical evaluation of current research strategies. *Journal of Marriage and the Family, 37,* 505–512.

Goodrich, D. W., & Boomer, D. S. (1963). Experimental assessment of modes of conflict resolution. *Family Process, 2,* 15–24.

Gottman, J. M. (1979). *Marital interaction: Experimental investigations.* New York: Academic Press.

Gottman, J. M. (1980). Consistency of nonverbal affect and affect reciprocity in marital interaction. *Journal of Consulting and Clinical Psychology, 48,* 711–717.

Gottman, J. M., Markman, H., & Notarius, C. (1977). The topography of marital conflict:

A sequential analysis of verbal and non-verbal behavior. *Journal of Marriage and the Family, 39*, 461–477.

Gottman, J. M., Notarius, C., Markman, H., Bank, S., Yoppi, B., & Rubin, M. E. (1976). Behavior exchange theory and marital decision making. *Journal of Personality and Social Psychology, 34*, 14–23.

Gottman, J. M., & Porterfield, A. L. (1981). Communicative competence in the nonverbal behavior of married couples. *Journal of Marriage and the Family, 43*, 817–825.

Griffin, K., & Patton, B. R. (1971). *Fundamentals of interpersonal communication.* New York: Harper & Row.

Griffin, W., & Crane, D. R. (1986). Nonverbal reciprocity in nondistressed marital partners: An examination of base rate change. *Journal of Marital and Family Therapy, 12*, 301–309.

Hahlweg, K., Reisner, L., Kohli, G., Vollmer, M., Schindler, L., & Revenstorf, D. (1984). Development and validity of a new system to analyze interpersonal communication: Kategoriensystem fur partnerschaftliche interaktion. In K. Hahlweg & N. S. Jacobson (Eds.), *Marital interaction: Analysis and modification* (pp. 182–197). New York: Guilford.

Haley, J. (1959a). The family of the schizophrenic: A model system. *Journal of Nervous and Mental Diseases, 129*, 357–374.

Haley, J. (1959b). An interactional description of schizophrenia. *Psychiatry, 22*, 321–322.

Haley, J. (1962). Family experiments: A new type of experimentation. *Family Process, 1*, 265–293.

Haley, J. (1964). Research on family patterns: An instrument measurement. *Family Process, 3*, 41–65.

Haynes, S. N., Follingstad, D. R., & Sullivan, J. C. (1979). Assessment of marital satisfaction and interaction. *Journal of Consulting and Clinical Psychology, 47*, 789–791.

Heinicke, C., & Bales, R. F. (1953). Developmental trends in the structure of small groups. *Sociometry, 16*, 7–38.

Hill, W. F. (1971). The Hill Interaction Matrix. *Personnel and Guidance Journal, 49*, 619–623.

Huntington, R. M. (1958). The personality-interaction approach to study of marital relationship. *Marriage and Family Living, 20*, 43–46.

Jacobson, N. S. (1978a). A review of the research on the effectiveness of marital therapy. In T. J. Paolino & B. S. McCrady (Eds.), *Marriage and marital therapy* (pp. 395–444). New York: Brunner/Mazel.

Jacobson, N. S. (1978b). Specific and nonspecific factors in the effectiveness of a behavioral approach to the treatment of marital discord. *Journal of Consulting and Clinical Psychology, 46*, 442–452.

Jacobson, N. S., Ellwood, R., & Dallas, M. (1981). The behavioral assessment of marital dysfunction. M. D. Barlow (Ed.), Behavioral Assessment of Adult Dysfunction. New York: Guilford.

Kahn, M. (1970). Nonverbal communication and marital satisfaction. *Family Process, 9*, 449–456.

Kenkel, W. F. (1959). Traditional family ideology and spousal roles in decision making. *Marriage and Family Living, 21*, 334–339.

Kenkel, W. F., & Hoffman, D. K. (1956). Real and conceived roles in family decision making. *Marriage and Family Living, 18*, 311–316.

Kennedy, D. L. (1976). Behavior of alcoholics and spouses in a simulation game situation. *Journal of Nervous and Mental Diseases, 162*, 23–34.

Klopfer, W. G. (1968). Discussion: The resurrection of the Rorschach as consensus. *Journal of Projective Techniques, 32*, 357.

Knapp, M. L. (1983). Dyadic relationship development. In J. M. Wiemann & R. P. Harrison (Eds.), *Nonverbal interaction* (pp. 179–207). Beverly Hills: Sage.

Kniskern, D., & Gurman, A. S. (1983). Future directions for family therapy research. In D. A. Bagarozzi, A. P. Jurich, & R. W. Jackson (Eds.), *Marital and family therapy: New perspectives in theory, research and practice* (pp. 209–235). New York: Human Sciences.

Komisar, D. D. (1949). A marriage problem story completion test. *Journal of Consulting Psychology, 13,* 403–406.

L'Abate, L. (1983). Intimacy is sharing hurt feelings: A reply to David Mace. In L. L'Abate (Ed.), *Family psychology: Theory, therapy and training* (pp. 101–122). Washington, DC: University Press of America. (Reprinted from *Journal of Marriage and Family Counseling,* 1977, *3,* 13–16.)

L'Abate, L. (1985). Descriptive and explanatory levels in family therapy: Distance, defeats, and dependence. In L. L'Abate (Ed.), *Handbook of family psychology and therapy* (pp. 1218–1248). Pacific Grove, CA: Brooks/Cole.

L'Abate, L. (1986). *Systematic family therapy.* New York: Brunner/Mazel.

L'Abate, L., & Frey, J. (1981). The E-R-A model: The role of feelings in family therapy reconsidered: Implications for a classification of theories of family therapy. *Journal of Marital and Family Therapy, 7,* 143–150. (Reprinted in L. L'Abate [Ed.] [1983], *Family psychology: Theory, therapy and training* [pp. 125–141]. Washington, DC: University Press of America.)

L'Abate, L., & McHenry, S. (1983). *Handbook of marital interventions.* New York: Grune & Stratton.

Landy, F. J. (1988). Stamp collecting versus science: Validation as hypothesis testing. *American Psychologist, 41,* 1183–1193.

Levy, J., & Epstein, N. B. (1964). An application of the Rorschach test in family investigation. *Family Process, 3,* 344–376.

Lewis, R. A., & Spanier, G. B. (1979). Theorizing about the quality and stability of marriage. In W. R. Burr, R. Hill, F. I. Nye, & I. L. Reiss (Eds.), *Contemporary theories about the family: General theories/theoretical orientations* (Vol. 1, pp. 268–294). New York: Free Press.

Liebowitz, B., & Black, M. (1974). The structure of the Ravich Interpersonal Game/Test. *Family Process, 13,* 169–183.

Loveland, N. (1967). The relation Rorschach: A technique for studying interaction. *Journal of Nervous and Mental Diseases, 145,* 93–105.

Loveland, N. T., Wynne, L. C., & Singer, M. T. (1963). The family Rorschach: A new method for studying family interaction. *Family Process, 2,* 187–215.

Margolin, G. (1978a). A multilevel approach to the assessment of communication positiveness in distressed marital couples. *International Journal of Family Counseling, 6,* 81–89.

Margolin, G. (1978b). Relationships among marital assessment procedures: A correlational study. *Journal of Consulting and Clinical Psychology, 46,* 1556–1558.

Margolin, G., & Wampold, B. E. (1981). Sequential analysis of conflict and accord in distressed and nondistressed marital partners. *Journal of Consulting and Clinical Psychology, 49,* 554–567.

Markman, H. J. (1979). The application of a behavioral model of marriage in predicting relationship satisfaction of couples planning marriage. *Journal of Consulting and Clinical Psychology, 4,* 743–749.

Markman, H. J., Notarius, C. I., Stephen, T., & Smith, R. J. (1981). Behavioral observation systems for couples: The current status. In E. E. Filsinger & R. A. Lewis (Eds.), *Assessing marriage* (pp. 234–262). Beverly Hills: Sage.

McCarrick, A. K., Manderscheid, R. W., Silbergeld, S., & McIntyre, J. J. (1982). Control patterns in dyadic systems: Marital group psychotherapy as a change agent. *American Journal of Family Therapy, 10,* 3–14.

Mehrabian, A. (1972). *Nonverbal communication.* Chicago: Aldine-Atherton.

Mehrabian, A. (1976). *Public places and private spaces*. New York: Basic Books.

Mishler, E. G., & Waxler, N. E. (1968). *Family process and schizophrenia*. New York: Wiley.

Navran, L. (1967). Communication and adjustment in marriage. *Family Process, 6*, 173–184.

Noller, P. (1980a). Gaze in married couples. *Journal of Nonverbal Behavior, 5*, 115–129.

Noller, P. (1980b). Misunderstanding in marital communication: A study of couples' nonverbal communication. *Journal of Personality and Social Psychology, 39*, 1135–1148.

Noller, P. (1981). Gender and marital adjustment level of differences in decoding messages from spouses and strangers. *Journal of Personality and Social Psychology, 41*, 272–278.

Noller, P. (1982). Channel consistency and inconsistency in the communications of married couples. *Journal of Personality and Social Psychology, 43*, 732–741.

Noller, P. (1984). *Nonverbal communication and marital interaction*. Oxford: Pergamon.

Notarius, C. I., Markman, H. J., & Gottman, J. M. (1983). Couple interaction scoring system: Clinical implications. In E. E. Filsinger (Ed.), *Marriage and family assessment: A sourcebook for family therapy* (pp. 117–136). Beverly Hills: Sage.

Olson, D. H. (1969). The measurement of family power by self-report and behavioral methods. *Journal of Marriage and the Family, 31*, 545–550.

Olson, D. H. (1981). Family typologies: Bridging family research and family therapy. In E. E. Filsinger & R. A. Lewis (Eds.), *Assessing marriage* (pp. 74–89). Beverly Hills: Sage.

Olson, D. H., & Ryder, R. G. (1970). Inventory of Marital Conflicts (IMC): An experimental interaction procedure. *Journal of Marriage and the Family, 32*, 443–448.

Olson, D. H., & Ryder, R. G. (1972). *Marital and Family Interaction Coding System (MFICS)*. Unpublished manuscript, University of Minnesota, St. Paul.

Patterson, G. R., & Reid, J. B. (1970). Reciprocity and coercion: Two facets of social systems. In C. Neuringer & J. Michael (Eds.), *Behavior modification in clinical psychology* (pp. 133–177). New York: Appleton-Century-Crofts.

Premo, B. E., & Stiles, W. B. (1983). Familiarity in verbal interactions of married couples versus strangers. *Journal of Social and Clinical Psychology, 1*, 209–230.

Raush, H. L. (1965). Interaction sequences. *Journal of Personality and Social Psychology, 2*, 487–499.

Raush, H. L., Barry, W. A., Hertel, R. K., & Swain, M. A. (1974). *Communication, conflict, and marriage*. San Francisco: Jossey-Bass.

Raush, H. L., Greif, A., & Nugent, J. (1979). Communication in couples' families. In W. R. Burr, R. Hill, E. I. Nye, & I. L. Reiss (Eds.), *Contemporary theories about the family: Vol. 1. Research-based theories* (pp. 468–489). New York: Free Press.

Ravich, R. A. (1969). The use of an interpersonal game test in conjoint marital psychotherapy. *American Journal of Psychotherapy, 23*, 217–229.

Ravich, R. A., Deutsch, M., & Brown, B. (1966). An experimental study of marital discord and decision-making. *Psychiatric Research Reports, 20*, 91–96.

Reddy, M. J. (1972). Interaction testing in the study of marital disturbance. Ohio State University: *Dissertation Abstracts International, 32*, 6659–6660.

Revenstorf, D., Vogel, B., Wegener, C., Hahlweg, K., & Schindler, L. (1980). Escalation phenomena in interaction sequences: An empirical comparison of distressed and nondistressed couples. *Behavioral Analysis and Modification, 4*, 97–115.

Rogers, L. E., & Bagarozzi, D. A. (1983). An overview of relational communication and implications for therapy. In D. A. Bagarozzi, A. P. Jurich, & R. W. Jackson (Eds.), *Marital and family therapy: New perspectives in theory, research and practice* (pp. 48–78). New York: Human Sciences.

Rogers-Millar, E. L., & Millar, F. E. (1979). Domineeringness and domination: A transactional view. *Human Communication Research, 5*, 238–246.

Rubin, M. E. (1977). Differences between distressed and nondistressed couples in verbal and nonverbal communication codes (Doctoral dissertation, Indiana University, 1977). *Dissertation Abstracts International, 38,* 1902B.

Russell, C., Bagarozzi, D. A., Atelano, R. B., & Morris, J.E. (1984). A comparison of two approaches to marital enrichment: Minnesota Couples Communication Program and structural behavior and change contracting. *American Journal of Family Therapy, 12,* 13–25.

Ryder, R. (1968). Husband-wife dyads versus married strangers. *Family Process, 7,* 233–238.

Ryder, R., & Goodrich, D. W. (1966). Married couples' responses to disagreement. *Family Process, 5,* 30–42.

Sackett, G. P., Holm, R., Crowley, C., & Henkins, A. (1979). A FORTRAN program for lag sequential analysis of contingency and cyclicity in behavioral interaction data. *Behavior, Research Methods & Instrumentation, 85,* 6–17.

Santa-Barbara, J., & Epstein, N. B. (1974). Conflict behavior in clinical families: Preasymtotic interactions and stable outcomes. *Behavioral Science, 19,* 100–110.

Schaap, C. (1984). A comparison of the interaction of distressed and nondistressed married couples in a laboratory situation: Literature survey, methodological issues and an empirical investigation. In K. Hahlweg & N. S. Jacobson (Eds.), *Marital interaction: Analysis and modification* (pp. 133–158). New York: Guilford.

Silbergeld, S., & Manderscheid, R.W. (1976). Dyadic free association. *Psychological Reports, 39,* 423–426.

Speer, D. C. (1972). Marital dysfunctionality and two-person non-zero-sum game behavior: Cumulative monadic measures. *Journal of Personality and Social Psychology, 21,* 18–24.

Strodtbeck, F. L. (1951). Husband-wife interaction over revealed differences. *American Sociological Review, 16,* 468–473.

Turkewitz, H. A. (1977). *A comparative study of behavioral marital therapy and communication therapy.* Unpublished doctoral dissertation, State University of New York at Stony Brook.

Vincent, J. P., Weiss, R. L., & Birchler, G. R. (1975). A behavioral analysis of problem solving in distressed and nondistressed married and stranger dyads. *Behavior Therapy, 6,* 475–487.

Vosk, B. N., Chelune, G. J., Sultan, F. E., Ogden, J. K., & Waring, E. M. (1981, March). *Differences in self-disclosure patterns in clinical and nonclinical couples.* Paper read at the annual meeting of the Southeastern Psychological Association, Atlanta.

Waxler, N. E., & Mishler, E. G. (1965). Scoring and reliability problems in interaction process analysis: A methodological note. *Sociometry, 29,* 32–49.

Weiss, R. L., & Summers, K. J. (1983). Marital Interaction Coding System—III. In E. E. Filsinger (Ed.), *Marriage and family assessment: A sourcebook for family therapy* (pp. 85–115). Beverly Hills: Sage.

Wieder, G. B., & Weiss, R. L. (1980). Generalizability theory and the coding of marital interactions. *Journal of Consulting and Clinical Psychology, 48,* 469–477.

Willi, J. (1969). Rorschach testing of partner relationships. *Family Process, 8,* 64–78.

Winter, W. D., & Ferreira, A. J. (1967). Interaction process analysis of family decision making. *Family Process, 6,* 155–172.

Winter, W. D., & Ferreira, A. J. (Eds.). (1969a). *Research in family interaction: Readings and commentary.* Palo Alto, CA: Science and Behavior Books.

Winter, W. D., & Ferreira, A. J. (1969b). Taking time as an index of intrafamilial similarity in normal and abnormal families. *Journal of Abnormal Psychology, 74,* 574–575.

Winter, W. D., Ferreira, A. J., & Bowers, N. (1973). Decision-making in married and unrelated couples. *Family Process, 12,* 83–94.

4

Behavioral Measures of Marital Interaction

In this chapter we review the main self-report measures that have been developed by behavioral marital therapists.

Jacobson and Margolin (1979), who typify behavioral marital therapists, believe that behavioral assessment must do the following: (1) describe the problems in the relationship, (2) identify variables that control the problem behaviors, (3) help the therapist select appropriate therapeutic interventions, and (4) help the therapist recognize when the intervention has been effective. Thus, assessment is seen as an integral part of therapy itself. A thorough assessment is essential to the development of effective and efficient treatment, and several objectives must be met to achieve these goals.

Assessment should examine discrete, observable behaviors. The problem behavior must be carefully defined, and global concepts must acquire behavioral referents. A thorough description of the problem behaviors can be obtained from the SORC (Stimulus-Organismic-Response-Consequences) analysis (Goldfried & Sprafkin, 1974). Here the following components are examined: (1) stimulus variables, which elicit or set the stage for the target behavior; (2) organismic variables, which act as mediating factors (cognitive and psychological) to a person's overt behaviors; (3) response variables, which are the specific samples of the maladaptive responses; and (4) consequent variables, which are changes in the environment that follow the response variables and affect their frequency. Each variable can be measured along three dimensions: (1) frequency, (2) duration, and (3) intensity.

According to behavior therapists, assessment should have a broad basis. Therefore, a wide range of couple interactions should be assessed so that the therapist obtains a detailed analysis that includes a couple's strengths and weaknesses. The primary reason for the wide-range approach is that spouses typically are not the most qualified judges of their own marital functioning: They tend to identify problems from a narrow perspective and have difficulty identifying behaviors that would enhance their relationship. Another reason for the broad-based approach is its therapeutic effect: It requires couples to look at their relationships in new ways since they are asked to respond to unanticipated questions.

More recently, sociobehavioral clinicians have begun to consider cognitive processes in marital and family assessments. Cognitions, which can take the form of assumptions; attributions; evaluations of the self, mate, or children; and attitudes about the quality of these relationships, can be viewed as internal responses that are part of a behavioral response chain. These cognitions are considered to be legitimate targets for modification since they often serve as antecedent stimulus cues for overt behavioral responses between spouses.

TYPES OF BEHAVIORAL ASSESSMENT

The two basic types of behavioral assessment are direct and indirect methods (Cone, 1978). Direct assessment methods require observations in natural environments, in analogue situations, and by self-monitoring (i.e., self-observations). Indirect assessment methods include interviews, self-reports, and ratings by others. In direct behavioral marital assessment, only the interactional coding systems (Gottman, 1979) have been systematized and researched well enough to provide measures of reliability and validity. (The interactional coding systems are evaluated in Chapter 3). Of the indirect behavioral marital assessment techniques, only the written self-report questionnaires and checklists have adequate reliability and validity measures (see Self-Report Questionnaires section to follow).

There are several advantages and several disadvantages both to self-report and to direct observational (interactional coding systems) procedures. The advantages of the self-report questionnaires are that they have face validity; they are inexpensive; they are quick and easy to administer, score, and interpret; and they are useful in collecting data too personal for direct observation. Their disadvantage is that the data collected may be biased and reactive, thus decreasing reliability and validity. Direct observational methods have the advantages of high reliability and completeness; however, they are very expensive and time-consuming. Nevertheless, because of social desirability, observers can affect reactions and thus affect reliability and validity.

Four interactional approaches form the basis of behavioral marital assessment (Margolin & Jacobson, 1981). These four approaches are: exchange theory, coercion theory, systems theory, and social learning theory. Some of the main assessment devices derived from these interactional approaches are reviewed below.

Self-Report Questionnaires

Spouse Observation Checklist (SOC)

Developed by the Oregon Research Group, the SOC (Patterson, 1976; Weiss, Hops, & Patterson, 1973; Weiss & Margolin, 1977) consists of 400 items designed to assess pleasing and displeasing behaviors in 12 areas of married life. These are companionship, affection, consideration, sex, communication process, couple activities, household management, financial decision making, employment and education, child rearing, personal habits, and self and spouse independence. The SOC was intended to obtain repeated measures of a couple's daily interaction. Spouses report about their own behavior as well as the behavior of their mates. Before retiring, each spouse completes the SOC.

In spite of its potential for reactivity, the SOC has shown little evidence of this occurrence. Two studies indicated no changes in please and displease frequencies over a 2-week period (Wills, Weiss, & Patterson, 1974; Robinson & Price, 1980).

Validity of the SOC has been addressed in several studies. Construct validity was offered by Birchler, Weiss, and Vincent (1975), who found that distressed couples had significantly fewer pleases and significantly more displeases than did nondistressed couples. Construct validity was also shown by Christensen and Nies (1980). Evidence for criterion-related validity has also been demonstrated (Margolin & Weiss, 1978; Patterson, Hops, & Weiss, 1974; Weiss et al., 1973).

Marital Status Inventory (MSI)

A 14-item true/false questionnaire, the MSI (Weiss & Cerreto, 1980) measures the degree to which spouses think about and behave in ways that may lead to separation and divorce. The following are examples of items on the scale.

(1) I have occasionally thought of divorce . . . (Item 1).
(2) I have discussed the question of divorce with someone other than my spouse . . . (Item 4).
(3) My spouse and I have separated . . . (Item 8).
(4) I have filed for divorce . . . (Item 14).

Weiss and Cerreto (1980) offered some initial data for reliability and validity.

Marital Happiness Scale (MHS)

A measure of the current level of happiness in a marital relationship, the MHS (Azrin, Naster, & Jones, 1973) is made up of 10 Likert-type items. Like the SOC, spouses are asked to complete the MHS before retiring each evening. The MHS has been shown to be sensitive to pre- and posttherapy change.

Area of Change Questionnaire (ACQ)

Adopted from the Willingness to Change Scale (Weiss et al., 1973), the ACQ assesses the amount of change spouses desire from each other in 34 areas of marital interaction (Patterson, 1976; Weiss & Birchler, 1975; Weiss & Perry, 1979). The ACQ differs from other brief, easily administered self-report measures by virtue of its precision in assessing specific behaviors. Discriminant validity has been demonstrated. The ACQ was able to discriminate among distressed and nondistressed couples (Birchler & Webb, 1977). The ACQ was also shown to correlate highly with other measures of marital adjustment, for example, the Marital Adjustment Scale (Margolin & Wampold, 1981; Weiss et al., 1973).

Mead and Vatcher (1985) have questioned whether the ACQ covers a sufficient range of problems, as claimed by its originators (Weiss & Birchler, 1975; Margolin, Talovic, & Weinstein, 1983). Mead and Vatcher (1985) were not able to replicate the earlier work done by those who constructed the measure. Only 13 of the original 29 categories could be reproduced through factor analyses.

Marital Precounseling Inventory (MPI)

Actually an assessment package, the MPI combines 13 separate scales (Stuart, 1980; Stuart & Stuart, 1980). Information is collected in nine target areas: identification of target problems, common interests, satisfaction with communication, rules for decision making, reinforcement power, general satisfaction, optimism about the future, positive aspects of spouse's behaviors, and resources for change. The MPI is used in two ways: (1) to identify specific behavioral changes and (2) to determine reinforcers and resources in the marriage.

Stuart described three purposes of the MPI: (1) It provides clients with socialization into therapy by directing their observations toward positive elements of their own and the spouse's behaviors; (2) It provides highly organized, comprehensive data relevant to therapeutic goals; and (3) It provides the therapist and the clients with a periodic evaluation of therapeutic goals.

Discriminant validity has been presented for only 2 of the 13 subscales, that is, Decision Making and General Satisfaction (Stuart & Stuart, 1973).

Marital Activities Inventory (MAI)

The MAI elicits information about how spouses distribute their time (alone, together, or with others outside the relationship) and how they would like to change the time distributions (Birchler et al., 1975; Weiss et al., 1973). Each spouse records social interactions and is asked to rate the frequency of recreational events.

The MAI is used to assess discrepancies between spouses' expectations. For example, a spouse expects his or her mate to provide reinforcement, while the partner expects to get most of his or her recreational needs met through independent activities. Birchler and Webb (1977) and Vincent, Weiss, and Birchler (1975) presented some data in support of discriminant validity (distressed versus nondistressed couples).

Feelings Toward Spouse Questionnaire (FTSQ)

Turkewitz and O'Leary (1975) developed the FTSQ, an 18-item questionnaire that evaluates the emotional quality of the marital relationship. The FTSQ assesses feelings that may not be communicated directly by spouses. Each spouse is asked to rate (on a 5-point Likert-type scale) frequency of feelings—for example, How often do you look forward to being alone with your spouse? How often do you think about particularly good experiences that you and your spouse have shared? Turkewitz and O'Leary (1975) reported adequate test-retest reliability and scores were shown to correlate significantly with the revised Locke-Wallace (Locke & Wallace, 1959). They also offered some data in support of predictive validity.

Goal Attainment Scaling (GAS)

The GAS has been used for assessment in behavioral marital therapy (Stuart, 1980) and in a variety of other settings. The GAS is a system for individualizing goals for each client instead of using a uniform set of criteria for all clients (Kiresuk & Sherman, 1968; Woodward, Santa Barbara, Lewis, & Epstein, 1978). With the GAS, therapists can construct specific scales to measure change that is specifically tailored for a particular couple.

Goals are identified during the initial interviews and attainments can be evaluated periodically and at the end of treatment. Each goal is behaviorally specified and attainment criteria are outlined. Although GAS has been used in work with individuals (Kiresuk & Sherman, 1977), no data are available for the use of GAS with couples.

Verbal Problem Checklist (VPC)

Thomas and his associates (Thomas, Walter, & O'Flaherty, 1974) developed the VPC, which contains guidelines that a clinician can use in surveying important aspects of couples communication. The VPC, comprising 49 categories (carefully defined) of verbal behavior, is a comprehensive catalog for the identification of verbal responses.

Spousal Inventory of Desired Changes and Relationship Barriers (SIDCARB)

Bagarozzi and his associates (Bagarozzi, 1983; Bagarozzi & Atilano, 1982; Bagarozzi & Pollane, 1983) have developed the SIDCARB, a 24-item self-report questionnaire using a 7-point Likert-type scale. Designed to gain the spouse's perception of the *conjugal exchange process*, the instrument measures the desired level of behavior change by spouse, commitment the willingness to separate or divorce, and the barriers to separation or divorce. A comparison of the scores of husbands and wives is used to examine relative power and influence in the relationship with respect to calling an end to the marriage.

To help spouses identify 10 areas of exchange where inequities might exist, the investigators asked respondents to indicate the degree to which changes were desired in expressive and in instrumental realms of exchange. To assess commitment, the investigators asked respondents to answer questions about commitment to the marriage, thoughts concerning separation and divorce, willingness to separate and divorce if equity could not be restored, and the degree to which they were willing to change their own behavior to improve the marriage. Finally, spouses were asked to evaluate the strength of the barriers that they believed would prevent their terminating an unsatisfactory marriage.

The psychometric properties of SIDCARB were assessed in two studies. Cronbach's alpha for the three factors ranged from .74 to .86 in the initial study and from .74 to .90 in the replication study. *T* tests were also conducted to determine whether significant differences existed between the responses of the husbands and the wives. No significant differences were reported.

This instrument, which came out of a social learning-behavioral philosophy, could also be used to measure the relative importance of some of the priorities stressed by L'Abate (1986): self, marriage, children, in-laws, work, friends, and leisure. The SIDCARB yields information that can also be useful to structural marital and family therapists.

Cognitive Measures

Although many of the self-report measures described in this chapter could be included in the next two chapters, we review them here because of their cognitive orientation and their close alliance to behavioral measures and to what has been called cognitive-behavioral marital therapy (Jacobson, 1984). In this section, we deal with instruments that reflect a clear cognitive bias.

Epstein and Eidelson (1981) administered to 47 clinical couples a battery composed of the following instruments: (1) Irrational Beliefs, (2) Relationship Beliefs Inventory (RBI), (3) the Locke-Wallace MAT, and (4) Therapy Goals and Expectations. As hypothesized, couples' unrealistic beliefs, especially those concerning their relationships, were negatively correlated with their estimate of improvement in therapy, desire to improve rather than terminate the relationship, preference for marital rather than individually oriented treatment, and overall marital satisfaction. The results were interpreted as supporting the importance of cognitive factors. The major contributor in this area has been Epstein (1985), who, in stressing the importance of cognitive factors in marital dysfunctionality, suggested that marital therapy should modify unrealistic expectations, correct faulty attributions, and use self-instructional procedures to decrease destructive interactions.

In the same vein, Epstein, Pretzer, and Fleming (1987) examined multidimensionally the extent to which dysfunctional cognitive patterns concerning marital relationships account for the link between self-report measures of marital communication and marital distress. A total of 156 couples participated in this study. Couples were defined as distressed if they had sought marital therapy or had been referred for marital evaluation and scored below 100 on Spanier's DAS. Volunteers who were not in therapy and who scored above 100 on the DAS were classified as nondistressed. The subjects answered the following questionnaires: (1) the VPC (Thomas et al., 1974), (2) the DAS, (3) the Rational Beliefs Inventory (RBI) (Eidelson & Epstein, 1982), and (4) the Marital Attitude Survey.

Scores on the VPC were found to be closely related to scores on the DAS, as well as to scores on the RBI and the Marital Attitude Survey. Cognitive measures accounted for a major proportion of the variance shared by the VPC and the DAS. A factor analysis of the VPC revealed three independent factors that accounted for 90.5% of the variance and were differentially related to the other measures of marital distress: (1) criticism/ defensiveness, (2) withdrawal, and (3) dominance. Again, the authors interpreted their results in terms of the importance of cognitive variables. Note, however, that none of these studies or the studies measuring behavioral factors included affective factors (rather like claiming to fish for bass with a lure for trout and then claiming that bass were not there!).

Fincham (1985) originally found that distressed couples, as most clinicians know well, blamed their spouses and their relationships for their difficulties, attributing more negative attitudes to their spouses and avoiding assuming responsibility for themselves. This process of externalization was further supported by Fincham and his coworkers (Fincham, Beach, & Nelson, 1987), who studied the role of attribution processes in 40 distressed and 40 nondistressed couples. They were administered the Marital Attribution Style Questionnaire (MASQ), which is based on the Feelings Questionnaire, developed by O'Leary, Fincham, and Turkewitz (1983).

The MASQ consists of ratings concerning the causes of positive and negative partner behaviors, making attributions for who was responsible for the behaviors, indicating the impact of these behaviors, and specifying the responses to these behaviors. Distressed couples saw the causes of negative partner behaviors as global and more negative in intent, more selfishly motivated and blameworthy, than did the nondistressed couples. An inverse pattern of results was obtained for positive behaviors: Only responsibility attributions predicted the affective impact and intended responses to the behavior. Attributions, therefore, are a product of cognitive factors that need to be considered in the process of therapy.

CONCLUSION

This chapter has described behavioral methods of evaluating marriage quality. The empirical approach, typically advocated by behavioral marriage therapists, assumes that all these procedures will be subjected to continual and rigorous checking and rechecking for validity and reliability.

REFERENCES

Azrin, N. H., Naster, B. M., & Jones, R. (1973). Reciprocity counseling: A rapid learning-based procedure for marital counseling. *Behavior Research and Therapy, 11,* 365–382.

Bagarozzi, D. A. (1983). Methodological developments in measuring social exchange perceptions in marital dyads: SIDCARB. A new tool for clinical intervention. In D. A. Bagarozzi, A. P. Jurich, & R. W. Jackson (Eds.), *Marital and family therapy: New perspectives in theory, research and practice* (pp. 79–104). New York: Human Sciences.

Bagarozzi, D. A., & Atilano, R. B. (1982). SIDCARB: A clinical tool for rapid assessment of social exchange inequities and relationship barriers. *Journal of Sex and Marital Therapy, 8,* 325–344.

Bagarozzi, D. A., & Pollane, L. (1983). A replication and validation of the Spousal Inventory of Desired Changes and Relationship Barriers (SIDCARB): Elaborations on diagnostic and clinical utilization. *Journal of Sex and Marital Therapy, 9,* 303–315.

Birchler, G. R., & Webb, L. J. (1977). Discriminating interaction behaviors in happy and unhappy marriages. *Journal of Consulting and Clinical Psychology, 45,* 494–495.

Birchler, G. R., Weiss, R. L., & Vincent, J. P. (1975). A multimethod analysis of social reinforcement exchange between maritally distressed and nondistressed spouse and stranger dyads. *Journal of Personality and Social Psychology, 31,* 349–360.

Christensen, A., & Nies, D. (1980). The Spouse Observation Checklist: Empirical analysis and critique. *American Journal of Family Therapy, 8,* 69–79.

Cone, J. D. (1978). The Behavioral Assessment Grid (BAG): A conceptual framework and a taxonomy. *Behavior Therapy, 9,* 882–888.

Eidelson, R. J., & Epstein, N. (1982). Cognition and relationship maladjustment: Development of a measure of dysfunctional relationship beliefs. *Journal of Consulting and Clinical Psychology, 50,* 715–720.

Epstein, N. (1985). Depression and marital dysfunction: Cognitive and behavioral linkages. *International Journal of Mental Health, 13,* 86–104.

Epstein, N., & Eidelson, R. J. (1981). Unrealistic beliefs of clinical couples: Their relationship to expectations, goals and satisfaction. *American Journal of Family Therapy, 9,* 13–22.

Epstein, N., Pretzer, J. L., & Fleming, B. (1987). The role of cognitive appraisal in self-reports of marital communication. *Behavior Therapy, 18,* 51–69.

Fincham, F. D. (1985). Attribution processes in distressed and nondistressed couples: 2. Responsibility for marital problems. *Journal of Abnormal Psychology, 94,* 183–190.

Fincham, F. D., Beach, S., & Nelson, G. (1987). Attribution processes in distressed and nondistressed couples: 3. Causal and responsibility attributions for spouse behavior. *Cognitive Therapy and Research, 11,* 71–86.

Floyd, F. J., & Markman, H. J. (1983). Observational biases in spouse observation: Toward a cognitive/behavioral model of marriage. *Journal of Consulting and Clinical Psychology, 51,* 450–457.

Goldfried, M. R., & Sprafkin, J. N. (1974). *Behavioral personality assessment.* Morristown, NJ: General Learning Press.

Gottman, J. M. (1979). *Marital interaction: Experimental investigations.* New York: Academic Press.

Jacobson, N. S. (1984). A component analysis of behavioral marital therapy: The relative effectiveness of behavior exchange and communication/problem-solving training. *Journal of Consulting and Clinical Psychology, 52,* 295–305.

Jacobson, N. S., & Margolin, G. (1979). *Marital therapy: Strategies based on social learning and behavior exchange principles.* New York: Brunner/Mazel.

Kiresuk, T. J., & Sherman, R. E. (1968). Goal attainment scaling: A general method for evaluating comprehensive community mental health programs. *Community Mental Health Journal, 4,* 443–453.

Kiresuk, T. J., & Sherman, R. E. (1977). A reply to the critique of goal attainment scaling. *Social Work Research Abstracts, 13,* 9–11.

L'Abate, L. (1986). *Systematic family therapy.* New York: Brunner/Mazel.

Locke, H. J., & Wallace, K. M. (1959). Short marital-adjustment and prediction tests. Their reliability and validity. *Marriage and Family Living, 21,* 251–255.

Margolin, G., & Jacobson, N.S. (1981). The assessment of marital dysfunction. In M. Hersen & A. S. Bellack (Eds.), *Behavioral assessment: A practical handbook* (pp. 389–426). New York: Pergamon.

Margolin, G., Talovic, S., & Weinstein, C. D. (1983). Areas of Change questionnaire: A practical approach to marital assessment. *Journal of Consulting and Clinical Psychology, 51,* 920–931.

Margolin, G., & Wampold, B. E. (1981). Sequential analysis of conflict and accord in distressed and nondistressed marital parners. *Journal of Consulting and Clinical Psychology, 49,* 554–567.

Margolin, G., & Weiss, R. L. (1978). Comparative evaluation of therapeutic components associated with behavioral marital treatments. *Journal of Consulting and Clinical Psychology, 46,* 1476–1486.

Mead, D. E., & Vatcher, G. (1985). An empirical study of the range of marital complaints found in the areas of change questionnaire. *Journal of Marital and Family Therapy, 11,* 421–423.

O'Leary, K. D., Fincham, F., & Turkewitz, H. (1983). Assessment of positive feelings toward spouse. *Journal of Consulting and Clinical Psychology, 51,* 949–951.

Patterson, G. R. (1976). Some procedures for assessing changes in marital interaction patterns. *Oregon Research Institute Bulletin, 16.*

Patterson, G. R., Hops, H., & Weiss, R. L. (1975). Interpersonal skills training for couples in early stages of conflict. *Journal of Marriage and the Family, 37,* 295–304.

Robinson, E. A., & Price, M. G. (1980). Pleasurable behavior in marital interaciton: An observational study. *Journal of Consulting and Clinical Psychology, 48,* 117–118.

Stuart, R. B. (1980). *Helping couples change: A social learning approach to marital therapy.* New York: Guilford.

Stuart, R. B., & Stuart, F. (1980). *Pre-marital Counseling Inventory, Family pre-counseling inventory program, and Marital Pre-counseling Inventory.* Champaign, IL: Research Press.

Thomas, E. J., Walter, C. L., & O'Flaherty, K. (1974). A verbal problem checklist for use in assessing family verbal behavior. *Behavior Therapy, 5,* 235–246.

Turkewitz, H. A., & O'Leary, K. D. (1975). *Positive feelings questionnaire: The relationship between positive feelings towards one's spouse and general marital satisfaction.* Unpublished manuscript, State University of New York at Stony Brook.

Vincent, J. P., Weiss, R. L., & Birchler, G. R. (1975). A behavioral analysis of problem solving in distressed and nondistressed married and stranger dyads. *Behavior Therapy, 6,* 475–487.

Weiss, R. L., & Birchler, G. R. (1975). *Areas of change.* Unpublished manuscript, University of Oregon, Eugene.

Weiss, R. L., & Cerreto, M. (1980). The Marital Status Inventory: Development of a measure of dissolution potential. *American Journal of Family Therapy, 8,* 80–85.

Weiss, R. L., Hops, H., & Patterson, G. R. (1973). A framework for conceptualizing marital conflict: A technology for altering it, some data for evaluating it. In L. A. Hammerlynck, L. C. Handy, & E. J. Marsh (Eds.), *Behavior change: Methodology, concepts and practice* (pp. 309–342). Champaign, IL: Research Press.

Weiss, R. L., & Margolin, G. (1977). Marital conflict and accord. In A. R. Ciminero, J. S. Calhoun, & H. E. Adams (Eds.), *Handbook for behavioral assessment* (pp. 555–602). New York: Wiley.

Weiss, R. L., & Perry, B. A. (1979). *Assessment and treatment of marital dysfunction.* Eugene: Oregon Marital Studies Program.

Wills, T. A., Weiss, R. L., & Patterson, G. R. (1974). A behavioral analysis of the determinants of marital satisfaction. *Journal of Consulting and Clinical Psychology, 42,* 802–811.

Woodward, C. A., Santa Barbara, J., Lewis, S., & Epstein, N. B. (1978). The role of goal attainment scaling in evaluating family therapy outcomes. *American Journal of Orthopsychiatry, 48,* 464–476.

5

Sexual Functioning and Sexual Relationships

To understand any sexual problem, to formulate the treatment of choice, and to estimate the prognosis of a particular sexual disorder, the clinician must first clarify the chief complaint, establish an accurate diagnosis, and determine the etiology of the problem (Kaplan, 1983). To arrive at an accurate diagnosis and discover the true cause (or causes) of the problem, Kaplan stressed that two types of data are required: "the differential diagnosis between organic and psychological causes and an analysis of the psychological elements of the problem" (p. 15).

For clinicians working with couples, the first question is whether the presenting sexual problem is organic or psychogenic in origin. To determine the difference, one must know which phase of the sexual response cycle is impaired, what the impairment is, and how this impairment affects the person's sexual experiences. The sexual response cycle can be divided into four distinct phases: desire, arousal and excitement, orgasm, and resolution. To rule out physiological causes, all clients with sexual problems should be thoroughly examined by a competent gynecologist or urologist.

When couples with sexual problems have not consulted a physician to rule out physiological causes, the marital therapist should be aware of some of the more common organic and chemical causes that might be responsible for the symptom. For example, there are no common organic causes for primary ejaculatory disorders in males; but secondary ejaculatory problems are associated with radical abdominal or pelvic surgery, trauma, and diseases of the lower spinal cord. Certain alpha adrenergic blocking drugs, such as thioridazine, also can be responsible for ejaculatory disorders. Similarly, there are no common organic causes of primary anorgasmia in females; but secondary anorgasmia can be a sign of advanced diabetes or the side effect of monoamine oxidase (MAO) inhibitors.

Impotence may also be caused by diabetes, penile circulatory problems, endocrine imbalances, and the presence of certain drugs in the body (e.g., antihypertensives, beta blockers, alcohol). Vaginal dryness and painful coitus can be brought about by female hormone deficiencies (e.g., low estrogen during menopause).

Difficulties during the desire phase of the sexual response cycle (e.g., total or partial loss of desire) in both men and women can be caused by diseases that reduce testosterone or by drugs that impair the sex circuits of the brain (e.g., beta blockers, narcotics, alcohol). Severe depression and severe stress may also impair a person's desire.

Infections of the urogenital tract (e.g., prostatitis, vesiculitis, herpes) and painful gynecologic conditions (e.g., pelvic inflammatory diseases, endometriosis, hymen obstruction, painful hymenal remnants) are common causes of ejaculatory pain and vaginismus and dyspareunia, two conditions that often result in secondary avoidance of intercourse. Because pain during intercourse is more frequently organically based than psychologically caused, organic factors should always be ruled out before psychological reasons are assumed.

Global sexual disorders that are frequently associated with organic causes are impotence, dyspareunia, vaginismus, unconsummated marriage, low or absent libido, secondary anorgasmia, secondary premature ejaculation, and secondary retarded ejaculation. Sexual disorders that are usually not associated with physical causes are primary premature ejaculation, primary impairment of female orgasm, and primary retarded ejaculation.

A number of potentially reversible conditions are organically or chemically caused:

(1) loss of sexual drive due to endocrine deficiencies (e.g., testosterone deficiency and thyroid deficiency);

(2) loss of sexual drive due to endocrine-secreting tumors (e.g., prolactin-secreting tumors of the pituitary gland and estrogen-secreting tumors of the testes and the adrenal glands);

(3) loss of sexual desire due to depression and stress;

(4) loss of sexual desire due to substances (e.g., centrally acting beta adrenergic blockers, centrally acting antihypertensive agents, excessive use of alcohol and narcotics);

(5) vaginal dryness or atrophy due to estrogen deficiency;

(6) impotence due to hypertensive drugs, blockage of large vessels supplying blood to the penis, deficits in the tunica albuginea of the penis, and organic impotence (which can be ameliorated through the use of surgically implanted prostheses);

(7) vaginal obstructions due to vaginal agenesis or to imperforate or rigid hymen;

(8) female dyspareunia due to vaginal infections, bladder infections, endometriosis, painful hymenal tags, episiotomy scars);

(9) male dyspareunia resulting from prostate infections, vesicular infections, urethral infections and tumors, hernia, chordee, penile infections, and herpes;

(10) orgasm and excitement-phase impairment caused by reversible neurological conditions resulting from vitamin deficiencies and neurotropic viral infections;

(11) delayed or absent orgasm caused by MAO inhibitors.

Other medical conditions are not reversible but can be managed and treated medically to prevent progression of the disease and further deterioration of sexual response. Some of the most common are diabetes (which causes impotence in males and anorgasmia in females), hypertension in males (which may cause arteriosclerosis of the small blood vessels of the penis and thus lead to impotence), and vaginal atrophy that is secondary to pelvic irradiation and surgery.

Finally, the therapist should also be aware of the medical conditions affecting sexual functioning for which no treatment is available. The following conditions are considered irreversible:

(1) small-vessel arteriosclerosis of the penile vessels and corpora cavernosa;

(2) diabetic damage to blood vessels and nerves involved in erection and in organ reflexes;

(3) degenerative neurological diseases and injuries to the central nervous system and surgical trauma to the nerves and the anatomic structure involved in the genital reflexes;

(4) impotence and diminished sex drive associated with renal dialysis;

(5) drug-related impotence when no effective substitute without sexual side effects is available.

Once physiological causes have been ruled out, the therapist must undertake a thorough evaluation of both partners, their relationship, and the problem for which they are seeking help. An outline for assessing these three domains follows (some of this material is taken from Bagarozzi & Anderson, 1989; Kaplan, 1983; Kolodny, Masters, & Johnson, 1979; Masters & Johnson, 1970).

HISTORY OF THE PROBLEM
(MALE AND FEMALE)

(1) What do you consider to be the problem?

(2) How do you think this problem came about?

(3) When does the problem occur?

(4) How frequently does it occur?

(5) In what situations and interpersonal contexts does the problem seem to be worst?

(6) In what situations and interpersonal contexts does the problem seem to trouble you least?

(7) When did you first become aware of this problem?

(8) Has the problem gotten worse since you first became aware of it?

(9) Were there times when the problem disappeared?

(10) How do you feel about the problem?

(11) Have there been times when the problem did not trouble you? (Have respondent explain this lack of concern.)

(12) What have you done to correct this problem?

(13) What have you done that seems to have been helpful?

(14) What have you done that has not been helpful?

(15) What have you done that has made the problem worse?

(16) What have been your current partner's reactions to the problem?

(17) What types of reactions have you gotten from previous (or other) sexual partners?

(18) How do you feel about these reactions?

(19) What has prompted you to seek help for this problem at this time in your life?

(20) How does this problem affect your feelings about yourself?

(21) How does this problem affect your feelings about your current partner?

(22) What significance does this problem have with regard to your sexual functioning?

(23) What significance does this problem have with regard to your partner's sexual functioning?

(24) Do you think that your partner has any sexual problems, inhibitions, anxieties, concerns?

(25) If your partner also has a sexual dysfunction, which problem do you recall as having developed first?

(26) How have you and your partner tried to handle this problem?

(27) What techniques or methods have you found helpful?

(28) What techniques or methods have you used that were not helpful or that made matters worse?

(29) What is your concept of effective sexual functioning for a male? for a female?

(30) On a weekly basis, how frequently do you desire to have sexual intercourse?

(31) How has this frequency changed over the years? during your teenage years? during adulthood? during courtship? during marriage? after the birth of children? after divorce? any other significant changes?

For Males

(32) Have you ever had erectile failure?

(33) How frequently has this occurred?

(34) Under what circumstances has this occurred?

(35) What have been your partners' reactions to your erectile failure?

(36) How do you feel about yourself when this happens?

(37) How do you feel about your partner(s) when this happens?

(38) What have you done to try to regain your erection? What have your partners done?

(39) What techniques have been helpful?

(40) What techniques have not been helpful?

(41) When was the first time you experienced erectile failure?

(42) Do you consider this a problem?

(43) Additional considerations in erectile failure: Is there alcohol abuse? Is there any other substance abuse that may contribute to erectile failure? Are you taking any medication that may produce erectile failure? Do you have any physical or medical conditions that may contribute to erectile failure (e.g., diabetes)? Do you have morning erections? Do you have erections when you masturbate? What do you think about during masturbation? What is most exciting? What do you think about during lovemaking? Are there any psychological conditions that may cause erectile failure (e.g., anxiety, depression, anger)? At what point during lovemaking do you lose your erection?

For Females

(44) Are you orgasmic?

(45) Have you ever been unable to achieve an orgasm?

(46) Under what conditions and interpersonal situations have you been unable to achieve an orgasm?

(47) How frequently has this occurred?

(48) What have been your partners' reactions to your not being able to achieve an orgasm?

(49) How do you feel about yourself when this happens?

(50) How do you feel about your partners when this happens?

(51) What have you done to try to bring about your own orgasm? What have your partners done?

(52) What techniques have been helpful?

(53) Do you lubricate during masturbation?

(54) Do you lubricate during sexual intercourse?

(55) What techniques have not been helpful?
(56) Do you consider this a problem?

For Males and Females

(57) How much time does your partner spend in foreplay?
(58) Is this time sufficient for you to become sexually aroused?
(59) How much time do you enjoy spending in foreplay?
(60) Do you need more or less time than your partner?
(61) Have you discussed with your partner your desire for more or less time in foreplay?
(62) What has been your partner's response to your request for a change?
(63) Do you feel comfortable asking your partner to engage in sexual acts that are pleasing to you?
(64) Are you able to ask your partner to refrain from sexual behaviors that are not pleasing to you?
(65) Do you enjoy your partner's lovemaking techniques?
(66) What do you like most?
(67) What do you like least?
(68) By what means, other than intercourse, has your partner sought to give you sexual pleasure?
(69) What do you enjoy most?
(70) What do you enjoy least?
(71) By what means, other than intercourse, have you tried to give your partner sexual pleasure?
(72) What do you enjoy most?
(73) What do you enjoy least?
(74) How long does lovemaking usually last between you and your partner?
(75) Do you find this duration satisfactory? Does your partner find this duration satisfactory?
(76) During lovemaking, how frequently do you have an orgasm?
(77) Is this frequency satisfying to you? Is this frequency satisfying to your partner?
(78) During lovemaking, how frequently does your partner have an orgasm?
(79) Is this frequency satisfying to your partner? Is this frequency satisfying to you?
(80) Do you experience any discomfort during intercourse?
(81) Do you experience any discomfort during orgasm?
(82) Do you ever have an orgasm during which you experience no feelings of pleasure?
(83) Have you discussed this with your partner?

(84) What has been your partner's reaction to this?
(85) How frequently does this occur?
(86) How long has this been going on?

For Males with Premature Ejaculation

(87) Does ejaculation occur before intromission?
(88) During what part of the lovemaking cycle does premature ejaculation occur? during the desire phase? during the arousal phase? during foreplay? when you are fully clothed? when you are partially clothed? when you are naked? when your partner is fully clothed? when your partner is partially clothed? when your partner is naked?
(89) If premature ejaculation occurs after intromission, how long after intromission do you have an orgasm?
(90) Is the problem situational or global?
(91) How do you feel about your sexual partner (partners) with whom premature ejaculation has occurred?
(92) What has been the usual length of time spent in masturbation before ejaculation occurs?
(93) Do you ever engage in a second or third (or more) round of intercourse in one evening?
(94) Does ejaculatory time change during the second and third (and other) rounds of sexual intercourse?
(95) Does the frequency of intercourse have any effect on ejaculatory time?
(96) Do any positions during intercourse give you more ejaculatory control than others?
(97) When you ejaculate prematurely, what are the typical sexual responses of you partner? Are the responses orgasmic? How does your partner achieve an orgasm?
(98) What are your thoughts and feelings about your partner's sexual response patterns?

For Males with Situational Anorgasmia (Retarded or Absent Ejaculation)

(99) Do you ever ejaculate with masturbation?
(100) What types of masturbation techniques do you use?
(101) Describe these techniques with respect to speed, amount of friction, roughness, manual or other stimulation.
(102) What are your fantasies during masturbation?
(103) Do you have any concerns about pregnancy, venereal diseases, the female genitals?

(104) What types of reactions and responses are typical for your sexual partner when ejaculation is retarded?

(105) What are your thoughts and feelings about your partner with whom you experience retarded ejaculation? Do you have any negative feelings about your partner that you are not expressing directly?

(106) Are negative feelings associated with other parts of your life interfering with your ability to have an orgasm?

(107) Under what conditions have you ejaculated with your partner's stimulation?

(108) What type of sexual stimulation is most helpful in bringing about orgasm (e.g., manual, oral, anal intercourse)?

HISTORY OF COUPLE'S SEXUAL RELATIONSHIP (MALE AND FEMALE)

(1) How long have you been married (living together)?

(2) How did you meet each other?

(3a) Where did you go on your first date? How was this decision made? How would each of you describe this first date? Was it successful or unsuccessful? What was it about your partner that made you want to date him or her again?

(b) What traits, behaviors, or characteristics about your partner did you find most sexually attractive when you first met?

(c) What sexual traits, behaviors, or characteristics about your partner did you dislike most when you first met? How did you deal with these undesirable traits, behaviors, and characteristics during courtship (or before you decided to live together)? How did you deal with them after marriage (or after you began to live together)? How do you deal with them now?

(4) If you had sexual relations together before you were married (or before you began to live together), how long after your first date did you wait before having sexual relations?

(5) How would each of you describe your first sexual intercourse together? Was it satisfying, disappointing, uneventful?

(6) How frequently (on a weekly basis) did you have sexual intercourse during dating and courtship (before moving in together)? How frequently (on a weekly basis) did you have sexual intercourse during the first year of your marriage (during the first year of living together)? Has the frequency of your sexual intercourse changed substantially over the years?

(7) When did you first notice this change?

(8) How did you feel about this change when you first noticed it? How do you feel about it now?

(9) How long did you date before deciding to marry (live together)?

(10) Were there any significant circumstances, in either of your personal lives, that you believe played a part in your decision to marry (live together)? For example, the death of a parent or sibling; disabling illness of a parent, sibling, grandparent; graduation from school; personal illness (physical or emotional); loss of steady employment; personal trauma?

(11) Did you marry because of pregnancy? If yes, how was this decision made?

(12) Which of you proposed marriage, and how was the proposal received?

(13) Did you have a formal engagement? How long was the engagement?

(14) How did your respective parents respond to your decision to marry?

(15) Were there any breakups before marriage? If yes, how many times did you break up? What were the reasons for the breakups? Did you date other people during these breakups? Did you have sexual intercourse with others during these periods? Who initiated reconciliation each time?

(16) How did your parents react to these breakups and reconciliations each time?

(17) Did you develop any of your present sexual difficulties during these breakups or reconciliations?

(18) How did you decide where you were going to live in relationship to where your parents were living at the time of your marriage (at the time you began to live together)?

(19) How did your friends and extended family members respond to your decision to marry (live together)?

(20) Do either of you still maintain friendships with people you knew and dated before you began to date each other? How does your partner feel about these relationships?

(21) Do you continue to have relationships with couples that you met together?

(22) Does either of you have friends (male or female) that your partner disapproves of? If yes, how do you deal with this disagreement?

(23) Are sexual relationships with persons other than your partner acceptable for either of you?

(24) If yes, how was this decision made and how does each of you feel about this arrangement?

(25) If both of you consider the marriage (relationship) monogamous and sexually exclusive, has there ever been an incident of infidelity? If yes, by whom? How was this infidelity treated? How did this infidelity affect the sexual relationship? What residue remains (in this relationship) as a result of this infidelity?

(26) If either of you has been married before, was there any infidelity in your previous marriage? If yes, by whom?

(27) How did you decide whether or not to have children and the number of children to have?

(28) What types of birth control have you used? Has there ever been a disagreement about birth control? If yes, how did you resolve it?

(29) Have you ever had any sexual difficulties associated with the use of birth control?

(30) Have you had any unwanted pregnancies? How have you dealt with these unwanted pregnancies?

(31) Have you ever had an abortion? How was this decision made? How did this decision and the abortion itself affect your sexual functioning and your sexual relationship?

(32) What legacy has each of you received from your family of origin that you brought into this marriage (relationship) and that you believe affects your sex life as a couple? For example, inheritances; values; spiritual or religious beliefs; traditions and commitments; emotional, psychological, or financial debts or loyalties; unresolved conflicts or unfinished business with members of your family of origin?

(33) What sexual traditions have you brought to this marriage (relationship) from your families of origin?

(34) What sexual rituals have your brought to this marriage (relationship)?

(35) Which of these traditions and rituals do you think are beneficial? Which traditions and rituals do you think are harmful to your sexual relationship?

(36) What sexual rituals or traditions have you developed as a couple that you believe to be special in your relationship?

(37) To characterize your sexual relationship as a couple, would you say that it is modeled more closely on the sexual relationship of your parents or the sexual relationship of your partner's parents?

(38) Have you ever been separated for long periods during your marriage (relationship)? If yes, was sexual fidelity expected of both of you?

(39) How satisfactory has the sexual component of your relationship been in comparison to other areas of your relationship?

(40) What were your expectations concerning sex, lovemaking, intercourse, before marriage (living together)? Were these expectations fulfilled at some point within the first year of marriage (living together)? If not, please discuss your disappointment.

(41) Describe your sexual experience on your honeymoon. Was it satisfying, dissatisfying, or uneventful?

(42) What has had the most influence on when or how often or under what circumstances you and your partner have intercourse?

(43) Does lovemaking always lead to intercourse? If not, give a percentage estimate. How does each of you feel about this?

(44) Does either partner have a preference for a particular time of day,

evening, night, or for a particular situation for lovemaking or inter-course? Are there discrepancies between you concerning time or situational preferences? If yes, explain how you reconcile these differences.

(45) Do both of you feel free to express sexual desires at any time, and do you anticipate warm receptivity?

(46) Describe the situations that you find sexually most attractive and desirable. Are there any discrepancies between your descriptions? If yes, how have you resolved these discrepancies?

(47) Describe the situation you find most sexually arousing and stim-ulating. If there are major differences, how have you resolved them?

(48) Is there a relationship between one partner's greatest sexual satisfac-tion and a particular time, setting, or sexual situation?

(49) In what areas of your sexual relationship and on what sexual subjects do you and your partner agree? disagree? Have the areas of disagree-ment ever caused you problems as a couple? How have you resolved these differences?

(50) Do either or both of you have a sense of humor? Can you use your sense of humor when everything seems to be going wrong? Do you use humor in sexual situations?

INDIVIDUAL SEX HISTORY (MALE AND FEMALE)

(1) How many children (siblings) were there in your family of origin when you were growing up?

(2) What is your birth order in your family of origin? If you grew up in a blended family, what was your birth order in this blended family?

(3) What circumstances, beliefs, values do you think played a part in your parents' decision to have the number of children they had?

(4) What circumstances, beliefs, values do you think played a part in your parents' decision to have you?

(5) How do you think your parents reacted to finding out that your mother was pregnant with you?

(6) What do you think your mother's reaction was to seeing you for the first time?

(7) What do you think your father's reaction was to seeing you for the first time?

(8) What do you think your siblings' reactions were to knowing your mother was pregnant with you?

(9) What do you think your siblings' reactions were to seeing you for the first time?

(10) How do you think your mother felt about your gender (sex)?

(11) How do you think your father felt about your gender (sex)?

(12) How do you think your siblings felt about your gender (sex)?

(13) Who named you, and why do you think you were given your name?

(14) Do you think your name is a particularly masculine or feminine name?

(15) Do you have a nickname? Do you think this nickname is more masculine or feminine than your given name?

(16) What is your first sexual memory?

(17) Describe the general feeling, tone, and atmosphere in your family of origin when you were growing up.

(18) Do you consider your father and mother sexual people? Which parent do you consider the more sexual?

(19) Did your parents openly display loving feelings toward each other in the presence of the children?

(20) Did your parents openly display sexual feelings toward each other in the presence of the children?

(21) Were you and your siblings allowed to ask questions about or discuss sexual topics with your parents? If yes, how did your parents respond to these questions?

(22) Do you remember playing sex games as a child? with friends? with siblings? with adults?

(23) Were you ever caught playing any of these sex games? By whom? What was that person's reaction to you?

(24) Did you ever have the opportunity to see animals involved in sexual activity? having their offspring? What were your reactions? If your parents, siblings, or other adults were also present during these times, what were their reactions?

(25) Did you ever observe anyone else, accidentally or otherwise, engaging in sexual activity? If yes, were they children or adults? What was your reaction?

(26) Have you ever observed your parents in sexual activity? If yes, what were your father's behavior and reactions? What were your mother's behavior and reactions? How did you feel about seeing your parents engaged in sexual activity? What did you think about them and this behavior? How old were you at the time?

(27) Did observing your parents in sexual activity change any of your feelings or attitudes toward either of them? If yes, explain this change.

(28) When do you recall first having any pleasurable genital or pelvic sensations or feelings?

(29) What thoughts, activities, situations, or people were connected with these pleasurable feelings?

(30) If people were connected with these feelings, how did you feel about these people?

(31) At what age did you first begin to experiment with masturbation or with any kind of solitary activity that produced a genital feeling of pleasure?

(32) With what frequency did you engage in this activity?

(33) How did you feel before, during, and after these activities?

(34) What were the contents of your masturbatory fantasies as a child, teenager, young adult, adult, and now?

(35) How have the contents of these fantasies changed over the years?

(36) How frequently do you masturbate now?

(37) What were the contents of your fantasies while having sexual intercourse as a teenager, young adult, adult, and now?

(38) How have the contents of these fantasies changed over the years?

(39) How often do you dream about sexual situations and sexual encounters? What are the usual contents of these dreams? Do these contents differ significantly from your conscious fantasies? How?

(40) As a child, did you first experiment sexually in the presence of another person? If so, who was that person? Was the person of your own sex or the opposite sex? Was it a family member or someone outside the family? Was the person your age, older, or younger?

(41) How did you feel before, during, and after this experience?

For Males

(42) How old were you when nocturnal emissions began?

(43) What was your reaction to these nocturnal emissions?

(44) Did you ever talk with anyone about these experiences?

(45) Did you ever talk with either parent about these experiences? What were their reactions?

For Females

(46) When did you first begin to menstruate?

(47) Had menstruation been functionally and accurately described to you in advance? By whom? Was the person comfortable discussing these issues with you?

(48) Did you and the person describing these experiences at the onset of menses perceive them as something positive, as something negative, or as something neutral?

(49) Have you ever had any menstrual difficulties? If so, describe them.

(50) By what term do you refer to menstruation?

Male and Female

(51) When did you learn "where babies come from" and how they are conceived? Who told you about this? What was your reaction to this revelation?

(52) When did you put the entire picture together, that is, ovulation, menses, erection, intercourse, sperm, ejaculation, conception, childbirth?

(53) At what age did you start to date?

(54) Did you date in groups or single-date?

(55) Did you ever go steady? For how long with each partner?

(56) In what type of petting did you participate?

(57) Did you engage in petting with all dates or only with certain persons?

(58) When did you first participate in manipulating your partner's genitals? When did your partner first manipulate your genitals and genital area?

(59) Did you ever engage in stimulation or sexual behavior other than intercourse? Explain.

(60) When did you experience your first sexual intercourse? How old were you? How old was your partner?

(61) Was your first sexual intercourse planned by you?

(62) How would you describe your first sexual intercourse? Was it pleasurable, unpleasurable, or uneventful?

(63) What means of contraception was used during your first sexual intercourse, and who took the responsibility for providing contraception?

(64) Under what circumstances did intercourse usually occur?

(65) How much pleasure and freedom from concern usually accompanied these initial experiences with intercourse?

(66) Did your parents ever suspect you of having sexual relations?

(67) Did you ever get caught in the act by a parent?

(68) How did you and your parents react?

SPECIFIC ISSUES RELATED TO THE SELF AND THE SELF IN RELATIONSHIP TO A SIGNIFICANT OTHER

(1) Have you ever engaged in homosexual activity?

(2) At what age did you first participate in homosexual activity?

(3) How old was your partner?

(4) How did you feel about this experience?

(5) Have you continued to have homosexual relationships throughout your life?

(6) Do you consider yourself primarily heterosexual, bisexual, or homo-

sexual? Are you pleased with your sexual identity and sexual orientation?

(7) Do you consider yourself sexually attractive?

(8) Do you feel sexually attractive?

(9) Would you like to change anything about yourself that you believe would make you more attractive to others or make you feel more attractive to yourself?

(10) Do you feel that you are attractive to your partner?

(11) Is your partner attractive to you?

SENSUAL AWARENESS

Touch

(1) Is the dimension of touch meaningful and stimulating for you? For instance, do you explore surfaces with your fingers and hands to feel their texture?

(2) Do you ever touch your partner similarly to derive pleasure?

(3) How does your partner respond when you touch him or her this way?

(4) Do you enjoy being touched by your partner in a similar manner?

(5) Do you and your partner ever use body contact to express your feelings toward each other? If yes, what form does this body contact usually take?

(6) Do you use body contact with your partner to express any of the following:
   (a) affection or desire for affection
   (b) sexual arousal or desire
   (c) identification or a need to be recognized, noticed
   (d) reassurance or a desire for reassurance
   (e) comfort
   (f) solace
   (g) affirmation
   (h) belonging
   (i) anger
   (j) resentment
   (k) sadness, unhappiness, depression

(7) Does your partner desire or initiate this kind of contact (for any of the above reasons) more or less than you do?

(8) Do you ever find touching or body contact irritating? If so, explain.

(9) Do you ever find touching embarrassing? Does your partner find touching embarrassing under certain circumstances?

(10) Are there certain types of touches or body contacts that you cannot

tolerate? If yes, what are the feelings associated with these kinds of touches or body contacts?

(11) Do you usually establish some form of body contact in social situations?

(12) Are you receptive to your partner's touches in social situations? Is your partner receptive?

(13) Do you and your partner have a pattern of exchanging personal touching in the form of massage, back rubs?

(14) Does being touched or held help you to relax, feel secure, fall asleep, overcome unpleasant feelings?

(15) Does your partner use touch or being held for any of these reasons?

(16) Do you feel the need to be physically close or held by your partner after intercourse? Does your partner?

(17) How do you feel and respond when your requests for physical closeness or body contact are ignored or denied by your partner?

(18) How does your partner react?

(19) Which do you prefer or enjoy more—touch and body contact or sexual intercourse?

(20) What is the most sexual kind of tactile sensation for you? for your partner?

(21) What is the most comforting or pleasing kind of tactile sensation you can remember from your childhood? Who was the person responsible for conveying these feelings to you?

Sight

(22) Is your visual pleasure in your partner enhanced when he or she is groomed or dressed in a particular way? Explain.

(23) Is your partner's visual pleasure in you enhanced when you are groomed or dressed in a particular way? Explain.

(24) Do either you or your partner ever wear special kinds of clothing during lovemaking and sexual activity? If yes, explain.

(25) Do you enjoy watching your partner on special occasions, when talking with others, while absorbed in some interest, while dressing or undressing?

(26) Does your partner enjoy watching you in any of these activities?

Smell

(27) Are you particularly aware of odors? If so, which odors? Describe your feelings and responses to these odors.

(28) Is your partner particularly aware of specific odors? If yes, which ones?

(29) Which of the following have the most pleasant connotation for you? Explain.
   (a) food-related odors
   (b) odors related to outdoors and the environment
   (c) scented products
   (d) other

(30) Are there any odors that you consider especially sexual?

(31) Are there any odors that your partner considers especially sexual?

(32) Is your pleasure in any particular odor related to a specific experience or an occasion in your past?

(33) Do you associate any particular odors or fragrances with any memorable occasion? If yes, explain.

(34) Were these pleasant or unpleasant occasions? Describe these as best you can.

(35) Have you noticed any significant changes in your awareness of odors or fragrances since you have been married (living together)?

(36) Have you noticed any major changes in your awareness of odors or fragrances since the sexual dysfunction developed?

(37) Do you or your partner respond to certain categories of odors or fragrances as masculine and others as feminine? If so, explain.

(38) Do you like your partner to use scented products? If so, which of the following do you prefer:
   (a) floral
   (b) musky
   (c) outdoor

(39) Does your partner prefer you to use any particular scented products? If so, describe.

(40) Is your preference for a particular odor, scent, or fragrance related to any experience or occasion?

(41) Are there any odors that you associate with your childhood home? Are these pleasing or unpleasing to you? Are they associated with specific memories?

(42) What odors or fragrances do you associate with your current home? Are these pleasing or displeasing to you?

(43) Do you enjoy the smell of your partner's body without the addition of scented products?

(44) Are you particularly aware of body odors and fragrances of other persons—strangers, persons who represent something or someone you dislike, persons who represent someone or something pleasant in your life?

(45) When faced with fear, anger, or anxiety in your partner, are you aware of any particular odors?

Sound

(46) Do extraneous sounds or noises tend to intrude upon your pleasure in whatever you are doing? Does this ever happen during sexual activity?

(47) Do extraneous sounds or noises intrude upon your partner's pleasure, specifically during sexual behavior and activity?

(48) Does music play a particularly important role in your life? in the life of your partner?

(49) Do you and your partner ever add the sounds of music to your sexual behavior together? If yes, explain.

(50) What kinds of music do you prefer? your partner?

(51) Do you or your partner play a musical instrument?

(52) Do you or your partner use music as a form of tension release or relaxation?

(53) Does your partner's voice please you or displease you?

(54) Do you do important work with the radio or television turned on?

(55) Do you or your partner find any particular kind of music sexually stimulating?

Movement

(56) Do you or your partner find any form of movement (e.g., exercising, dancing, running, swimming) particularly enjoyable?

(57) Do you or your partner find any form of movement particularly sexually stimulating? If so, explain.

(58) Do you or your partner find that certain activities reduce your sexual desires? If so, explain.

ADDITIONAL CONSIDERATIONS: SEXUAL EXPERIENCES OUTSIDE NORMAL LIFE CYCLE EXPECTATIONS

Inquire about the following:

(1) Incest

(2) Illegitimate pregnancies

(3) Abortions

(4) Rapes (including date rape)

(5) Infidelities

(6) Homosexuality

(7) Sexual obsessions

(8) Other

It is our contention that the clinical interview consisting of (1) a thorough personal evaluation and sex history, (2) an in-depth examination of the dynamics of the couple's sexual relationship, and (3) a comprehensive investigation of the factors associated with the presenting problem is a sine qua non for understanding and treating the sexual realm of a couple's relationship. Although a number of instruments have been developed to explore various aspects and dimensions of a couple's sexual activity, none can be considered a substitute for the comprehensive clinical interview presented earlier in this chapter. In the following section, we provide an overview of some of the most frequently used instruments and questionnaires employed by sex therapists as adjuncts to the clinical interview. For a more detailed and in-depth discussion, analysis, and critical evaluation of many of the instruments reviewed here, consult the excellent paper written by Talmadge and Talmadge (1990).

Instruments and procedures designed to investigate sexual dysfunctioning fall into two main groups: unidimensional and multidimensional. Unidimensional tools help a sex therapist (1) assess the amount and kind of measures sexual knowledge, (2) measure sexual experience, (3) assess sexual drive and desires, (4) explore sexual attitudes and affects, (5) assess sexual and gender role expectations, and (6) measure sexual satisfaction. Multidimensional instruments can measure any combination within the domain of sexual functioning. Both are reviewed in the next section.

ASSESSMENT OF SEXUAL KNOWLEDGE

The extent of one's knowledge about human sexuality and the type of knowledge one possesses are critical components in the assessment of sexual dysfunctioning. Masters and Johnson (1973) postulated a causal relationship between information deficits in clients and their sexual dysfunctioning. Derogatis and Meyer (1979) found severe gaps in the sexual knowledge of sexually dysfunctional men and women who participated in their research. The success of some of the contemporary treatment approaches that stress sex education as a central component of therapy add support to Masters and Johnson's original conceptions (Kilmann, Wanlass, Sabalis, & Sullivan, 1981; Mills & Kilmann, 1982; Sabalis, Gleaving, Burshel, & Scoveri, 1982).

Sex Knowledge Inventory

The Sex Knowledge Inventory, developed in 1955 by Gegolo, McHugh, Schiavi, Derogatis, Kuriansky, O'Conner, and Sharpe (cited in L'Abate & McHenry, 1983), was designed to be a basic teaching tool to assess individual levels of sexual knowledge. The Sexual Knowledge Inventory appears in two forms: Form X, an 80-item version, was revised in 1968 so that it could be used for adults; Form Y, consisting of 100 items, was developed for youth groups and is used for high school sex education classes. No information about reliability and validity is available.

Sexual Experience

Sexual experience has been shown to correlate positively with one's success and satisfaction in sexual relationships (Derogatis & Meyer, 1979). Levels of sexual experience also have been shown to influence dating and the choice of a mate (Istvan & Griffitt, 1980).

Heterosexual Behavior

Two Guttman-type scales—Heterosexual Behavior Assessment I (for males) and Heterosexual Behavior Assessment II (for females)—were developed to assess the extent of heterosexual experience, developmental precocity or retardation, and the degree of heterosexuality in homosexuals (Bentler, 1968a, 1968b). Both scales arrange heterosexual behavior hierarchically from *most experienced* to *least experienced*. Both scales have 21 items. Kuder-Richardson reliability for each scale was found to be .95.

The Bentler coefficient of homogeneity, indicating the extent of ordinality among the items, reached .99. The Loevinger (Loevinger, 1947) coefficient for homogeneity, or scalability, is .76. A 10-item form (male or female) correlates .98 with the total scale. The instrument was standardized by using a college-educated population.

Sex Experience Scales for Males and Females

Another Guttman-type scale for assessing sexual experience in males and females is the Human Sexuality Questionnaires, developed by Zuckerman (1973). The scales (one for men, one for women) consist of 12 items for which forced-choice responses indicate whether the subject has engaged in a particular behavior. The items range from kissing behavior to coital positions and oral-genital behaviors.

Coefficients of reproducibility are .97 for both males and females. The rank-order correlation between the ordering of items in male and female scales is .95.

Guttman Scale of Sexual Experience

A self-report inventory (Cowart-Steckler, 1984) describing heterosexual experience, this instrument consists of 30 items for females and 31 items for males, in a forced-choice format. Coefficients of reproducibility were .85 for males and .88 for females in the 1979 cross-validation samples used in the development of the scale.

Sexuality Experience Scales (SES)

A group research inventory, the SES (Schiavi, Derogatis, Kuriansky, O'Connor & Sharpe, 1979) is composed of four scales that relate to a hypothetical dimension of sexual experience—acceptance or rejection of sexuality. A factor analysis identified three factors: Traditional Restrictive Sex Morals (acceptance versus rejection); Psychosexual Stimulation (seeking, allowing or avoiding, rejection); and Sexual Motivation (appetitive versus aversive). A fourth subscale measures the degree of attraction to marriage.

The SES contains 83 questions and multiple-choice responses. For example: Some women have very little need for intercourse. Others have a strong need. How often would you prefer to have intercourse? (1) less than once a month; (2) once a month; (3) two to three times a month; (4) once a week. Reliability for each of the subscales ranges from .86 to .92 (mean, .89).

Although the SES was designed to be a research tool, it can be used in intake interviews in clinical settings when the exact value of the score is not stressed. Focusing on the respondent's answers to specific items can provide insights into the respondent's sexual problems.

ASSESSMENT OF SEXUAL DRIVE

Drive is an imprecise concept. Kinsey and his associates (Kinsey, Pomeroy, & Martin, 1948) operationalized drive so that it reflected contributions from autoerotic, heterosexual, and homosexual activities. The following instruments address the cognitive aspects of drive as measured by one's stated interests and desires.

Questionnaire Measure of Sexual Interest

Harbison, Graham, Quinn, and McAllister's (1974) Questionnaire Measure of Sexual Interest, a 140-item test, was designed to assess the degree of interest a male or a female shows in heterosexual and homosexual situations. Subjects mark statements that best describe their response to a stim-

ulus sexual situation. The five subscales measure aspects of sexual behavior:
(1) Kissing, (2) Being Kissed, (3) Touching Sexually, (3) Being Touched Sexually, and (5) Sexual Intercourse. These behaviors are assessed on four bipolar adjectival scales: (1) *seductive-repulsive*, (2) *sexy-sexless*, (3) *exciting-dull*,
and (4) *erotic-frigid*. For each scale, five scale positions are used: (1) *very
erotic*, (2) *quite erotic*, (3) *neither erotic nor frigid*, (4) *quite frigid*, and (5) *very
frigid*. Completing and scoring the test takes a long time unless it is scored
by computer.

The internal consistency of the responses of 40 subjects showed that on
each of the five subscales, 90% to 95% of the subjects made one or more
mistakes. Data from 35 clinical subjects showed that 83% to 94% of this population made one or more mistakes. Test-retest ($n = 15$) reliability over a
3- to 5-month interval showed rank order correlations ranging from .68 to
.92 for the five subscales.

Validation studies have compared the means of the total scores for three
different groups—nonsymptomatic subjects, impotent men, and women
suffering from orgasmic dysfunction ($n = 15$)—and have compared
means along the five subscales for each group. All groups differed significantly on t test ($p < .001$) on all comparisons except Touching Sexually,
where the difference between normal and impotent males was significant
at the .05 level.

Body Contact Questionnaire

Consisting of 12 items scored on a 5-point Likert scale, the Body Contact
Questionnaire (Hollender, Luborsky, & Scavanella, 1969) measures one's
desire for body contact. A sample question reads, "If you have trouble falling
asleep, is it helpful to have someone hold you?" Options range from *never*
(1) to *always* (5).

In testing for internal consistency, the reliability coefficient was .82. The
test-retest reliability coefficient was .94 over 1 to 14 days. No information
on validity is available.

ASSESSMENT OF SEXUAL ATTITUDES AND AFFECTS

Some evidence suggests that sexual attitudes predict sexual functioning.
Athanasiou and Shaver (1971) reported that persons who score high on lib-
eralism show high arousal to sexually explicit material. Persons who score
high on conservatism tend to react to sexually explicit material with dys-
phoria and disgust. No data have shown any relationship between sexual
attitudes and sexual functioning.

Negative Attitudes Toward Masturbation Scale (NATMS)

The NATMS (Abramson & Mosher, 1975) is a 30-item, 5-point Likert scale that measures responses to statements such as "When I masturbate, I am disgusted with myself" or "Masturbation is a normal sexual outlet." Factor analysis produced three factors: (1) Positive Attitude Toward Masturbation, (2) False Beliefs about Masturbation, and (3) Personally Experienced Negative Effects Associated with Masturbation.

Split-half reliability was calculated to be .75. Validation of this instrument is based upon correlations between the NATMS and the average number of masturbations reported per month by both males and females. Significant negative correlations were found for men ($r = -.26$) and for women ($r = -.40$).

Attitudes Toward Homosexuality Scale (ATHS)

The ATHS (MacDonald, Huggins, Young, & Swenson, 1973) was developed to measure subjects' attitudes about homosexuality, regardless of their sexual orientation. Three forms are available: (1) general (Form G), (2) lesbian (Form L), and (3) male (Form M). The scale has been used mainly in studies with college students and faculty, although it was developed for use with widely divergent populations. The ATHS contains 28 items, each item having nine scale positions.

Reliability has been demonstrated in a number of independent studies. For example, internal consistency was found to be .94 in a sample of 94 undergraduate males and .93 in a sample of 103 undergraduate females. A sample of 104 students and faculty members produced an alpha coefficient of .93. A split-half reliability of .93 was reported for 188 students with whom a 22-item version of this scale was used.

Sexual Irrationality Questionnaire (SIQ)

Jordan and McCormick (1988) developed the SIQ to assess irrational beliefs about sex. The SIQ is based upon Ellis's views on sexual matters. The irrational beliefs tapped in this instrument include sexual performance to win approval and expectations that sexual encounters should pose no problems. Factor analysis produced six factors: Frustration Tolerance, Sex-Role Stereotyping, Conformity of Partner, Rules about Sexual Fantasies, Spontaneity-Adequacy, and Cautious Control of One's Sexual Responses.

Sexual Arousability Inventory

In 1976 Hoon, Hoon, and Wincze developed the Sexual Arousability Inventory. This behavioral self-report questionnaire consists of 28 items depicting specific sexual scenes to which the subject is asked to respond on a 7-point Likert-type scale. Response options range from *adversely affects arousal* to *always causes sexual arousal*. A 14-item short form was developed at the same time. Alpha coefficients for validation and cross-validation samples were .91 and .92, respectively; Spearman-Brown split-half reliabilities for both samples were .92. The test-retest reliability, .69, was not as high. Convergent validity was shown through significant correlations between the Sexual Arousability Inventory and ratings of satisfaction of sexual responsivity-awareness of physiological changes during sexual arousal and reported frequency of intercourse before marriage and during marriage for both samples.

The expanded version of the Sexual Arousability Inventory, developed by Chambliss and Lepshetz in 1984, was designed to measure a person's anxiety as experienced during specific sexual behaviors. It will also assess which types of sexual behaviors are most arousing and least arousing and which behaviors produce aversive reactions in the respondent. Female undergraduate students at the University of Georgia ($n = 252$) and 90 women from the university community served as subjects. The expanded inventory consists of 56 items scored on a 7-point Likert-type scale. Each item is answered twice, once for arousability and once for the amount of anxiety it engenders in the respondent. Factor analysis of responses resulted in five factors: Preparation for and Participation in Intercourse, Pornography and Masturbation, Nongenital Sex Play, Breast Stimulation, and Other Sex Play.

Reliability and validity are available only for females. Spearman-Brown coefficients of .92 for Arousal and .94 for Anxiety were found. Discriminant validity was shown by the absence of a positive correlation between the Arousal and the Anxiety subscales ($r = .04$, p > .52). Convergent validity was also demonstrated by a significant negative correlation between sexual arousal and anxiety level.

Rating of Sexual Arousal and Affective Sexual Arousal

The Rating of Sexual Arousal and Affective Sexual Arousal (Mosher, 1980; Mosher, Barton-Henry, & Green, 1988) was developed to assess three areas of sexual arousal: Sexual Arousal, Genital Sensations, and Affective Sexual Arousal. Acceptable levels of internal consistency have been reported for all three subscales.

Mosher Guilt Inventory

The Mosher Guilt Inventory (Mosher, 1966, 1968) was developed to investigate three aspects of guilt: Sex Guilt, Hostility Guilt, and Guilty Conscience. The revised version of this measure came out in 1985 (Mosher & Vonderheide). Reliability for the revised version has not yet been reported. However, the split-half reliabilities for the original version are reported to average .90. Numerous published studies have offered solid empirical support for this instrument's validity (Mosher, 1979).

Sex Anxiety Inventory

The Sex Anxiety Inventory (Janda & O'Grady, 1980) was developed to help distinguish guilt from anxiety. This self-report inventory, made up of 25 forced-choice items, taps behavioral, attitudinal, and affective dimensions. Factor analysis produced three factors: Discomfort in Social-Sexual Situations, Socially Unacceptable Sexual Behavior, and Sexuality Experienced in Private. Internal consistency and test-retest reliabilities range from .84 to .86. The Sex Anxiety Inventory is a short, concise instrument that gives relevant data concerning the respondent's anxieties in social-sexual situations.

Sexual Orientation Method and Anxiety Questionnaire

Another instrument that was developed to assess anxiety associated with sexual problems is the Sexual Orientation Method and Anxiety questionaire (Patterson & O'Gorman, 1986). This 112-item questionnaire investigates problems in four distinct areas: heterosexuality, heterosexual anxiety, homosexuality, and homosexual anxiety. Factor analysis produced three factors: Sexual Orientation, Heterosexual Anxiety, and Homosexual Anxiety. Reliability data and validity data are considered acceptable. The Sexual Orientation Method and Anxiety questionnaire is thought to be a better measure of anxiety than the Sex Anxiety Inventory (Janda & O'Grady, 1980) because it permits the clinician to measure the degree of anxiety experienced by the respondent and yields more specific information about the types of sexual behaviors and experiences that cause the respondent to become anxious (Talmadge & Talmadge, 1990).

Semantic Differential as a Measure of Sexual Attitudes

The Semantic Differential as a Measure of Sexual Attitudes (Marks & Sartorius, 1968) was devised to assess attitudinal change during treatment for sexual deviation. The scale consists of 20 sexual and nonsexual concepts rated on 13 bipolar semantic differential scales. Factor analysis revealed three factors: (1) General Evaluation, (2) Sex Evaluation, and (3) Anxiety. Adequate stability has been reported on test-retest within 24 hours.

Passionate Love Scale

In 1986, Hatfield and Sprecher developed the Passionate Love Scale, defining passionate love as "a state of intense longing for union with another" that encompasses sexual desire and physiological arousal. This scale is a behavioral self-report measure consisting of 30 items arranged on a 9-point Likert-type scale. The scale assesses cognitive and emotional as well as behavioral domains of the love experience. Coefficient alpha reliabilities for both the long and the short versions are acceptable. Studies attesting to validity (discriminant and convergent) are also available (Hatfield & Sprecher, 1986).

Sexual Anxiety Scale (SAS)

The SAS (Obler, 1973) measures cognitively experienced social and sexual anxieties. The content of the 22-item forms (one form for males, one for females) ranges from anxiety experienced during contact with a member of the opposite sex to that experienced during vaginal penetration. The SAS shows a .92 reliability coefficient and a .62 validity coefficient with intensity of sexual dysfunction.

Sex Knowledge and Attitude Test (SKAT)

The SKAT (Schiavi et al., 1979), which is used mostly by educators in gathering information from students, has been administered to approximately 35,000 students (Miller & Lief, 1979). The instrument was designed to be of value both as a teaching aid in courses dealing with human sexuality and as a research instrument for the social sciences, as well as to determine whether or not the treatment of sexual dysfunction affects the individual's sexual attitudes or knowledge.

The instrument comprises 149 items about sexual knowledge, sexual attitudes, and sexual experience. The SKAT yields five scores: one knowledge score and four attitude scores. The internal consistency reliability (coefficient alpha) estimates for the four attitude scales range from .68 to .86. A reliability of .87 on the knowledge scale has been reported from the original and cross-validational studies.

Sexual Response Profile

The Sexual Response Profile (Schiavi et al., 1979), an 80-item questionnaire, has been reported to be useful in pinpointing problem areas related to patients' sexual history. The questionnaire assesses past and present sexual knowledge, attitudes, and behaviors. Reliability has not been reported.

Sex Inventory

The Sex Inventory (Thorne, 1966) is a 200-item questionnaire especially constructed for the investigation of sex delinquency. Of the items, 40 are subtle and indirect, and 160 are obvious-direct items relating to all aspects of sexuality (e.g., interests, drives, attitudes, adjustment, conflict, cathexis, controls, and sociopathic tendencies). The inventory comprises nine distinct subscales derived from factor analysis: Factor A: Sex Drive and Interest; Factor B: Sexual Maladjustment and Frustration; Factor C: Neurotic Conflict Associated with Sex; Factor D: Sexual Fixation and Cathexis; Factor E: Repression of Sexuality; Factor F: Loss of Controls; Factor G: Homosexuality; Factor H: Sex Role Confidence; and Factor I: Promiscuity.

The instrument is intended to measure *state* phenomena, which may be in constant flux or change. According to the author, reliability in this kind of instrument need not be regarded as methodologically important (as in instruments of "presumably" fixed factors). Despite Thorne's suggestion, the instrument demonstrated good reliability when tested by Allen and Haupt (1966). Test-retest reliability over a 3-month interval by the interclass correlation method revealed test-retest ratios for all scales (except Scale C, $r = .67$) of .75 and above. All correlations were significant beyond the .01 level.

Sexual Attitudes and Beliefs Inventory

The Sexual Attitudes and Beliefs Inventory (Schiavi et al., 1979) is a 250-item scale for collecting information about sexual attitudes, behaviors, and knowledge. The content headings on the inventory include contraception, psychosexual development, disorders, anatomy, and physiology. The scale includes true-false questions and Likert-type responses. Test-retest reliability coefficients for a population of medical students have been reported as .75 to .85. There is no information concerning validity.

Sex Questionnaire

The Sex Questionnaire (Zuckerman, Tushup, & Finner, 1976), designed to evaluate sexual attitudes and behaviors, comprises 91 items that make up 10 subscales: (1) Parental Attitudes, (2) Heterosexual Experience, (3) Number of Partners, (4) Homosexual Experience, (5) Number of Homosexual Partners, (6) Masturbation, (7) Orgasmic Experience, (8) Social Relationship Attitudes, (9) Emotional Relationship Attitudes, and (10) Volunteering for a Film, which measures the strength of the desire to view erotic materials.

The scales were evaluated for test-retest reliability over a 15-week period. Of 234 students who were pre-and posttested, 47 males and 50 females were from a control group, and 41 males and 96 females were from an experimental group. Test-retest reliability coefficients were given for each of the four samples on all 10 subscales. Coefficients of reproducibility and scalability were reported for four subscales, reflecting scores from 221 females and 331 males.

ASSESSMENT OF GENDER ROLE DEFINITION

The notion that masculinity and feminity exist as polar opposites on a conceptual continuum has been supplanted by the conceptualization of masculinity and feminity as orthogonal dimensions. Derogatis and Melisaratos (1979) suggested that gender role definition, through a related process of identification and complementation, plays a significant part in sexual functioning.

Safir, Peres, Lichtenstein, Hoch, and Shepher (1982) tested the hypothesis that persons who have androgynous personalities would be more competent sexually than would individuals who have stereotyped personalities. Using the Sex Role Inventory (Bem, 1974), the researchers found a higher percentage of androgynous subjects in their control group than in the dysfunctional group. In a similar study, Hoch, Safir, Peres, and Shepher (1981) found that more couples in their control group ($n = 60$) showed androgynous traits than did clinical couples ($n = 120$). In addition, a significant number of clinical subjects showed sex-stereotyped character traits.

Sex Role Inventory

The Sex Role Inventory (Bem, 1974) measures gender role definition by characterizing a person according to two independent dimensions—

masculinity and femininity. Masculinity and femininity scores reveal how many of the masculine and feminine personality characteristics are self-descriptive. An androgyny score (defined as student's t ratio for the difference between a person's masculine and feminine self-endorsement) indicates the relative amount of masculinity and femininity that the person includes in his or her self-description.

Internal consistency (coefficient alpha) has been shown to range from .80 to .82 for femininity and .86 for masculinity. Reliabilities for androgyny range from .85 to .86. Test-retest reliability after a 4-week interval ($n = 56$; 28 males, 28 females) revealed the following scores: $r = .90$ (masculinity); $r = .90$ (femininity); $r = .93$ (androgyny).

Sex Role Survey (SRS)

The SRS (MacDonald, 1974) measures attitudes toward sex roles. It consists of four factors: (1) Equality in Business and the Professions, (2) Sex Role Appropriate Behavior, (3) Equal Involvement in Social and Domestic Work, and (4) Power in the Home. This measure is composed of 53 items (a 20-item short form is available). Reliabilities are Factor 1, .94; Factor 2, .85; Factor 3, .85; Factor 4, .86; total, .96.

SEXUAL FUNCTIONING AND SATISFACTION

Sexual Interaction Inventory (SII)

The SII (LoPiccolo & Steger, 1974) measures the level of sexual functioning and satisfaction in relationships. Standardization of the SII was based on four samples totaling 191 couples (clinical couples, paid volunteers, and unpaid volunteers). This instrument is a behavioral self-report measure composed of 17 items, 15 of which are explicit drawings of heterosexual couples engaged in various sexual behaviors. The two additional items consist of statements, unaccompanied by drawings, having to do with sexual intercourse. In response to each drawing, the participant is asked to give the following information: current frequency of the behavior under consideration, the level of satisfaction experienced while engaged in the target behavior, the desired frequency, the level of partner satisfaction as perceived by the respondent, the ideal level of satisfaction for self, and the ideal level of satisfaction as perceived for one's partner.

Moderate levels of test-retest reliabilities have been reported. Some data in support of convergent and discriminant validity are also presented, but these findings are based upon small sample sizes. Taking into consideration the less than robust empirical support, the SII should not be used for research purposes. However, it is a valuable clinical aid that offers a wealth of information about a couple's sexual relationship and functioning.

Derogatis Sexual Functioning Inventory

The Derogatis Sexual Functioning Inventory (Derogatis, 1975) is an instrument designed to measure the level of one's sexual functioning and global sexual satisfaction. It is also a measure of psychological symptoms and affects as they relate to sexual functioning. The Derogatis measure, comprising 245 items, is lengthy and assesses 10 areas of sexual functioning: information, experience, drive, attitudes, symptoms, affects, gender roles, fantasies, body image, and sexual satisfaction. Both male and female profiles can be developed from each of the subscales, from which *t* scores and percentile ranks can be determined.

Administration takes approximately 1 hour and scoring requires an additional 45 minutes. Obviously, this instrument may be too time-consuming for regular use. In reviewing the range of reliability coefficients (.50 to .97) and test-retest reliabilities (.42 to .96), the wisdom of spending so much valuable time administering and scoring this instrument is questioned.

Sexual Function Questionnaire (SFQ)

The SFQ (Miller, McLaughlin, & Murphy, 1982) is another fairly comprehensive tool that helps the clinician gather significant amounts of information in a standard fashion. However, the SFQ, takes less time to complete than the Derogatis measure (approximately 25 minutes). However, no reliability or validity data are available.

Although less experienced sex therapists and students in training may find the Derogatis and the Miller et al. (1982) questionnaires of some value, all the areas covered in these two measures can be assessed more easily through the use of a well-organized and thorough evaluation of both partners' sexual histories, the history of the couple's sexual relationship, and a systematic examination of the presenting problem as outlined earlier in this chapter.

Index of Sexual Satisfaction (ISS) and Golombok-Rust Inventory of Sexual Satisfaction

We close this section by mentioning two short instruments designed to assess sexual satisfaction: the ISS (Hudson, Harrison, & Grosscup, 1981) and the Golombok-Rust Inventory of Sexual Satisfaction (Golombok, Rust, & Pickard, 1984). The ISS, a 25-item self-report questionnaire that can be used with both heterosexual and homosexual couples, offers a relatively quick qualitative assessment of a couple's sexual relationship (i.e., it takes approximately 5 to 6 minutes to score). Internal consistencies for three independent samples are very good (.90, .91, and .92), and the evidence of discriminant and convergent validity is also impressive. The ISS has one important characteristic: It is very sensitive to changes produced through treatment and can therefore serve as an excellent outcome measure of therapeutic effectiveness.

The Golombok-Rust Inventory contains 28 items, takes about 6 to 7 minutes to complete, and requires even less time to score. An overall score of global sexual functioning is computed. There are two subscales for males (Impotence and Premature Ejaculation) and two for females (Anorgasmia and Vaginismus). Split-half reliabilities for males and females are .94 and .87, respectively; internal consistency scores range from .61 to .83; and test-retest reliabilities are .47 to .84. Discriminant validity data are also reported. This instrument seems to be sensitive to changes that result from planned intervention. It offers some poignant insights into a couple's functional as well as dysfunctional sexual interrelatedness.

MISCELLANEOUS TESTS

Male Impotence Test (MIT)

The MIT can discriminate psychogenically impotent men, organically impotent men, and sexually potent men (Schiavi et al., 1979). The MIT includes reaction to female rejection, flight from male roles, reaction to male inadequacy, an organic factor, and a total score. The test was standardized on a sample of 30 psychogenically impotent males, 10 organically impotent males, and a control group of 20 males who had no problems with sexual potency.

Ellis (1972) questioned the validity of the test as a diagnostic instrument on several grounds. First, many of the questions concern feelings about general rather than sexual inadequacy. Thus, the test undoubtedly produces many false positives. Second, questions that are typically used to help discriminate psychogenic and organic impotence are not asked (e.g., Does the client have morning and sleeping erections? Does he become aroused while reading or while viewing sexy pictures or films?).

One study (Beutler, 1975) failed to show that the MIT was of value in discriminating organically impotent males from psychogenically impotent males.

Sexual Development Scale for Females (SDSF)

The SDSF (Schiavi et al., 1979) is an attempt to measure the "relative degree of sexual frigidity" and to identify the causes of it. The inventory consists of 177 items, which make up seven subscales: (1) Lack of Feminine Identity, (2) Free-Floating Anxiety, (3) Unpleasant Sexual Encounter, (4) Passive Sex Aversion, (5) Flight Into Sex, (6) Sexual Insufficiency, and (7) Early Negative Conditioning.

The SDSF was also reviewed by Ellis (1972), who found it to have many of the problems identified in the MIT (that is, questions are too general). The SDSF was standardized on 100 volunteer subjects.

CONCLUSION

There is no question that there exist many and various ways to measure sexual functioning and sexual relationships. The major task of the future for those who are interested in evaluating these behaviors will be to find their correlates with other measures of personality functioning, marital satisfaction, intimacy, and overall interpersonal competence. Furthermore, they will need a theoretical framework on which to hang their findings. Without a comprehensive and relevant theoretical framework, many of these measures will be like actors in search of a play. For instance, many measures of sexual behavior relate to sex as a physical act of performance and/or production. How do these measures relate to sex as an act of love? What is the relationship between sexual activity and satisfaction with measures of emotional intimacy and availability?

REFERENCES

Abramson, P. R., & Mosher, D. L. (1975). Development of a measure of negative attitudes toward masturbation. *Journal of Consulting and Clinical Psychology, 43,* 485–490.

Allen, R. M., & Haupt, T. D. (1966). The Sex Inventory: Test-retest reliabilities of scale scores and items. *Journal of Clinical Psychology, 22,* 375–378.

Athanasiou, R., & Shaver, D. (1971). Correlates of heterosexuals' reactions to pornography. *Journal of Sex Research, 7,* 298–311.

Bagarozzi, D. A., & Anderson, S. A. (1989). *Personal, marital and family myths: Theoretical formulations and clinical strategies.* New York: Norton.

Bem, S. (1974). The measurement of psychological androgyny. *Journal of Consulting and Clinical Psychology, 42,* 155–162.

Bentler, P. M. (1968a). Heterosexual behavior assessment: 1. Males. *Behavior Research Therapy, 6,* 21–25.

Bentler, P. M. (1968b). Heterosexual behavior assessment: 2. Females. *Behavior Research and Therapy, 6,* 27–30.

Beutler, L. E. (1975). MMPI and MIT discriminators of biogenic and psychogenic impotence. *Journal of Consulting and Clinical Psychology, 43,* 899–908.

Chambliss, D. L., & Lepshetz, J. L. (1984). Self-reported sexual anxiety and arousal: The expanded Sexual Arousability Inventory. *Journal of Sex Research, 20,* 241–254.

Cowart-Steckler, D. (1984). A Guttman scale of sexual experience. *Journal of Sex Education and Therapy, 6,* 3–7.

Derogatis, L. R. (1975). *Preliminary scoring manual: Derogatis sexual functioning inventory, clinical.* Baltimore: Psychometric Research.

Derogatis, L. R., & Melisaratos, N. (1979). The DSFI: A multidimensional measure of sexual functioning. *Journal of Sex and Marital Therapy, 5,* 244–281.

Derogatis, L. R., & Meyer, J. K. (1979). A psychological profile of the sexual dysfunctions. *Archives of Sexual Behavior, 8,* 201–223.

Ellis, A. (1972). The male impotence test. In O. K. Buros (Ed.), *The seventh mental measurements yearbook* (Vol. 2). Highland Park, NJ: Gryphon.

Golombok, S., Rust, J., & Pickard, C. (1984). Sexual problems encountered in general practice. *British Journal of Sexual Medicine, 11,* 65–72.

Harbison, J. J., Graham, P. J., Quinn, J. T., & McAllister, H. A. (1974). A questionnaire measure of sexual interest. *Archives of Sexual Behavior, 3,* 357–366.

Hatfield, E., & Sprecher, S. (1986). Measuring passionate love in intimate relationships. *Journal of Adolescence, 9,* 383–410.

Hoch, Z., Safir, M. P., Peres, Y., & Shepher, J. (1981). An evaluation of sexual performance: Comparison between sexually dysfunctional and functional couples. *Journal of Sex and Marital Therapy, 7,* 195–206.

Hollender, M. H., Luborsky, L., & Scavanella, T. J. (1969). Body contact and sexual excitement. *Archives of General Psychiatry, 20,* 188–191.

Hoon, E. F., Hoon, P. W., & Wincze, J. (1976). An inventory for the measurement of female sexual arousability: The SAI. *Archives of Sexual Behavior, 5,* 291–300.

Hudson, W. W., Harrison, D. F., & Grosscup, P. C. (1981). A short-form scale to measure sexual discord in dyadic relationships. *Journal of Sex Research, 17,* 157–174.

Istvan, J., & Griffitt, W. (1980). Effects of sexual experience on dating desirability and marriage desirability: An experimental study. *Journal of Marriage and the Family, 42,* 377–384.

Janda, L. H., & O'Grady, K. E. (1980). Development of a sex anxiety inventory. *Journal of Consulting and Clinical Psychology, 48,* 169–175.

Jordan, T. J., & McCormick, N. B. (1988). Development of a measure of irrational beliefs about sex. *Journal of Sex Education and Therapy, 14,* 28–32.

Kaplan, H. S. (1983). *The evaluation of sexual disorders: Psychological and medical aspects.* New York: Brunner/Mazel.

Kilmann, P. R., Wanlass, R. L., Sabalis, R. F., & Sullivan, B. (1981). Sex education: A review of its effects. *Archives of Sexual Behavior, 10,* 177–205.

Kinsey, A. C., Pomeroy, W. E., & Martin, C. E. (1948). *Sexual behavior in the human male.* Philadelphia: Saunders.

Kolodny, R. C., Masters, W. H., & Johnson, V. E. (1979). *Textbook of sexual medicine.* Boston: Little, Brown.

L'Abate, L., & McHenry, S. (1983). *Handbook of marital interventions.* New York: Grune & Stratton.

Loevinger, J. (1947). A systematic approach to the construction and evaluation of tests of ability. *Psychological Monographs, 4,* 61.

LoPiccolo, J., & Steger, J. C. (1974). The Sexual Interaction Inventory: A new instrument for assessment of sexual dysfunction. *Archives of Sexual Behavior, 3,* 585–595.

MacDonald, A. P., Jr. (1974). Identification and measurement of multidimensional attitudes toward equality between the sexes. *Journal of Homosexuality, 1,* 165–178.

MacDonald, A. P., Jr., Huggins, J., Young, S., & Swenson, R. A. (1973). Attitudes toward homosexuality: Preservation of sex morality or the double standard? *Journal of Consulting and Clinical Psychology, 40,* 161.

Marks, I. M., & Sartorious, N. H. (1968). A contribution to the measurement of sexual attitude in sexual deviations. *Journal of Nervous and Mental Diseases, 154,* 442.

Masters, W. H., & Johnson, V. E. (1970). *Human sexual inadequacy.* Boston: Little, Brown.

Masters, W. H., & Johnson, V. E. (1973). Current status of the research programs. In J. Zubin & J. Money (Eds.), *Contemporary sexual behavior: Critical issues in the 1970s* (pp. 276–292). Baltimore: Johns Hopkins University Press.

Miller, G. D., McLaughlin, C. S., & Murphy, N. C. (1982). Personality correlates of college students reporting sexual dysfunction. *Psychological Reports, 51,* 1075–1082.

Miller, W. R., & Lief, H. I. (1979). The Sex Knowledge and Attitude Test (SKAT). *Journal of Sex and Marital Therapy, 5,* 282–287.

Mills, K. H., & Kilmann, P. K. (1982). Group treatment of sexual dysfunctions: A methodological review of the outcome literature. *Journal of Sex and Marital Therapy, 8,* 259–296.

Mosher, D. L. (1966). The development of a multitrait-multimethod matrix analysis of three measures and three aspects of guilt. *Journal of Consulting and Clinical Psychology, 30,* 35–39.

Mosher, D. L. (1968). Measurement of guilt in females by self-report inventories. *Journal of Consulting and Clinical Psychology, 32,* 690–695.

Mosher, D. L. (1979). The meaning and measurement of guilt. In N. E. Izard (Ed.), *Emotions and personality and psychopathology.* New York: Plenum.

Mosher, D. L. (1980). Three dimensions of depth involvement in human sexual responses. *Journal of Sex Research, 16,* 1–42.

Mosher, D. L., & Vonderheide, S. L. (1985). Contributions of sex guilt and masturbation guilt to women's contraceptive attitudes and use. *Journal of Sex Research, 21,* 24–39.

Mosher, D. L., Barton-Henry, M., & Green, S. E. (1988). Subjective sexual arousal and involvement: Development of multiple indicators. *Journal of Sex Research, 25,* 412–425.

Obler, M. (1973). Systematic desensitization in sexual disorders. *Journal of Behavior Therapy and Experimental Psychiatry, 4,* 93–101.

Patterson, D. G., & O'Gorman, E. C. (1986). The SOMA: A questionnaire measure of sexual anxiety. *British Journal of Psychiatry, 149,* 63–67.

Sabalis, R. F., Gleaving, M. L., II, Burshel, C. H., & Scoveri, A. W. (1982). The treatment of sexual paraphilias: A review of outcome research. *Journal of Sex Research, 18,* 193–252.

Safir, M. P., Peres, Y., Lichtenstein, M., Hoch, Z., & Shepher, J. (1982). Psychological androgyny and sexual adequacy. *Journal of Sex and Marital Therapy, 8,* 228–238.

Schiavi, R. C., Derogatis, L. R., Kuriansky, J., O'Connor, D., & Sharpe, L. (1979). The assessment of sexual function and marital interaction. *Journal of Sex and Marital Therapy, 5,* 179–224.

Talmadge, L. D., & Talmadge, W. C. (1990). Sexuality assessment measures for clinical use: A review. *American Journal of Family Therapy, 18,* 80–105.

Thorne, F. C. (1966). The Sex Inventory. *Journal of Clinical Psychology, 22,* 367–374.

Zuckerman, M. (1973). Scales of sex experiences for males and females. *Journal of Consulting and Clinical Psychology, 41,* 27–29.

Zuckerman, M., Tushup, R., & Finner, F. (1976). Sexual attitudes and experience: Attitude and personality correlates and changes produced by a course in human sexuality. *Journal of Consulting and Clinical Psychology, 44,* 7–19.

6

Nonbehavioral Self-Report Measures of Marital Quality

Although the term *adjustment* is often used synonymously with *satisfaction*, we believe that these two constructs are conceptually different and distinct. The Random House Dictionary of the English Language (2nd ed.) defines the verb *to satisfy* as a person's ability "to fulfill the desires, expectations, needs or demands of (another) person." Furthermore, to satisfy means to "give full contentment to" or "to put an end to desire by sufficient or ample provisions." *Adjustment*, on the other hand, is defined as "the act of adjusting; adaptation to a particular condition, position or purpose." Secondly, adjustment is also defined as "the state of being adjusted" and "orderly relation of parts or elements."

If one accepts these definitions, marital satisfaction is said to occur in relationships where a spouse is able to fulfill most, if not all, of his or her partner's needs, desires, expectations, and demands. Such a definition closely approximates the popular ideal of a romantic relationship. Marital dissatisfaction will be experienced whenever a spouse fails to gratify his or her mate in any of the aforementioned areas.

According to the definition offered above, marital adjustment is a condition or state that may come about once a spouse reaches the realization that his or her mate cannot meet every one of his or her needs, fulfill each and every expectation (especially expectations that have not been verbalized), quench all of his or her desires, and accede to all of his or her demands (regardless of how unreasonable these demands might be). We say that marital dissatisfaction may follow because, in some cases, the spouse may be unable or unwilling to adjust to the realities of the honeymoon being over. The dissatisfied spouse may then seek satisfaction in another relationship that is perceived to offer the promise of satisfaction.

MEASURES OF MARITAL ADJUSTMENT

In the first section of this chapter we review the most commonly used measures of marital adjustment. We then take a look at those empirically developed instruments that assess some of the critical dimensions of marital satisfaction. It is important to understand that no one instrument can be said to cover all aspects of marital satisfaction. It is also important to keep in mind that such assessment tools focus on the insider's subjective appraisals. This is one area of marriage where an outsider's views of what is satisfying are of little importance. The sole judge of one's satisfaction is the spouse, not his or her mate, not some objective expert (therapist or researcher).

Locke-Wallace Marital Adjustment Test (LWMAT)

The Locke-Wallace Marital Adjustment Test (LWMAT) (Locke & Wallace, 1959) is cited in numerous reviews of scales and indices dealing with marital relations (Bonjean, Hill, & McLemore, 1967; Schiavi, Derogatis, Kuriansky, O'Connor, & Sharpe, 1979; Straus, 1969; Touliatos, Perlmutter, & Straus, 1990). The following aspects of the LWMAT are reviewed in this first section: history and development, confusion with other Locke scales, psychometric analysis, reliability, and scale weaknesses. Those seeking a review of the literature on marital adjustment and satisfaction will find it very adequately covered in other sources (Barry, 1970; Burr, 1973; Hicks & Platt, 1971; L'Abate & Goodrich, 1980; Urdy, 1974).

History and Development

The LWMAT (Locke & Wallace, 1959) was developed to provide a reliable and valid test of marital adjustment that would overcome problems of length in the measures available at that time. These earlier marital adjustment/satisfaction measures included the Terman Happiness Test—75 items (Terman, 1938); the Burgess-Cottrell Marital Adjustment Test—26 items (Burgess & Cottrell, 1939); the modified Terman-Oden—103 items (Terman & Oden, 1947); the Karlsson Index of Marital Satisfaction—40 items (Karlsson, 1951); the Locke Marital Adjustment Test—29 items (Locke, 1951); and the Burgess-Wallin Marital Success Schedule—89 items (Burgess & Wallin, 1953). Using selected, nonduplicated, statistically significant items from previous measures that had the highest levels of discrimination and that covered what the authors considered to be important areas of marriage, Locke and Wallace composed their 15-item marital adjustment scale. Marital adjustment is defined by Locke and Wallace as the accommodation of husband and wife to each other at a given time (1959).

The scale was standardized on 96 unrelated subjects divided into two matched groups on the basis of age, sex, and marital adjustment. Of the subjects, 48 were judged maladjusted according to one of the following four criteria: recently divorced, separated, presently in marital therapy, or assessed to be maladjusted through extensive case study. The remaining 48 subjects, judged by close friends to be exceptionally well adjusted in marriage, were assigned to the adjusted group.

Although these selection criteria are open to debate, the scores of the individuals in each group were highly discriminating. The mean adjustment scores (the test has a possible score range of 2–158 points) were *71.7* and *135.9*, respectively, for the maladjusted and adjusted groups. The difference in group scores was significant (critical ratio of 17.5, $p < .001$); only 17% of the maladjusted group scored 100 or higher. Therefore, the LWMAT differentiated between persons considered well adjusted and persons considered adjusted in marriage. This offered initial support for construct validity.

Discussion of the LWMAT is often clouded because many researchers and clinicians confuse the LWMAT with other adjustment measures developed by Locke and his associates. Those measures are the Locke-Wallace Short Form (Cole, Cole, & Dean, 1980), the Locke Marital Adjustment Scale (Locke, 1951), the Marital Relationship Inventory (Locke & Williamson, 1958), and the Short Form Marital Adjustment Questionnaire (Kimmel & van der Veen, 1974).

Psychometric Analysis of the LWMAT

In reviewing the literature on marital evaluation and research, one finds that the use of the LWMAT has been much more widespread than has the evaluation of its psychometric properties. Very few studies analyzed specific test properties of the LWMAT for the population being studied.

Item weighing. The item weights for scoring the LWMAT derive from the weights assigned to the items in the earlier marital adjustment studies used to construct the 15-item scale. These studies added weights to the item alternatives according to the percentage from each group (maladjusted and adjusted) who answered the item in a particular way. When one uses these original weights, the range of possible scores on the scale is 2–158 points.

Hunt (1978) investigated the effect of using the original weights versus using an unweighted, or continuous, scale (e.g., the choices for Item 4 have original weights of 0, 1, 2, 4, 6, and 8; continuous weights would be 0, 1, 2, 3, 4, 5) on LWMAT scores. When one uses continuous weights, the range of scores becomes 0-60 points. He found the two weighing methods to correlate highly for LWMAT scores for both husbands ($r = .94$) and wives ($r = .92$).

Hunt also investigated the relationship of weighing method on score correlations between the LWMAT and a subset of 11 MAS items, which appear in almost identical format on the Spanier Dyadic Adjustment Scale (Spanier, 1976). He found that the original weights of the MAS correlated $r = .77$ with the Spanier scale for husbands and $r = .73$ for wives. When continuous weighing was used, Hunt found the correlations of LWMAT scores and the Spanier items to be much higher: $r = .93$ for husbands and wives. Hunt concluded that using continuous weighing on the LWMAT brings it into very close similarity with the Spanier scale. When Spanier (1976) published correlations between his scale, the DAS, and the MAS, he used the original weights for the MAS.

Discriminant, item, and factor analyses. Cross and Sharpley (1981) investigated three psychometric properties of the LWMAT: discriminant analysis, item analysis, and factor analysis. Their Australian sample consisted of 95 individual males and females who had been married at least 3 years (average: 10 years) and whose ages ranged from 22 to 63 years (average: 33); 63% of the subjects had one or more children. When the *101*-point cutoff (suggested by Locke and Wallace) of high-versus-low marital adjustment was used, 62% of the sample scored in the high range.

Cross and Sharpley found that all 15 items discriminated between high and low marital adjustment group placement. Items 1, 7, 9, 10, 12, and 14 were the major contributors to the discriminant function when standardized canonical coefficients were computed. Items 1 ($r = .43$) and 14 ($r = .43$) correlated highest with this discriminant function (Item 1: The degree of happiness, everything considered, of your present marriage; Item 14: If you had your life to live over, do you think you would marry the same person, marry a different person, or not marry at all?). But correlation coefficients for these two items were low. Cross and Sharpley (1981) believe that these measure two relatively independent areas of marital adjustment.

Item analysis revealed between-item correlations to range from $r = .04$ for Items 5 and 15 to $r = .61$ for Items 1 and 13, with an overall mean of $r = .38$. Corrected item-total correlations were high, ranging from $r = .38$ for Item 9 to $r = .81$ for Item 1. Internal consistency was found to be $r = .83$.

In a factor analysis of the scale, two main factors were extracted. All items loaded heavily on the first factor, which accounted for 89% of the variance. This factor was interpreted as a global measure of "marital adjustment." Only three items (5, 7, and 15) loaded on the second factor.

Reliability and internal consistency. Initial reliability coefficients for the LWMAT range from .73 to .90 (Locke & Wallace, 1959).

Cross and Sharpley (1981) found the corrected item-total correlations to range from $r = .38$ to $r = .81$. Internal consistency was found to be .83. Edmonds, Withers, and Dibatista (1972), Spanier (1976), and Spanier and Thompson (1982) found similar item-total correlation ranges ($r = .39$ to .73

and $r = .37$ to $.77$, respectively). However, Spanier (1973) argued that the items at the lower end of this range of correlations raised important questions about the validity of these dimensions as applied to contemporary marriages.

Validity. Gottman (1979), using a modification of the Locke-Williamson Marital Relationship Inventory (MRI), found that it correlated highly with LWMAT scores for husbands ($r = .89$) but not so well for wives ($r = .56$). He concluded that, although the two scales have a great deal of common variance, they may be to some degree different, especially when one considers the wives' scores.

Locke and Wallace (1959) found that 4% of the couples assigned to their high marital adjustment group scored below the suggested cutoff score of 100 for marital adjustment; 17% of the maladjusted group scored above this cutoff. Although no replications of these initial findings have been reported, researchers continue to use the LWMAT to discriminate adjusted from maladjusted couples. Haynes et al. (1979) reported that they were able to discriminate between clinical and nonclinical couples at a rate of 92%. ANOVA of the scores of the two groups revealed significant differences, $F(1, 24) = .962, p < .01$. Fineberg and Lowman (1975), using as criteria for group selection: (1) couples (10) in the initial stages of marital therapy and (2) couples (10) who indicated separately that their marriages were as happy as most marriages, found similar results, $F(1, 18) = 7.21, p < .001$.

Wackowiak and Bragg (1980) assessed the relationship between scores on the LWMAT and scores on the 40-item Marital Contract Assessment Blank (MCAB), a measure of marital openness (O'Neill & O'Neill, 1972). Using a nonclinical volunteer university population, they found that LWMAT scores significantly correlated with scores on the MCAB only for the wives in their sample ($r = .36, p < .05$). Dividing the sample into two groups, those with no children and those with children, the authors found a significant relationship between LWMAT and MCAB scores ($r = .33, p < .05$) only for the latter group of couples, who were older and had been married longer. Additionally, spousal discrepancy in scores on the MCAB was significantly correlated with scores on the LWMAT only for wives ($r = -.49, p < .01$). The data suggest that, for this population, spousal consensus concerning marital openness, as measured by the MCAB, was a significant factor in LWMAT scores for the wives but not for husbands.

Two studies involving depression and marital maladjustment (Coleman & Miller, 1975; Weiss & Aved, 1978) found significant relationships between scores on the LWMAT and scores on the Beck and the Zung inventories of depression. They found a significant negative relationship between LWMAT scores and depression scores on the Beck and the Zung depression scales for husbands. This relationship was not as strong for wives.

Scores of exchange orientation, measured by the F scale, and scores on the LWMAT correlated negatively both for men ($r = -.63$, $p < .01$) and women ($r = -.27$, $p < .06$) (Murstein, Cerreto, & MacDonald, 1977). Correlations between a spouse's F-scale score and the partner's LWMAT score were also significant ($r = -.31$, $p < .05$, for husbands' F-scale scores and wives' MAS scores; $r = -.39$, $p < .02$, for wives' F-scale scores and husbands' LWMAT scores).

Hawkins (1966) explored the extent to which subjects report degrees of marital adjustment thought to be socially appropriate. Using both clinical and nonclinical samples matched for length of marriage, number of children, occupational prestige, educational level, and age, Hawkins found no differences between groups. A small but significant positive correlation was found between scores on the Marlowe-Crown Social Desirability Scale and scores on the LWMAT for both husband and wives. Hawkins concluded that the correlations ($r = .32$ and $r = .37$) were too small for responding in a socially desirable fashion to be the sole determinant of the variance in marital adjustment scores.

However, Edmonds et al. (1972), using three nonclinical volunteer sample populations and the short form of the Edmonds Marital Conventionalization Scale (EMCS), measured the extent to which subjects distort the appraisal of their marriage in the direction of social desirability. He found the EMCS and LWMAT scores to correlate ($r = .63$, .53, and .70, $p < .01$, for the respective samples). Correlation coefficients between item scores on the LWMAT and total scores on the EMCS ranged from $r = .37$ to $r = .59$ for the married-student sample. Using just the sample population of 152 married persons, Edmonds et al. (1972) found that scales of traditional family morality (using items from Terman's Marital Happiness Scale) and religious activity substantially correlated with scores on the LWMAT ($r = .44$ and .41, p not given); when marital conventionalization was held constant, the correlations were reduced to $r = .15$ and $-.02$ (p's not given).

If one accepts the definition of marital adjustment given at the beginning of this chapter, the findings concerning the relationship between marital adjustment and social desirability should not be surprising. Accepting one's mate and one's marriage for what they are may not only be a sign of social desirability, it may also be an indication of maturity (Cole et al., 1980).

Discussion

The Locke-Wallace Marital Adjustment Test has been used extensively in family studies research as well as in clinical outcome investigations. Because of its widespread use, it can be regarded as a recognized standard for comparing samples and outcomes in meta-analytical studies. However, it is important to remember that Locke and Wallace (1959) stressed that their scale was best suited for use with middle-class couples—an issue that some researchers have ignored. This fact should be taken into account in any attempts to compare findings from various studies.

Dyadic Adjustment Scale (DAS)

Another measure of marital adjustment that is currently in use—the Dyadic Adjustment Scale—also comes from the discipline of family sociology (Spanier, 1976).

Development

The following procedures were used in the development of the DAS. A pool of 300 items was developed by identifying all items ever used in scales for measuring adjustment. Duplicate items were eliminated. Three judges, other than the principal researcher, reviewed all items for content validity, eliminating those judged unacceptable. Items had to be relevant for use in the 1970s, as well as judged to be indicators of marital adjustment. The 200 remaining items, plus some new items, were included in a questionnaire administered to 218 married persons and mailed to every person in the county who had obtained a divorce during the prior 12-month period. In addition, the questionnaire was given to a small sample of never-married cohabiting couples.

Frequency distributions were analyzed. Items with low variance and high skew were removed. Remaining items were analyzed by use of a *t*-test for significance of difference between means of the married and of the divorced individuals. After elimination of those items that were not significant at .001 level and that had the lowest *t*-value when they were the same question with alternative wording, 40 items were retained. A factor analysis was conducted on these 40 items to assess adequacy of definition and to make a final determination of items to be included in the scale. Eight items were dropped for having factor loading below .30. A decision was made against item weighting. The final scale of 32 items has a theoretical range of 0-151; the higher the score, the higher the rating of adjustment.

In addition to providing an adjustment score, the DAS yields subscale scores for four interrelated dimensions of adjustment: cohesion, consensus, satisfaction, and affection.

Validity. Content validity was achieved by having three judges maintain items for inclusion only if they considered the items relevant measures of dyadic adjustment for contemporary relationships, consistent with definitions for adjustment, satisfaction, cohesion, and consensus, and well worded with appropriate fixed-choice responses.

Criterion-related validity was considered satisfactory since each of the 32 items in the scale correlated significantly with the external criterion of marital status. Using a *t*-test for differences between married and divorced samples, each item's mean difference between groups was significant at the .001 level.

Construct validity was obtained by correlating the DAS with the LWMAT, which is the most frequently used scale for assessing marital adjustment. The correlation between these scales was .86 among married respondents and .88 among divorced respondents. Factor analysis of the final scale produced four interrelated components, three of which were hypothesized as components of adjustment. The DAS seems to partially measure the theoretical construct of marital adjustment.

Reliability. Reliability was determined for each of the four component scales of the DAS using Cronbach's Coefficient Alpha measure of internal consistency, which is a variant of the basic Kuder-Richardson. The Dyadic Consensus subscale of 13 items has a reliability coefficient of .90. The 10 items of the Dyadic Satisfaction subscale yield a reliability estimate of .94. The Dyadic Cohesion subscale containing 5 items had a .86 reliability coefficient. The subscale of 4 items measuring affectional expression had a .73 coefficient. Total scale reliability is .96.

Weighting. The decision not to use weighting in the DAS was determined as follows. Each respondent was asked to rate each item on the questionnaire on a dimension of importance and in terms of partnership level of agreement. The importance variable was highly skewed in the direction of *very important*. The issue that is of lesser consequence to a relationship, if a couple disagrees on a matter of no importance, would not easily be resolved by assigning different weights to different items because only two items rated *not important*. Since Locke and Wallace (1959) didn't explain how they determine the weighting of the items on their scale and since the evidence in Spanier's (1976) research did not suggest a compelling need for weighting, the DAS does not weight items differently.

The sum of the four DAS subscales comprises the total DAS score. Respondents answer most questions in terms of gradations of agreement or frequency.

Use of the DAS

The DAS has been used in numerous studies since it first appeared in 1976 despite scanty evidence of construct validity. For example, it has been used in studies investigating the relationship between marital quality and environmental-social variables (Bergen and Bergen, 1978); values (Medling & McCarrey, 1981; Stallman, 1979); individual developmental variables and stages of the family life cycle (Balswick, 1979; Houseknecht, 1979;

Houseknecht & Macke, 1981; Selzer, 1978); and the relationship between DAS scores and response set biases (Hansen, 1981).

Two attempts at factor structure replication were undertaken (Sharpley & Cross, 1982; Spanier & Thompson, 1982). Sharpley and Cross found only one underlying adjustment factor in a sample of 95 married individuals. Spanier and Thompson found support for the first three factors—consensus, satisfaction, and cohesion—but not for affectional expression in their sample of 205 divorced and separated individuals.

Essentially, the DAS has not held up well under empirical scrutiny. Empirical findings are mixed. More empirical work is needed to find out precisely what dimensions of marriage are being tapped by the DAS.

Marriage Adjustment Balance Scale (MABS)

The MABS (Orden & Bradburn, 1968) has 18 items that assess a marriage in terms of satisfactions and tensions. Satisfactions are determined by the degree to which activities are shared (e.g., "shared a good laugh"). Tensions are determined by the complaints about the marriage (e.g., "not showing love).

The scale has no items designed to measure sexual satisfaction directly. According to the authors, "not showing love" and "being tired" (in the tensions category) and "showing affection" (in the satisfactions category) were designed to tap into sexual problems. This light treatment of the sexual dimension is a major weakness of the MABS.

Content validity was tested by correlating the two dimensions with an individual's response to the question, "Taking all things into consideration, would you say your marriage is very happy, pretty happy, or not too happy?" Satisfactions were positively correlated to the marital happiness question ($r = .29$ for men and .41 for women); tensions were negatively correlated ($r = -.24$ for men and $-.26$ for women; $N = 1,738$). These correlations are quite low. In his initial factor analytic study of SIDCARB, Bagarozzi (1983) found two 1-item, Likert-style questions—"In general how satisfied are you with your marriage?" and "In general how satisfied are you with your spouse?"—to correlate ($r = .73$ and $r = .71$) respectively with the Locke-Wallace Marital Adjustment Test. The small magnitude of MABS correlations with the LWMAT should be kept in mind when considering the MABS as an indicator of marital satisfaction. The MABS is a product of family sociology. Its continued use in the discipline, despite its questionable validity, may be a reflection of political bias rather than sound empirical judgment.

In the first uses of this measure, the authors found that the answers in the satisfactions dimension fell into two clusters—companionship and sociability. This clustering indicates a differentiation of satisfactions into satisfaction with what goes on within the dyad and satisfaction with what a couple does together, external to the dyad (e.g., "entertaining friends").

Although the clinical utility of MABS is limited, it may serve a diagnostic function by focusing on the separate dimensions of satisfaction and tensions. Clinically, it may be helpful to know how different mixes of satisfactions and tensions affect the marital relationship.

Holmes Social Readjustment Rating Scale (SRRS)

A 43-item self-report questionnaire, the SRRS is used to evaluate the amount of stress in a person's or a couple's life and to evaluate the amount of readjustment needed. Frederickson (1977) hypothesized "that couples experiencing marital dysfunction would show a greater amount of accumulated life stress units than would non-dysfunctioning couples for the previous 12-month period" (p. 43). Subjects were 20 Caucasian married couples (10 nondistressed couples, not receiving or not having received therapy, and 10 conflicted couples, with one or both partners receiving counseling). Their ages ranged from 22 to 56; their incomes ranged from $10,000 to $40,000 per year. The hypothesis was confirmed: The mean life stress score for the nondistressed couples was 260; the mean score for the conflicted couples was 571. The t score was 2.365, significant at the .05 level.

These results seem to indicate a significant relationship between stress and marital adjustment (i.e., a couple's need for therapy). The higher the stress, the greater the need for help in adjusting and relieving the stress. However, the conclusions are certainly limited because of the small sample, the absence of replication, and the paucity of validity data. Additional research is needed.

AFFECT

After years of neglect and the relative hegemony of behavioral and cognitive schools, the importance of feelings and emotions in intimate relationships is finally being given its due (Bradbury & Fincham, 1987; Greenberg & Johnson, 1988; O'Leary, Fincham, & Turkewitz 1983). Historically, feelings and emotions have defied attempts at measurement (Shibles, 1974). As a result, efforts to define feelings and emotions in ways that differentiate the two have been mainly linguistic. Although the scope of this chapter does not permit in-depth discussion of these issues, it is important to recognize the role they play in marriage (Frey, 1980). Feelings describe internal states of individuals. How feelings are dealt with is a matter of choice (Ellis & Harper, 1975). The expression of feeling is "one of the principal sources of information regarding other people" (Heller, 1979, p. 122).

As a topic of research, feelings seem to have received paltry attention. According to L'Abate and Frey (1981), "emotionality has been 'mistreated' in how it is applied to 'everyday psychology,' probably owing to misconceptions stemming from a cognitive-rationalistic perspective in both psychology (clinical and experimental) and western philosophy" (p. 143). This comment applies also to the study of self-disclosure of feelings and intimacy. In fact, 5 years ago, a search on the psychology data base using the descriptors *self-disclosure* and *emotions* uncovered only 16 articles published in the preceding 18 years. Fortunately, both topics have received a great deal of attention during the past 5 years.

One of the most relevant studies to evaluate the role of feelings in marital quality was undertaken by Eidelson (1983) who evaluated 25 distressed and 25 nondistressed couples in an effort to test his affiliation-independence model. Eidelson hypothesized that (1) a person's feeling of emotional uninvolvement in a marriage would be negatively correlated with his or her affiliation motivation; (2) feeling emotionally neglected by one's partner would be negatively correlated with the partner's affiliation motivation; (3) feeling controlled by one's partner would be negatively correlated with the partner's independence motivation; and (4) feeling confined in the marriage would be positively correlated with one's own independence motivation. Results confirmed all four hypotheses. In addition, Eidelson found that "regardless of overall relationship quality, low-affiliators displayed less emotional involvement in their marriages than high-affiliators" (p. 687).

The theoretical implications of this study relate to the possibility that dependence (i.e., affiliation) is essentially and ultimately an emotional condition that pervades the life cycle of the individual, the marriage, and the family (L'Abate 1993). The results of this study were strengthened by another study, in which agreement (i.e., consensus) and feeling understood were significant predictors of communicative satisfaction (Allen & Thompson, 1984).

The same support for the primacy of affect was also found in the laboratory (Gottman & Levenson, 1985) and in therapy (Beutler, Engle, Oro-Beutler, Daldrup, & Meredith, 1986; Guttman & Eaton, 1986; Johnson & Greenberg, 1985a, 1985b).

Dissatisfaction, Instability, and Dissolution

What are the factors that predict marital dissatisfaction, eventually leading to marital dissolution? The answer, of course, is multifaceted. In addition to socioeconomic and other factors, personality characteristics may account for breakup and divorce. Although Counts and Sacks (1986) based their assumptions strictly on clinically impressionistic observations, their conclusions may allow a more focused, hypothesis-testing approach to identifying personality factors in divorce-prone individuals. They studied 12 individuals who had been divorced two or more times. These cases fell into three broad and overlapping groups: (1) self-involved narcissists, (2) compliant depressed persons, and (3) casualties of life's vicissitudes. Counts and Sacks maintained that these three groups demonstrated different etiologies, different treatment effects, and three different diagnoses.

In view of the sheer number of divorces and the effects on the family in general, it would be very worthwhile to follow up these conclusions empirically and to confirm the extent to which intrapersonal characteristics interact with relational characteristics to produce a divorce. The importance of including intrapersonal assessment measures in the evaluation of family systems functioning has been described in detail by Bagarozzi (1985). It is pure folly to leave out the intraindividual dimensions of interpersonal relationships and still claim to be systematic in one's theoretical/clinical approach.

Crane, Newfield, and Armstrong (1984) created the Marital Status Inventory (MSI) to evaluate divorce potential. Two hundred forty-one couples were studied. The MSI was found to adequately meet the criteria of reliability, discriminant validity, and predictive validity. The MSI was able to identify couples who would later divorce.

Intimacy and Self-Disclosure

A byproduct of the increased interest in feelings has been the upsurge of interest in intimacy as a crucial variable in marriage and the family (L'Abate, 1986; Sloan & L'Abate, 1985). Gilbert (1976) defined intimacy as "the depth of exchange, both verbally and nonverbally, between two persons which implies a deep form of acceptance of the other as well as a commitment to the relationship" (p. 221). Intimacy has been cited as an important component in the marital relationship (Berman & Lief, 1975; Waring, 1981) and is considered one of several interpersonal dimensions of a close and prolonged relationship (Waring, Tillman, Frelick, Russell, & Weisz, 1980). Much has been written about the concept of intimacy in interpersonal behavior (e.g., Dahms, 1972, 1974; Derlega & Chaikin, 1975; Feldman, 1979; L'Abate & L'Abate, 1979). On the other hand, empirical approaches to the study of intimacy have been limited. (A thorough review of the literature of intimacy can be found in Sloan and L'Abate, 1985.)

Jourard (1959) believes that self-disclosure is "an index of 'closeness' . . . affection, love or trust that [exists] between two people" (p. 428). Self-disclosure is believed to facilitate intimacy. This idea has been examined by Waring and associates (Waring et al., 1980; Waring, McElreath, Lefcoe, & Weisz, 1981).

In 1983 Waring and Chelune developed a content coding system to score and predict self-disclosure on 10 dimensions of intimacy. This coding system, the Self-disclosure Coding System (Chelune, Skiffington, & Williams, 1981), was combined with a standardized structured interview, the Victoria Hospital Intimacy Interview. The results of a multiple regression analysis performed on the two measures suggest that self-disclosure and intimacy are not synonymous. However, the significant positive empirical relationship between self-disclosure and intimacy lends support to hypotheses that facilitating self-disclosure may increase a couple's level of intimacy and that self-disclosure is a determinant of intimacy.

Hall (1979) found a positive correlation between degree of intimacy and a couple's self-disclosure behavior. She also suggested support for the idea that the positive valence dimension of a disclosure is predictive of intimacy.

Foster (1981) presented a case study of eight older couples who had been married to the same partner for 35 years or longer. She sought to determine the changes that occur in an individual's perception of self-disclosure and intimacy in marriage. The study suggested that all couples had reached levels of self-disclosure at which everything was disclosed and at which intimacy was highest. Intimacy was reported to be more affective (than instrumental) in style.

The reciprocity of self-disclosure is one component of intimacy. Reciprocity of disclosure is believed to operate through the medium of social exchange. Exchange and reciprocity of self disclosure have been conceptualized in a number of ways. For example, Hill and Stull (1982) have identified four types of exchange: equivalent exchange, invariant exchange, turn taking, and trading in futures. The development of intimacy is said to occur along a continuum of these forms, moving from the equivalent exchange of disclosures, as in a quid pro quo relationship (Jackson, 1965), to trading in futures. Trading in futures may be exemplified by processes such as symbolic exchange (Stephen, 1981).

Social penetration theory seems to have grown from the recognition that self-disclosure and reciprocity do not take place in a vacuum. Essentially, social penetration theory is the study of interpersonal exchange, referring to "(1) overt interpersonal behaviors which take place in social interaction and (2) internal subjective processes which precede, accompany, and follow overt exchange" (Altman & Taylor, 1973, p. 4). A "system" involves "many levels of behaviors, which operate together—complementing one another, substituting for one another, and influencing one another" (p. 6).

The theoretical framework of social penetration theory involves two hypotheses.

The first is that interpersonal exchange gradually progresses from superficial, nonintimate areas to more intimate, deeper layers of the self. We get to know others by gradually revealing more and more information about ourselves.

The second hypothesis is that from interaction with others, we assess rewards and losses. The process of the first hypothesis is heavily dependent on the costs and the rewards. If the rewards are fair, in relation to the costs, the level of intimacy will increase, not only in depth but also in breadth.

Disclosure operates according to a norm of reciprocity. Among the findings concerning long-term relationships is the finding that reciprocity of disclosure seems to decrease over time (Altman, 1973). Morton (1978) conducted a study whose primary purpose was to compare the intimacy and reciprocity of overt, ongoing communication among strangers and spouses. Using a content coding system of scoring, Morton divided self-disclosure into a 2×2 matrix of high and low forms of evaluative and discriminative intimacy, replicating the earlier findings concerning reciprocity, these findings suggest "a gradual increase in the intimacy of information shared, that this increase operates through a reciprocity effect, and that reciprocity begins to decline as a relationship advances" (p. 79). Morton concluded by suggesting that reciprocity may be said to function as a regulator of intimacy during the initial acquaintance process but this function diminishes as the acquaintance process progresses.

A *reciprocity effect* has been found consistently (Altman, 1973; Hedges, 1981), but the explanations for it have not been well developed, neither theoretically nor empirically. The importance of reciprocity is that it is interpersonal and has been studied in long-term relationships. What remains are questions concerning the nature of social exchange in committed relationships.

One answer is found in the study of symbolic exchange (Stephen, 1981). In symbolic exchange, reciprocity occurs idiosyncratically at the communication and metacommunication levels. This exchange process lends itself well to L'Abate, Sloan, Wagner, and Malone's (1980) triangle of living made up of Being, Doing, and Having. For instance, a husband's reciprocation of a spouse's disclosure at the affective level (Being) may be his providing for her materially (Having) or performing chores in the house (Doing). A measure of this kind of exchange has been designed (Stephen, 1981).

MEASURES OF INTIMACY

Interpersonal Relationship Scale (IRS)

The IRS was designed by Schlein (1971), along with Guerney and Stover. It is a measure of marital quality in terms of trust and intimacy. The measure was constructed with 106 items but was trimmed to 52 Likert-type items selected as suitable by eight judges who were experts in the field of marriage and the family. Sample items include the following: "I feel comfortable expressing anything to my partner"; "In my relationship I feel I am able to expose my weaknesses"; "I tell my partner some things which I am very ashamed of." A number of the items thus address a person's willingness to disclose vulnerability to the partner.

The IRS has been used in a number of studies. Reliability was assessed by Rappaport (1976), who used a test-retest procedure after a 2-month interval and produced a test-retest Pearson Product Moment correlation of .92. Construct validity was also afforded by this study, which found positive results in assessing the effects of a training procedure (Guerney, 1977). Validity was tested by comparing the IRS with several other measures (Guerney, 1977). Using a sample of 96 subjects, significant correlations were found between the IRS and the Premarital Communication Inventory (.69, $p < .001$), Relationship Scale-Self (.79, $p < .001$), and the Relationship Scale-Partner (.70, $p < .001$).

The IRS has been used in several studies to evaluate various programs. It was used by Ridley, Jorgensen, Morgan, and Avery (1982) to assess the effects of a Relationship Enhancement (RE) program on aspects of relationship quality, such as adjustment, trust, and intimacy. This study compared 25 couples in the program to 29 couples in a relationship discussion group. Rappaport (1976) also used the IRS to assess the outcome of an Intensive Relationship Enhancement program, which uses a sequence of alternating 4- and 8-hour sessions in a total of four sessions. Schlein sought to determine whether dating couples participating in a program could learn to communicate through empathy and self-disclosure (Guerney, 1977). Jessee and Guerney (1981) also used the IRS in a study that compared 36 couples (randomly assigned to either a Relationship Enhancement or to a Gestalt Relationship Facilitation treatment) on the variables of marital adjustment, communication, trust and harmony, rate of positive change in the relationship, relationship satisfaction, and ability to handle problems.

Milholland and Avery (1982) evaluated the effectiveness of Marriage Encounter in increasing self-reports of disclosure, trust, and marital satisfaction. This study used an experimental group of 17 couples and a waiting-list control group of 23 couples. Pre- and posttest measures were taken, as was a 5-week follow-up. Ginsberg and Vogelsong (1977) reported the use of the IRS in a premarital Relationship Enhancement program that was designed to improve a couple's communication by improving their empathy with and self-disclosure to each other. One hypothesis was that trust and intimacy would show a measured improvement as couples were trained in empathy and self-disclosure. The results were not significant, though a favorable trend was indicated.

In a study using intimacy training in marital enrichment (Sloan, 1983), the IRS was again used to measure change in a pre- and posttest format. The results from an intimacy enrichment workshop were significant ($p <$

.05). Yarborough (1983) used the IRS to assess change in a pre- and posttest format in Structured Enrichment (L'Abate, 1975) negotiation training to groups of couples. The null hypothesis of no change of the level of intimacy was rejected ($p < .05$) for the treatment group.

Personal Assessment of Intimacy in a Relationship Inventory (PAIR)

The PAIR Inventory (Schaeffer & Olson, 1981) examines the five areas of intimacy—emotional, social, sexual, intellectual, and recreational. Individuals describe their relationships with significant others according to their current perceptions of them and how they would like the relationships to be. The design is intended for use in marital therapy and enrichment. The rationale of this study began with the idea that "intimacy is sometimes assumed to be characteristic of the ideal type of marriage and family relationship" (p. 47).

Intimacy is said to be a process that occurs over time but is never fully completed or accomplished. This process was originally described as occurring across seven dimensions, including spiritual intimacy and aesthetic intimacy in addition to the five dimensions already listed. However, these two were later dropped. The measure uses the five remaining types in two ways. The first use is to identify the partner's perception of how intimate the relationship is ("realized"). The second use is to identify how intimate a partner would like the relationship to be ("expected") (p. 51). The measure is easily scored, allowing immediate and direct feedback to the respondents.

The construction of the measure began with statements about intimacy solicited from students and professionals. Marriage and family professionals trimmed an initial pool of 350 items drawn from the statements to 113 items. Following a pilot study, the test was subjected to a number of psychometric test criteria. The final version contains 36 items, chosen for brevity and clarity, which are answered on a 5-point Likert-type scale. Subscales were balanced positively and negatively in terms of the responses to them. The test is taken twice—once for the realized dimension and once for the expected dimension. The scoring allows a profile to be made of a partner's weaknesses.

A post hoc correlational analysis was made with a version of the Jourard Self-Disclosure Questionnaire and the PAIR. The results suggest a positive relationship between the two measures. In addition, a highly significant correlation was found between the PAIR inventory and the LWMAT (Locke & Wallace, 1959), offering evidence of construct validity. Finally, reliability and internal consistency were demonstrated by Cronbach's alpha; however, no test-retest trials were presented.

The six subscales (Schaeffer & Olson, 1981) are defined as follows.

(1) Emotional Intimacy: the experiencing of closeness of feeling; the ability to share openly in a nondefensive atmosphere of supportiveness and understanding.
(2) Social Intimacy: the experience of having common friends and a social network.
(3) Sexual Intimacy: the experience of sharing affection, touching, physical closeness, sex.
(4) Intellectual Intimacy: the sharing of ideas, talking about events, discussing job-related issues, beliefs.
(5) Recreational Intimacy: shared pastimes or hobbies, mutual involvement in sports, leisure and recreational activities.
(6) Social Desirability: the extent to which people respond desirably irrespective of the content of the question.

Schaeffer and Olson (1981) have done much to shatter the myth that intimacy is a undimensional construct by empirically demonstrating that intimacy consists of at least six interrelated components. Waring and his associates (1981) have also identified eight components of intimacy: (1) the ability to resolve interpersonal conflict, (2) the ability to experience sexual satisfaction, (3) individual autonomy within the dyad and vis-à-vis other dyadic relationships, (4) couple identity, (5) affection and the expression of positive feelings, (6) dyadic commitment, (7) expression of private thoughts, and (8) compatibility with one's partner.

L'Abate (1977) has also shown how the expression and sharing of negative emotions, especially hurt feelings, is an important component of intimacy. To tap into this dimension of intimacy, Stevens and L'Abate (1989) began work on the Sharing of Hurts Questionnaire. This first version of the SOH was a 28-item true-false self-report measure. It was drawn from a 260-item marital questionnaire designed to measure attitudinal differences in relation to being a functional and effective spouse and parent.

The scoring of the test has a numerical range of 1–28; the higher the score, the greater the indication of psychological health. Test-retest reliability has been reported by Sloan (1983); however, her study offers no evidence of construct validity.

The first version has been used as a covariant measure of self-differentiation (Frey, 1980) and as a measure of intimacy change (Sloan, 1983). The results of these studies suggest that the original form of the SOH scale is equivocal. Reviewing the findings of Frey and of Sloan shows that scores among various groups—sex, religious preference, socioeconomic status, stage of testing (pre/post), and degree of dysfunctionality—ranged from 16.00 to 17.60. These high scores suggest a lack of content validity. As a measure of self-differentiation, the SOH scale demonstrated a low correlation with the Likeness Scale (L'Abate, 1976) in the Frey study. Thus, the record for the use of the SOH scale is less than remarkable. To demonstrate the empirical validity of the construct of the SOH concept, a revision of the SOH scale was necessary.

Because of the shortcomings of the first version of the SOH scale, Stevens and L'Abate (1989) developed a revision that was found to correlate significantly with selected aspects of the other three roles of intimacy already reviewed, the IRS, the PAIR, and the WIQ subscales of Affection and Cohesion.

The SOH concept deserves further study. Specifically, the establishment of the concept as an empirical measure must be attempted so that interventions may be designed and theories may be tested (e.g., the Sloan study, 1983).

The Marital Intimacy Questionnaire

In a series of theoretical articles, clinical papers, and empirical studies spanning the years from 1977 to 1989, Bagarozzi and his associates (Bagarozzi, 1981, 1983, 1986, 1990; Bagarozzi & Anderson, 1989; Bagarozzi & Pollane, 1983) have examined the intricate dynamics of social exchanges between spouses and among family members. For Bagarozzi et al., behavioral reciprocity represents only the surface level of the conjugal exchange process. To gain a more accurate and in-depth understanding of how social exchange systems develop and how a particular social exchange arrangement has come to characterize a given conjugal relationship, a number of issues must be taken into consideration. Some of these include (1) each spouse's definition of the relationship; (2) each spouse's conceptions about the nature of distributive justice in intimate relationships; (3) the symbolic meaning and significance of behaviors exchanged by spouses; (4) each spouse's personal rules for sending and receiving messages that communicate caring, valuing, and validation of the self and other; (5) each spouse's idiosyncratic rules for power sharing and power distribution within the marital dyad; and (6) intraindividual differences between spouses in the area of personal intimacy needs.

For Bagarozzi (1990), there are at least 10 intimacy need dimensions that can be identified. These include (1) physical intimacy, (2) emotional intimacy, (3) sexual intimacy, (4) intellectual intimacy, (5) psychological intimacy, (6) spiritual intimacy, (7) aesthetic intimacy, (8) temporal intimacy, (9) recreational intimacy, and (10) intimacy in the areas of information disclosure, information exchange, and social sharing.

Bagarozzi (1981, 1983, 1986, 1990) postulates that it is highly unlikely for a spouse's need levels to be constant across all 10 dimensions and that it is also highly unlikely for both spouses to experience and share precisely the same need level strength in all 10 intimacy dimensions. Romantic expectations are thought to be a major contributor to marital dissatisfaction. These generally are that a spouse-to-be will have the same strength of need in all 10 dimensions and that a spouse-to-be will be ready, willing, and able to fulfill all of one's desires, as well as to satisfy all of one's needs in every area of intimacy. Therefore assessment of these need expectations failures is considered to be an important aspect of clinical evaluation. To this end, Bagarozzi (1981, 1983, 1986, 1990) developed the Marital Intimacy Questionnaire (MIQ), which is currently undergoing testing and standardization. Bagarozzi (1981, 1983, 1986, 1990) believes that a valid, reliable, and multidimensional measure of intimacy needs may also help clinical researchers gain more insight into the dynamics of dyadic cohesion.

CONCLUSION

As has been said so often throughout this volume, the proliferation of instruments designed to gain both insider's and outsider's views of marriage and family dynamics is commendable. However, such instruments must be conceptually linked to theories of marital/family development if they are to be considered useful to clinicians as well as to researchers. Many of the instruments reviewed in this chapter and elsewhere in this book, even those that have empirical support, lack a theoretical rationale. Without any theoretical underpinning, any instrument or method will only widen the gap between theory and practice, a consequence we can ill afford. We hope that in the future much more attention will be given to healing this clinical/theoretical parting of the ways.

REFERENCES

Allen, A., & Thompson, T. (1984). Agreement, understanding, realization, and feeling understood as predictors of communicative satisfaction in marital dyads. *Journal of Marriage and the Family, 46,* 915–921.

Altman, I. (1973). Reciprocity of interpersonal exchange. *Journal of a Theory of Social Behavior, 3,* 249–261.

Altman, I., & Taylor, D. (1973). *Social penetration: The development of interpersonal relationships.* New York: Holt, Rinehart & Winston.

Bagarozzi, D. A. (1981). The symbolic meaning of behavioral exchanges in marital therapy. In A. S. Gurman (Ed.), *Questions and answers in the practice of family therapy* (pp. 173–177). New York: Brunner/Mazel.

Bagarozzi, D. A. (1983). Methodological developments in measuring social exchange perceptions in marital dyads: SIDCARB. A new tool for clinical intervention. In D. A. Bagarozzi, A. P. Jurich, & R. W. Jackson (Eds.), *Marital and family therapy: New perspectives in theory, research and practice* (pp. 79–104). New York: Human Sciences.

Bagarozzi, D. A. (1985). Family measurement techniques: The Family Coping Strategies Scale. *American Journal of Family Therapy, 13,* 67–71.

Bagarozzi, D. A. (1986). Some issues to consider in the assessment of marital/family functioning. *American Journal of Family Therapy, 14,* 84–86.

Bagarozzi, D. A. (1990). Spousal inventory of desired changes and relationship barriers. In J. Touliatos, B. F. Perlmutter, & M. Straus (Eds.), *Handbook of family measurement techniques* (pp. 469–470). Newbury Park, CA: Sage.

Bagarozzi, D. A., & Anderson, S. A. (1989). *Personal, marital and family myths: Theoretical formulations and clinical strategies.* New York: Norton.

Bagarozzi, D. A., & Pollane, L. (1983). A replication and validation of the Spousal Inventory of Desired Changes and Relationship Barriers (SIDCARB): Elaborations on diagnostic and clinical utilization. *Journal of Sex and Marital Therapy, 9,* 303–315.

Balswick, J. K. (1979). The importance of developmental task achievement to early marital adjustment. *Family Therapy, 6,* 145–153.

Barry, W. A. (1970). Marriage research and conflict: An integrated review. *Psychological Bulletin, 73,* 41–54.

Bergen, G. R., & Bergen, M. B. (1978). Quality of marriage of university students in relation to sources of financial support and demographic characteristics. *Family Coordinator, 27,* 245–250.

Berman, E. M., & Lief, H. I. (1975). Marital therapy from a psychiatric perspective. *American Journal of Psychiatry, 132,* 583–592.

Beutler, L. E., Engle, D., Oro-Beutler, M. E., Daldrup, R., & Meredith, K. (1986). Inability to express intense affect: A common link between depression and pain? *Journal of Consulting and Clinical Psychology, 54,* 752–759.

Bonjean, C. M., Hill, R. J., & McLemore, S. D. (1967). *Sociological measurement: An inventory of scales and indices.* San Francisco: Chandler Publishing.

Bradbury, T. N., & Fincham, F. D. (1987). Assessment of affect. In K. D. O'Leary (Ed.), *Assessment of marital discord* (pp. 59–108). Hillsdale, NJ: Erlbaum.

Burgess, E. W., & Cottrell, L. S., Jr. (1939). *Predicting success or failure in marriage.* Englewood Cliffs, NJ: Prentice Hall.

Burgess, E. W., & Wallin, P. (1953). *Engagement and marriage.* Philadelphia: Lippincott.

Burr, W. R. (1973). *Theory construction and the sociology of the family.* New York: Wiley.

Chelune, G. J., Skiffington, S., & Williams, C. (1981). Multi-dimensional analysis of observer's perceptions of self-disclosing behavior. *Journal of Personality and Social Psychology, 41,* 599–606.

Cole, C. L., Cole, A. L., & Dean, D. G. (1980). Emotional maturity and marital adjustment: A decade replication. *Journal of Marriage and the Family, 42,* 533–539.

Coleman, R. E., & Miller, A. G. (1975). The relationship between depression and marital maladjustment in a clinic population: A multitrait-multimethod study. *Journal of Consulting and Clinical Psychology, 43,* 647–651.

Counts, R. M., & Sacks, A. (1986). Personality characteristics of divorce-prone individuals: A preliminary clinical study. *Contemporary Family Therapy, 8,* 111–121.

Crane, D. R., Newfield, N., & Armstrong, D. (1984). Predicting divorce at marital therapy intake: Wives' distress and the Marital Status Inventory. *Journal of Marital and Family Therapy, 10,* 305–312.

Cross, D. G., & Sharpley, C. F. (1981). The Locke-Wallace Marital Adjustment Test reconsidered: Some psychometric findings as regards its reliability and factorial validity. *Educational and Psychological Measurement, 41,* 1303–1306.

Dahms, A. H. (1972). *Emotional intimacy.* Denver, CO: Pruett.

Dahms, A. H. (1974). Intimate hierarchy. In E. A. Powers & M. W. Lees (Eds.), *Process in relationship : Marriage and family* (pp. 73–92). St. Paul, MN: West.

Derlega, V. J., & Chaikin, A. L. (1975). *Sharing intimacy: What we reveal to others and why.* Englewood Cliffs, NJ: Prentice Hall.

Edmonds, V. H., Withers, G., & DiBatista, B. (1972). Adjustment, conservatism, and marital conventionalization. *Journal of Marriage and the Family, 34,* 96–103.

Eidelson, R. J. (1983). Affiliation and independence issues in marriage. *Journal of Marriage and the Family, 43,* 687–688.

Ellis, A., & Harper, R. A. (1975). *A new guide to rational living.* Hollywood, CA: Melvin Power Wilshire.

Feldman, L. B. (1979). Marital conflict and marital intimacy: An integrative psychodynamic, behavioral-systemic model. *Family Process, 18,* 69–78.

Fineberg, B. L., & Lowman, J. (1975). Affect and status dimensions of marital adjustment. *Journal of Marriage and the Family, 37,* 155–159.

Foster, B. G. (1981). Self-disclosure and intimacy in long-term marriages: Case studies (Doctoral dissertation, Kansas State University, 1980). *Dissertation Abstracts International, 41,* 4947A–4948A.

Frederickson, C. (1977). Life stress and marital conflict: A pilot study. *Journal of Marriage and Family Counseling, 3,* 41–47.

Frey, J. (1980). *Personal correlates of emotional masking.* Unpublished doctoral dissertation, Georgia State University, Atlanta.

Gilbert, S. (1976). Self-disclosure, intimacy, and communication in families. *Family Process, 25,* 221–231.

Ginsberg, B. G., & Vogelsong, E. (1977). Premarital relationship improvement by maximizing empathy and self-disclosure: The PRIMES Program. In B. G. Guerney, Jr (Ed.), *Relationship enhancement: Skill training programs for therapy, problem prevention and enrichment* (pp. 268–288). San Francisco: Jossey-Bass.

Gottman, J. M. (1979). *Marital interaction: Experimental investigation.* New York: Academic Press.

Gottman, J. M., & Levenson, R. W. (1985). A valid procedure for obtaining self-report of affect in marital interaction. *Journal of Consulting and Clinical Psychology, 53,* 151–160.

Greenberg, L. S., & Johnson, S. M. (1988). *Emotionally focused therapy for couples.* New York: Guilford.

Guerney, B. G., Jr. (1977). *Relationship enhancement: Skill training programs for therapy, problem prevention, and enrichment.* San Francisco: Jossey-Bass.

Guttman, H. A., & Eaton, W. (1986). Variables differentiating affective interaction in a family therapy and a control group: Father-child welfare and mother-child emergency affect. *Contemporary Family Therapy: An International Journal, 8,* 316–327.

Hall, J. C. (1979). Self-acceptance and self-disclosure as predictors of intimacy in the marital relationship. (Doctoral dissertation, University of Denver, 1979). *Dissertation Abstracts International, 40,* 2983A.

Hansen, G. L. (1981). Marital adjustment and conventionalization: A reexamination. *Journal of Marriage and the Family, 43,* 855–863.

Hawkins, J. L. (1966). The Locke-Wallace Marital Adjustment Test and social desirability. *Journal of Marriage and the Family, 28,* 193–195.

Haynes, S. N., Follingstad, D. R., & Sullivan, J. C. (1979). Assessment of marital satisfaction and interaction. *Journal of Consulting and Clinical Psychology, 47,* 789–791.

Hedges, N. A. (1981). Reciprocity-orientation and the developmental course of relationships. (Doctoral dissertation, Temple University). *Dissertation Abstracts International, 42,* 2130B–2131B.

Heller, A. (1979). *A theory of feelings.* The Netherlands: Van Gorcum Assen.

Hicks, M. W., & Platt, M. (1971). Marital happiness and stability: A review of the research in the sixties. *Journal of Marriage and the Family, 32,* 553–574.

Hill, C. T., & Stull, D. E. (1982). Disclosure reciprocity: Conceptual and measurement issues. *Social Psychology Quarterly, 45*, 238–244.

Houseknecht, S. K. (1979). Childlessness and marital adjustment. *Journal of Marriage and the Family, 41*, 259–265.

Houseknecht, S. K., & Macke, A. S. (1981). Combining marriage and career: The marital adjustment of professional women. *Journal of Marriage and the Family, 43*, 651–661.

Hunt, R. A. (1978). The effect of item weighting on the Locke-Wallace Marital Adjustment Scale. *Journal of Marriage and the Family, 40*, 249–256.

Jackson, D. D. (1965). Family rules: The marital *quid pro quo. Archives of General Psychiatry, 12*, 589–594.

Jessee, R. E., & Guerney, B. G. (1981). A comparison of gestalt and relationship enhancement treatments with married couples. *American Journal of Family Therapy , 10*, 41–48.

Johnson, S. M., & Greenberg, L. S. (1985a). Differential effects of experiential and problem-solving interventions in resolving marital conflict. *Journal of Consulting and Clinical Psychology, 53*, 175–184.

Johnson, S. M., & Greenberg, L. S. (1985b). Emotionally focused couples therapy: An outcome study. *Journal of Marital and Family Therapy, 11*, 313–317.

Jourard, S. M. (1959). Self-disclosure and other cathexis. *Journal of Abnormal Social Psychology, 59*, 428–431.

Karlsson, G. (1951). *Availability and communication in marriage: A Swedish prediction study of marital satisfaction.* Upsala, Sweden: Almquist & Wiksells, Boktrycheri Aktiebolag.

Kimmel, D., & van der Veen, F. (1974). Factors of marital adjustment in Locke's marital adjustment test. *Journal of Marriage and the Family, 36*, 57–63.

L'Abate, L. (1975). A positive approach to marital and familial intervention. In L. R. Wolberg & M. L. Aronson (Eds.), *Group therapy 1975: An overview* (pp. 63–75). New York: Stratton Intercontinental Medical Book Corp.

L'Abate, L. (1976). *Understanding and helping the individual in the family.* New York: Grune & Stratton.

L'Abate, L. (1977). *Enrichment: Structured interventions with couples, families, and groups.* Washington, DC: University Press of America.

L'Abate, L. (1986). *Systematic family therapy.* New York: Brunner/Mazel.

L'Abate, L. (1993). *A theory of personality development.* (Submitted for publication).

L'Abate, L., & Frey, J. (1981). The E-R-A model: The role of feelings in family therapy reconsidered: Implications for a classification of theories of family therapy. *Journal of Marital and Family Therapy, 7*, 143–150. (Reprinted in L. L'Abate [Ed.] [1983], *Family psychology: Theory, therapy and training* [pp. 125–141]. Washington, DC: University Press of America.)

L'Abate, L., & Goodrich, M. (1980). Marital adjustment. In R. Woody (Ed.), *Encyclopedia of clinical evaluation* (pp. 60–73). San Francisco: Jossey-Bass.

L'Abate, L., & L'Abate, B. L. (1979). The paradoxes of intimacy. *Family Therapy, 6*, 175–184.

L'Abate, L., Sloan, S., Wagner, V., & Malone, K. (1980). The differentiation of resources. *Family Therapy, 7*, 238–246.

Locke, H. J. (1951). *Predicting adjustment in marriage: A comparison of a divorced and a happily married group.* New York: Holt, Rinehart & Winston.

Locke, H. J., & Wallace, K. M. (1959). Short marital-adjustment and prediction tests. Their reliability and validity. *Mariage and Family Living, 21*, 251–255.

Locke, H. J., & Williamson, R. C. (1958). Marital adjustment: A factor analysis study. *American Sociology Review, 23*, 562–569.

Medling, J. M., & McCarrey, M. (1981). Marital adjustment over segments of the family life cycle: The issue of spouses' value similarity. *Journal of Marriage and the Family, 43*, 195–203.

Milholland, T. A., & Avery, A. W. (1982). Effects of marriage encounter on self-disclosure, trust, and marital satisfaction. *Journal of Marital and Family Therapy, 8*, 87–97.

Morton, T. L. (1978). Intimacy and reciprocity of feelings: A comparison of spouses and strangers. *Journal of Personality and Social Psychology, 36*, 72–81.

Murstein, B. I., Cerreto, M., & MacDonald, M. (1977). A theory and investigation of the effect of exchange-orientation on marriage and friendship. *Journal of Marriage and the Family, 39*, 543–549.

O'Leary, K. D., Fincham, F., & Turkewitz, H. (1983). Assessment of positive feelings toward spouse. *Journal of Consulting and Clinical Psychology, 51*, 949–951.

O'Neill, N., & O'Neill, G. (1972). *Open marriage: A new life style for couples.* New York: Evans.

Orden, S. R., & Bradburn, N. M. (1968). Dimensions of marriage happiness. *American Journal of Sociology, 73*, 715–731.

Rappaport, A. F. (1976). Conjugal relationship enhancement program. In D. H. L. Olson (Ed.), *Treating relationships* (pp. 41–66). Lake Mills, IA: Graphic Publishing.

Ridley, C. A., Jorgensen, S. R., Morgan, A. G., & Avery, A. W. (1982). Relationship enhancement with premarital couples: An assessment of effects on relationship quality. *American Journal of Family Therapy, 10*, 41–48.

Schaeffer, M. T., & Olson, D. H. (1981). Assessing intimacy: The PAIR inventory. *Journal of Marriage and the Family, 7*, 47–60.

Schiavi, R. C., Derogatis, L. R., Kuriansky, J., O'Connor, D., & Sharpe, L. (1979). The assessment of sexual function and marital interaction. *Journal of Sex and Marital Therapy, 5*, 179–224.

Schlein, S. P. (1971). *Training dating couples in emphatic and open communication: An experimental evaluation of a potential mental health program.* Unpublished doctoral dissertation, Pennsylvania State University, University Park.

Selzer, T. (1978). Selected factors and combination of factors which predict marital satisfaction for married women within selected stages across the family life cycle. *Dissertation Abstracts International, 38*(10-A), 6025.

Sharpley, C. F., & Cross, D. G. (1982). A psychometric evaluation of the Spanier Dyadic Adjustment Scale. *Journal of Marriage and the Family, 44*, 739–741.

Shibles, W. (1974). *Emotion: The method of philosophical therapy.* Whitewater, WI: Language Press.

Sloan, S. Z. (1983). *Assessing the differential effectiveness of two enrichment formats in facilitating marital intimacy and adjustment.* Unpublished doctoral dissertation, Georgia State University, Atlanta.

Sloan, S. Z., & L'Abate, L. (1985). Intimacy. In L. L'Abate (Ed.), *The handbook of family psychology and therapy* (Vol. 1, pp. 405–427). Pacific Grove, CA: Brooks/Cole.

Spanier, G. B. (1973). Whose marital adjustment? A research note. *Sociological Inquiry, 43*, 95–96.

Spanier, G. B. (1976). Measuring dyadic adjustment: New scales for assessing the quality of marriage and similar dyads. *Journal of Marriage and the Family, 38*, 15–28.

Spanier, G. B., & Thompson, L. (1982). A confirmatory analysis of the Dyadic Adjustment Scale. *Journal of Marriage and the Family, 44*, 731–738.

Stallman, L. S. (1979). Personal values, family values and central values: The interpersonal perception of these values to marital adjustment. Temple University: *Dissertation Abstracts International, 39*(11-B), 5528.

Stephen, T. D. (1981). Longitudinal and cross-sectional tests of a theory of symbolic exchange in developing intimate relationships (Doctoral dissertation, Bowling Green State University, 1980). *Dissertation Abstracts International, 41*(3-4), 2830B.

Stevens, F. E., & L'Abate, L. (1989). Validity and reliability of a theory-derived measure of intimacy. *American Journal of Family Therapy, 17*, 359–368.

Straus, M. A. (Ed.). (1969). *Family measurement techniques.* Minneapolis: University of Minnesota Press.

Terman, L. M. (1938). *Psychological factors in marital happiness.* New York: McGraw-Hill.

Terman, L. M., & Oden, M. H. (1947). *Genetic studies of genius: Vol. 4. The gifted child grows up.* Stanford, CA: Stanford University Press.

Touliatos, J., Perlmutter, B. F., & Straus, M. A. (Eds.). (1990). *Handbook of family measurement techniques.* Newbury Park, CA: Sage.

Urdy, J. R. (1974). *The social context of marriage.* Philadelphia: Lippincott.

Wackowiak, D., & Bragg, H. (1980). Open marriage and marital adjustment. *Journal of Marriage and the Family, 42,* 57–62.

Waring, E. M. (1981). Facilitating marital intimacy through self-disclosure. *American Journal of Family Therapy, 9,* 33–42.

Waring, E. M., & Chelune, G. J. (1983). Marital intimacy and self-disclosure. *Journal of Clinical Psychology, 39,* 183–190.

Waring, E. M., McElreath, P., Lefcoe, P., & Weisz, G. (1981). Dimensions of intimacy in marriage. *Psychiatry, 44,* 169–175.

Waring, E. M., Tillman, M. P., Frelick, L., Russell, L., & Weisz, G. (1980). Concepts of intimacy in the general population, *Journal of Nervous and Mental Diseases, 168,* 471–474.

Weiss, R. L., & Aved, B. M. (1978). Marital satisfaction and depression as predictors of physical health status. *Journal of Consulting and Clinical Psychology, 46,* 1379–1384.

Yarborough, D. M. (1983). *Effects of structured negotiation training on dyadic adjustment, satisfaction, and intimacy.* Unpublished doctoral dissertation, University of Georgia, Athens.

7

Some of the Most Commonly Used Nonbehavioral Measures of Marital Quality

Many of the instruments reviewed in this chapter were developed by family sociologists and family studies experts for research purposes rather than for clinical assessment. Nevertheless, some clinicians have used these non-behavioral measures in their work. For this reason, we have included several instruments whose validity is questionable. In all cases where construct validity is in doubt, we ask that researchers seriously consider whether they should continue to use these instruments, especially if more valid and reliable instruments and procedures are known to be available.

TWO FREQUENTLY USED MEASURES

Marital Communication Inventory (MCI)

Of all the self-report inventories in marital communication, the MCI is probably the one most frequently used in research. Bienvenu (1970) developed this inventory from a review of the literature and from experience in marriage and family counseling. He attempted to establish construct validity by submitting the MCI to scrutiny by sociologists, social workers, and psychologists. Also, groups of married couples reviewed the inventory to make sure the items were understandable. The MCI is designed for people with a seventh-grade reading level.

In a pilot study, Bienvenu (1970) administered the MCI to a group of 176 middle-class married couples, who completed the inventory at their homes. Assuming the procedure outlined above was a valid one, he used a quartile comparison to determine the discrimination between good and poor communication. Of the items, 40 discriminated at the .001 level and 45 items at the .01 level. Use of the Mann-Whitney U test resulted in a significant difference between the groups' scores (good communicators and poor communicators). Reliability of the instrument was tested by the split-half technique. The Spearman-Brown formula revealed a coefficient of .93 after correction.

The attention given to the relationship between marital communication and marital adjustment gave rise to research that used the MCI to measure adjustment. In one study (Murphy & Mendelson, 1973), the MCI and the Interpersonal Checklist (ICL) were compared. The subjects were 15 "adjusted" couples and 15 "maladjusted" couples, as determined by scores on the Locke-Wallace Marital Adjustment Test (LWMAT).

The first hypothesis was that there would be no significant correlation between the scores of the MCI and the LWMAT. This hypothesis was rejected: The instruments correlated at .84, $p = .05$ (Spearman ranking). This correlation adds to the validity of the MCI as a measure of marital communication. Since the MCI purports to measure patterns of communication, it is significant that destructive patterns of communication were found in maladjusted couples and constructive patterns in adjusted couples.

In a well-designed factor analytic study Schumm, Figley, and Jurich (1979) were able to demonstrate that the MCI is not a valid measure of marital communication. These researchers believe that what the MCI actually measures is something akin to marital conventionality, that is, the tendency of respondents to give traditional and generally accepted answers to questions regarding husband/wife relationships. It is no wonder that the MCI was found to correlate .84 with the LWMAT in the Murphy and Mendelson (1973) study since the LWMAT is a measure of conventional marital adjustment. Based upon these findings, we cannot accept the MCI as a valid measure of marital communication.

Primary Communication Inventory (PCI)

Developed by Locke, Sabagh, and Thomas (1956) to measure a couple's verbal and nonverbal communication, the PCI is a 25-item questionnaire designed to be answered on a 5-point scale (*very frequently, frequently, occasionally, seldom,* and *never*). Correlations ranged from .36 to .72, significant at the .01 level.

Navran (1967) used the Marital Relationship Inventory (MRI) to measure marital adjustment and the PCI to determine the relationship of adjustment to communication in marriage. The subjects were 24 couples who took the MRI and the PCI at home. The result was an intercorrelation between the PCI and the MRI of .82.

Kahn (1970) also used the PCI, along with the MAS and the Marital Communication Scale (MCS) to study marital adjustment and communication. The MAS and the PCI are self-report measures; the MCS is an observational, behavioral measure of the accuracy of marital communication. Two groups—21 satisfied and 21 dissatisfied couples—were selected on the basis of their scores on the MAS, which was taken at home. The PCI and the MCS were completed in the research setting.

It was predicted that the PCI scores of the satisfied couples and the dissatisfied couples would differ significantly. This proved to be true: The satisfied couples' mean score was 57.38; the dissatisfied couples' mean score was 52.86, producing a $t = 2.76$, $p > .005$, one-tailed. Correlation between the MCS and the PCI was significant only for the satisfied couples (.61, $p > .01$). These findings offered limited support for the validity of the PCI as a measure of functional communication between spouses.

Beach and Arias (1983) factor-analyzed the PCI with 45 clinical and 50 nonclinical couples who were also administered the LWMAT. They found two major factors: (1) the individual's perceptions of his or her communication ability and (2) the spouse's perceptions of the individual's communication ability. Beach and Arias found that within dyads the discrepancy was greater in nondistressed than in distressed couples. This raised additional questions about the validity of this measure and the "potentially adaptive nature of positive perceptual distortion within the marital dyad" (p. 309).

CONFLICT AND DISCORD

Marital discord comprises a number of interchangeable terms, including *dissatisfaction*, *conflict*, and *tension*. The instruments reviewed in this section assume that dissatisfaction and conflict arise from deficits in communication and problem-solving skills (Swenson & Fiore, 1982; Yelsma, 1981). Integral to this assumption is the idea that a person's predisposition for conflict arises from both intrapsychic and interpersonal factors. The ability to resolve conflict is considered to be an important determinant of marital satisfaction.

Communication Conflict Instrument (CCI)

The CCI (Yelsma, 1981) was developed to measure the relationship between a person's internal behavior and value conflicts and his or her ability to manage interpersonal conflicts. The CCI contains 105 items in six subscales of conflict management that were developed by Brown and Keller (1979) and by Brown, Yelsma, and Keller (1979). These scales operationalize six predispositional factors that are assumed to relate to conflict management: (1) the degree to which a person lives in joy or distress, (2) the amount of energy a person has to get tasks done, (3) a value orientation that reflects how much a person respects the rights of others, (4) a community-value orientation, (5) a measure of how much one feels that one can influence others, and (6) a measure of how much a person values the preservation and the development of his or her own uniqueness.

In addition to these six subscales, the CCI includes a measure of a person's aggressiveness. The items were designed to assess the relationship between a person's conflict management ability and marital dissatisfaction. Results suggest that persons in discordant relationships tend to be less productive in conflict management. The authors proposed that a spouse's values concerning communication determine how well conflict is managed.

Test-retest reliability for each of the six subscales ranged from $r = .48$ to $r = .68$. Internal consistency for the six constructs ranged from $r = .37$ to $r = .78$. In the initial study, the MRI and the CCI were correlated. The results showed that the CCI was able to differentiate happy couples from distressed clinical couples. While offering some data in support of reliability, the authors present no evidence for the validity of the CCI. At this point, we do not know what the CCI actually measures that correlates with the MRI.

DIFFERENTIATION

L'Abate's theory of personality development in the family in its original version (1976) contains three postulates: (1) self-differentiation, (2) priorities, and (3) congruence. The three postulates form the bases for the scales of the Marital Evaluation Questionnaire (MEQ). The first postulate deals with the self, the second deals with the relationship between the self and others, and the third deals with how individuals relate to themselves and one another.

Self-differentiation means setting boundaries on one's own feelings, role allocations, responsibilities, and marital, parental, and work functions. It involves an individual's clarity about self in being able (1) to distinguish various emotional states within the self; (2) to differentiate between what is part of one's own perceptions, opinions, roles, and those of others; (3) to reject that which does not belong to the self; (4) to maintain authority and control over one's own feelings; and (5) to be able to assert one's self positively.

The second postulate—priorities—deals with how the family will structure itself over the life cycle. Priorities can be demonstrated in one's expenditure of time and energy on self, marriage, family, work, friends, and leisure.

Congruence, the third postulate, is based on Satir's (1972) communication model. A dichotomous variable dealing with the consistency of an individual's communications across all behavioral levels, congruence was called "leveling". Congruence reflects trust and feelings of self-worth. A lack of congruence reflects a fear of rejection and feelings of low self-worth. The four types of incongruent communications—blaming, placating, computing, and distracting—hide feelings. Satir viewed these four patterns as discrete categories; but L'Abate has reduced them to two continuous dimensions: the punitiveness dimension, with blaming and placating as the polarities, and the emotional control dimension, with computing and distracting as the polarities. This reduction to two dimensions was done to aid empirical testing and comparative evaluation. This postulate was later collapsed into one of three styles in intimate relations (L'Abate, 1986).

The three postulates represent different aspects of development, with some overlap or interrelatedness. Although self-differentiation affects mate selection, how one asserts one's self after marriage also affects priorities and ultimately the congruence in expression of feelings. Consequently, pathology in self-differentiation and in family priorities shows itself in incongruent behavior. If self is not asserted positively, priorities will be dysfunctional.

> If the self is asserted aggressively (through blaming), or passively (through placating), or smugly (through computing), or actively (through distracting), its assertion would produce the overuse of one of the four incongruent patterns and the consequent overuse of the other three remaining patterns in the other members of the family. A blamer, for instance, may marry a placator, producing a computer or a distractor in the children.

Additionally, if priorities are dysfunctional, an overuse of one of the communication dysfunctions occurs in the family. The level of self-differentiation and the setting of appropriate priorities are positively related to marital satisfaction.

Similarity is seen as basic to mate selection and family functioning, and spouses are thought to be at similar levels of differentiation. Also, priorities are described to be related both to level of differentiation and to communication congruence. Similarity between spouses in terms of the three postulates can be expected. Complementarity can be expected on the communication scales.

L'Abate and Goodrich (1980) hypothesized that marital satisfaction and stability are related through the variable of self-differentiation, which is an intraindividual concept; Lewis and Spanier (1979) postulated that intradyadic factors directly affect the quality of marriage and that extradyadic factors affect the stability of marriage. Lewis and Spanier suggested that a marital pair may fall into one of four categories defined by combinations of marital quality and stability: high quality-high stability, high quality-low stability, low stability-low quality, and low quality-high stability. The combination that characterizes the marriage may change over time, depending upon the push and pull between attractions to the marriage and tensions within the marriage, as well as the balance between external attractions and pressures.

There are two important aspects to L'Abate's (1976) theory. First, the theory is linked to issues of therapeutic concern and thus has the potential to guide clinical practice. Second, this theory has led to the development of an instrument that can be used for diagnostic and evaluative purposes.

The scales of the MEQ define areas through which treatment should be ordered, starting with attention to congruence, followed by work on setting priorities, and ending with attention to the differentiation of self. One's level of differentiation determines one's ability to benefit from specific treatment approaches. Persons with a high level of differentiation might be able to benefit from unstructured intervention of undetermined length, as well as structured or programmed interventions of predetermined duration; those with lower levels of differentiation might be more appropriately treated with structured interventions.

One difficulty in the validation of the MEQ is that L'Abate's theory has not described environmental contingencies that may influence the relationships between postulates and the dependent measures of level of marital satisfaction. The dependent variables, which L'Abate has related to his postulates, may themselves be interdependent. For example, the level of marital satisfaction would seem to influence therapeutic outcome. Validation of the theory with level of marital satisfaction seems to be a logical step before treatment variables are considered as the criteria for validation.

Highly differentiated individuals or those striving for greater self-differentiation may be more able to ask for help than less differentiated individuals (L'Abate, 1976, p. 251). He, in fact, found partial support for this premise. Yet a highly differentiated person who seeks help with a marriage may do so because of either a dysfunction in the marriage or a desire for growth within a functional relationship. Thus, two extremes of marital satisfaction may be present in highly differentiated persons who seek help.

The relationship between communication dysfunctions and marital satisfaction implies that the greater the incongruence, the less the marital satisfaction. L'Abate views self-differentiation along a continuum of likeness (symbiosis, sameness, similarity, differentness, oppositeness, and autism), which he conceptualized as a dialectical rather than a linear model. This dialectical approach "considers the nature of feedback as going back and forth from one polarity to another or from an aspect of a problem, the thesis, in conflict with its antithesis, allowing for change and growth" (L'Abate, 1976, p. 96). The most undifferentiated individuals can be classified as functioning within the symbiotic-autistic range (the least healthy), less differentiated individuals within the sameness-oppositeness range, and the most differentiated within the different-similar range (the most healthy). He hypothesized that although marital satisfaction may be greatest in the most differentiated group (similar-different), marriages in extremely undifferentiated individuals (symbiosis-autism) would also be stable because "misery loves company" (L'Abate & Goodrich, 1980). Thus, marital satisfaction and marital stability may be related but not always in a positive direction. Level of self-differentiation influences the relationship between marital satisfaction and marital stability.

L'Abate (1983, 1986, 1993) later refined his theory and expanded the meanings and definitions of the three levels of differentiation. The autistic-symbiotic level was redefined as abuse-apathy; the sameness-oppositeness level was redefined as reactivity-repetitiveness; and the similar-different level was redefined as conductivity-creativity. This change was an effort to link an internal state of personality differentiation to external interpersonal styles.

Apathy stands for such behaviors as autism, alienation, and isolation. Reactivity means immediate reaction and repetition of the same or opposite patterns. Conductivity, however, stands for creativity, congruence, and commitment to change in intimate relationships. The postulate of communication congruence has thus been subsumed under the postulate of differentiation. The reactive group (formerly called same-opposite) is characterized by incongruent communications such as blaming, placating, distracting, and computing. The conductive group (formerly called similar-different) is characterized by the ability to form intimate relationships and to be congruent in communication.

In summary, the studies of Hutton (1974), Del Monte (1976), and Jessee (1978) provide positive evidence of the validity of L'Abate's instrument; the studies of Cohen (1975), Wright (1976), and Bryson (1978) suggest qualifications about the validity of the Likeness scale. Wagner's (1980) study did not provide evidence regarding the validity of the Likeness subscale. Cohen (1975) and Wright (1976) found sex differences in the concurrent validation of the Likeness subscale; Bryson (1978) did not find a significant correlation of the Likeness subscale with the other subscales.

The research on the Priorities subscale before Wagner's (1980) study was incidental, almost nonexistent. Cohen (1975) found a positive correlation between the Priorities subscale and the Likeness subscale of the MEQ for women. L'Abate & Wagner (1988) found evidence for the convergent and discriminant validity of the Priorities scale.

The four subscales measuring the communication dysfunctions are the Blaming, Placating, Computing, and Distracting scales, based on the postulate of congruence. Because all six subscales are coded so that the higher scores mean healthier psychological functioning, the higher scores on the Blaming, Placating, Computing, and Distracting scales mean that the individual is less likely to take one of these stances.

Using the *What Would You Do Test* to validate the four communication dysfunction or congruence scales, L'Abate & Wagner (1988) found evidence for the convergent validity of the Blaming, Placating, Distracting, and Computing scales and evidence for the discriminant validity of the Distracting and Computing scales. Earlier, Cohen (1975), incidental to her study on sex differences in differentiation, found negative correlations between the Blaming and Placating scales and between the Computing and Distracting scales. These findings provided evidence for L'Abate's bipolar model, with Blaming-Placating at the extremes of one dimension and Distracting-Computing at the extremes of another dimension. However, L'Abate & Wagner (1988) found no meaningful relationship between these four variables on the MEQ, which supported Satir's notion of four independent dimensions. There is justification for additional research concerning the MEQ and its relationship to criteria relevant to marital quality.

Exchange-Orientation

The Exchange-Orientation instrument contains 44 items scored on a 5-point scale ranging from *agree completely* to *strongly disagree*. Examples of the items are "If I do the dishes three times a week, I expect my spouse to do them three times a week" and "It does not matter if the people I love do less for me than I do for them" (Murstein, Cerreto, & MacDonald, 1977, p. 546). Of 34 married couples, each spouse was given the Exchange scale (E scale), as well as the Locke-Wallace short-form Marital Adjustment Scale (1959) and a background questionnaire. The spouses were to return the instruments to the researchers without discussing or even looking at each other's answers.

Of four hypotheses, however, only the following two dealt with marital adjustment: (1) the E score and marital adjustment would be negatively associated and (2) two E-oriented persons married to each other would be significantly less happy in marriage than would the three other combinations (p. 546).

A significant correlation was found between exchange and marital adjustment for men ($-.65$, $p < .01$) and for women ($-.27$, $p < .06$). The first hypothesis was confirmed strongly for the men, but no significance was found for the women. The second hypothesis was only partially confirmed, in that the E-oriented men showed a significantly smaller mean than the pooled group of other men, yielding a t score of 2.78, $p < .01$. The wives' scores, however, were not significant ($t = 1.01$, $p < .01$).

The authors concluded that a great deal more research is needed on the concept of exchange-orientation, especially the E personality. This theory does seem to hold promise for the study of marital adjustment and satisfaction. It should be noted that construct validity for the Exchange Orientation questionnaire still remains to be demonstrated. It cannot be assumed that significant correlations with LWMAT are a measure of Exchange Orientation. The EO may simply be another measure of marital quality as marital satisfaction.

Inventory of Marital Conflicts (IMC)

The Inventory of Marital Conflicts, or IMC (Olson & Ryder, 1970), is one of the oldest measures of conflict. Although both self-report and observation are used in this inventory, the written self-report is discussed here. The self-report section of the IMC consists of 18 short vignettes. In each vignette, a question is asked: "Who is responsible?" Scoring deals with who "wins" the argument. The IMC requires respondents to take a zero sum game approach to conflict resolution. The IMC has been used as a measure of power, authority, and complementarity.

The husband and the wife receive separate tests. For the wife, 12 of the 18 vignettes are slanted to make the husband seem to be at fault. For the husband, these same vignettes are slanted to make the wife seem to be at fault. The vignettes include themes such as a visit by a friend of the husband, satisfaction with sex, and the amount of time the husband spends at his job. For the observation section, the husband and wife are brought together to discuss the vignettes.

Split-half reliability was .46 and was significant at a level of $p < .001$. Validity was assessed by asking spouses to indicate whether their mates reacted in their usual manner while attempting to resolve differences. Of the spouses, 77% answered affirmatively. Another data analysis based on a sample of 200 couples indicated that at least one partner perceived each item on the IMC as identical to problems that had been experienced in the marriage or experienced by friends. These results offer some support for validity.

Scale of Marriage Problems (SMP)

The SMP (Swenson & Fiore, 1982) assumes that a couple's inability to solve problems is the major soure of marital discord. Drawn from a total of 100 common marital problems, six scales have been assembled: (1) problem solving, decision making, goal setting; (2) child rearing and home labor; (3) relations and in-laws; (4) personal care and appearance; (5) money arrangements; and (6) expression of affection and relationships with people outside the marriage. The 43-item, multiple-choice scale is easy to complete.

Cronbach's alpha reliabilities for the subscales ranged from .32 to .78, and reliability for the total scale was .85. No demonstrated validity was reported.

DYADIC FORMATION

This section takes a brief look at some of the measures that concern specific dynamics of the dyadic relationship, including sex roles and role norms and validation by other. Marital role behaviors may be defined as a broad combination of the past influences of the traditional marriage in contrast to the consequences of the industrial age and the women's movement (Minuchin, 1974). A typical result of this contrast is a need for the husband and father to alter his rigid role expectations. This view may be considered the cutting edge of marital trends for the rest of this decade in urban America. As a consequence of this trend, measures of sex roles and marital roles are, by implication, the means by which this movement may be monitored.

Maferr Inventory of Masculine and Feminine Values

The Maferr Inventory of Masculine and Feminine Values (Steinmann, 1975) assesses the balance between a spouse's personal interests and the interests of the family. The measure may be used to determine the differences between what partners want and expect for themselves and what they want and expect from their mates. The measure contains 68 items answered on a Likert scale—34 masculine values and 34 feminine values. There are 17 items on the Masculine Values scale that describe a "family-oriented man" (i.e., the degree to which a man sees his own satisfaction as no more important than his family's satisfactions). The other 17 items describe a man who sees his personal satisfactions as more important than his wife's or his family's satisfactions.

The 34 items on the Feminine Values scale are also divided: the first 17 items express the degree to which a woman places her needs and satisfactions second to those of her family and her husband; the other 17 items evaluate the degree to which a woman places her needs and satisfactions ahead of those of her husband and her family.

The measure was designed to investigate a spouse's perceptions about appropriate sex-role behavior. Intended for use in individual therapy, the measure has also been used in couples and in family therapy. It is useful in determining discrepancies between sex role expectations between husbands and wifes.

The Maferr Foundation, which began this research project in 1957, has collected a pool of more than 40,000 subjects from the United States and abroad. However, no data concerning reliability and validity have been presented.

SEX ROLE AND MARITAL ROLE NORMS

Scanzoni (1975) constructed a measure consisting of 39 items designed to assess the degree of traditionalism existing within a marriage. There are 10 subscales: (1) traditional wife; (2) traditional husband; (3) self-actualizing wife; (4) religious legitimation of the mother's role; (5) problematic husband, measuring a husband's acceptance of nontraditional marital roles; (6) institutionalized husband-wife equality, a more specific measure of the husband's willingness to accept specific changes in the wife's work role; (7) abilities evaluation, measuring how well a spouse performs particular tasks; (8) traditional mother; (9) self-concept; (10) expressive self-concept.

Although the measure may be slightly out of date, it may have some value with more conservative populations or in places where conventional marriages are the norm. As with many of the measures we have reviewed, this one also lacks data on validity and reliability.

Marital Problem-Solving Scale (MPSS)

The MPSS (Baugh, Avery, & Sheets-Haworth, 1982) is a measure of problem-solving ability. The MPSS has nine items that are answered on a 7-point Likert scale ranging from *very unhappy* to *very happy*; for example, "How happy are you with the decision making within your marriage?" Internal consistency was estimated to be $r = .95$ by Cronbach's alpha coefficient. Item correlations were computed and found to be significant ($p < .006$). Test-retest reliability was computed to yield a Pearson product moment correlation of $r = .86$ ($p < .001$).

Validity was established through correlation with the Spanier Dyadic Adjustment Scale and yielded $r = .61$ ($p < .0001$). Further correlation was performed between the MPSS and the Interpersonal Relations Scale, yielding $r = .55$ ($p < .0003$). Discriminant validity was also established.

This measure was also designed to alleviate the poor cost-benefit ratio of behavioral coding methods. The demonstration of reliability and validity is remarkable when one considers the simplicity of the nine-item MPSS. Although opinions diverge about the validity of self-report measures and of behavioral assessment via coding, this instrument, in a most thorough effort to bridge the two schools of assessment, has demonstrated significant correlation with a behavioral coding assessment scheme. In short, the MPSS has demonstrated concurrent validity with behavioral coding assessments, enabling one to say that it is just as good as the time-consuming and expensive methods of behavior coding. In conclusion, the MPSS has demonstrated itself to be the sine qua non in assessing problem-solving ability.

MARITAL ROLE EXPECTATIONS

The tests reviewed here measure different aspects of marital relationships, and focus on marital role expectations and performance.

Index of Marital Integration

The Index of Marital Integration was developed by Farber (1957) to study the effects of a severely retarded child on the parents' marital integration. Marital integration consists of two components: an integration of ends, which is the consensus between husband and wife on the rank ordering of domestic values, and an integration of means, which is the mutual coordination of domestic roles. Marital integration is partly determined by the extent to which the couple agrees on the rank ordering of 10 domestic values (ranked according to their perceived importance to family success). The extent of agreement is measured by the Spearman rank correlation coefficient, and the size of this coefficient is used as an index of the degree of consensus. Integration is also determined by the degree of coordination of domestic roles; a failure to coordinate is regarded as a cause of marital tension. The tension in the marital roles system is measured by the sum of the ratings by both spouses on 10 personality traits selected on the basis of a factor analysis. The sum provides a role tension score, a high score indicating low marital role tension and high integration.

The index of consensus and the index of role tension are combined to form a marital integration index by assigning a score to each couple according to the quartile in which their score for each index is found (top quartile scores 3; lowest quartile scores 0). Each couple's quartile scores are then added to form the marital integration score for the couple (possible range, 0–6). Couples with a score of 4, 5, or 6 are classified as having high marital integration; scores of 0, 1, 2, or 3 indicate low integration.

The extent to which the Index of Marital Integration accurately summarizes marital integration was examined in three ways: consistency with current theory and knowledge, consistency with personal experience, and consistency with two indexes of marital success (Farber, 1957). The validity of the index was measured by examining the consistency of the index with the theory and findings in (1) the social and emotional aspects of interaction and (2) the perceived similarity of family members. Using a sample of 99 white, urban, middle-class families, Farber found that marital integration, as measured by the Index of Marital Integration, was related to (1) the husband's emphasis on companionship, (2) the degree of the husband's identification with his spouse, (3) the degree of the wife's identification with the child, and (4) the personal adjustment of the husband and wife in the marriage (using a different sample).

Farber (1959) reported the effects of a severely mentally retarded child on the integration of the family. The sample consisted of 240 families, each with one mentally deficient child under age 16. The marital integration of lower-class parents was more adversely affected when the mentally deficient child was a boy, but this difference tended to disappear when the child was institutionalized. Although frequent interaction with the wife's mother was supportive, frequent interaction with the husband's mother was associated with low marital integration.

Crain, Sussman, and Weil (1966) studied the effects of a diabetic child on the parents' marital integration. The sample consisted of the families of 54 diabetic children and a control group of 76 families without a diabetic child. The amount of role tension was significantly greater among the parents of diabetic children, and the presence of a diabetic child was associated with lower marital integration and greater marital conflict.

Fowle (1969) also studied the effects of a retarded child on the parents' marital integration, comparing parents who kept their child at home and parents who placed their child in an institution. The sample comprised 35 families who had hospitalized their child and 35 families who had not hospitalized their child. The difference between the marital integration scores for the parents in the two groups was not statistically significant. When the data were reanalyzed to compare the scores of parents whose children had been institutionalized for 2 years or more with those whose children had been hospitalized for less than 2 years, the former group scored significantly higher on marital integration. It was also noted that the marital role tension of the wives was considerably greater than that of the husbands in both groups. Lacking a control group of parents without a retarded child, this later finding is not conclusive.

The Index of Marital Integration was also used in a study that examined marital integration as a factor in parents' agreement on their satisfaction with the behavior of their child (Farber & McHale, 1959). One result that supports the validity of this index is that when there was a high degree of role tension and a low degree of consensus on domestic values, there was little correlation between marital integration and satisfaction with the child's behavior. This suggests that when either the values are in conflict or the roles are in a state of tension, the development of consistent child-raising patterns by the husband and wife seems inhibited.

Farber's index of consensus was used in a longitudinal study examining the relationship between progress toward permanence in couples seriously considering marriage and measures of need complementarity and homogamy (value consensus) (Kerckhoff & Davis, 1962). In a sample of 94 couples, value consensus was significantly related to progress toward permanence during a 7-month period for the total sample. Complementarity was related to progress only in the couples who had gone together for 18 months or more. As a result of these findings, a series of "filtering factors" was proposed: Social status variables operate in the early stages of the relationship, consensus on values somewhat later, and need complementarity still later.

Using essentially the same data, Kerckhoff and Bean (1967) tested the following hypothesis: "Given a high need for value reinforcement, the greater the agreement in values between the perceiver and the other, the more positively will the other be evaluated" (p. 177). This relationship was expected to be more apparent when the perceiver is the female of the dyad. The findings for the women supported this hypothesis, but a negative relationship between consensus and person perception was found for high expressed inclusion men. The authors realized that this hypothesis would hold only for those who seek interaction for value reinforcement, not necessarily for those who seek to exert power over others. A reexamination of the data showed that persons who expressed a greater need to control others responded more favorably to value disagreement and that those who expressed a need to be controlled responded more favorably to value agreement.

Farber, Jenne, and Meyerowitz (as reported by Kirkpatrick, 1978) established the reliability for this measure through test-retest, internal consistency, and comparison of responses for married couples and randomly matched husbands and wives. Reliability estimates for role tension were .64 and .72 for the two samples; consensus reliability was .31 and .20. When the married and randomly matched couples were compared, the real consensus scores were considerably higher than the synthetic scores. In a test-retest comparison of 60 couples, made after 9 months, 52 couples scored within 2 units of their pretest scores (1 couple had separated during the interim). Of the other 7 couples, reasons for the shift in scores were recognized (Farber, 1960).

A 1-year longitudinal study of 43 newly married couples was conducted in Australia to assess the relationship between different patterns of marital role expectations and changes in levels of goal-value consensus (Craddock, 1980). The original goals contained in Farber's index of value consensus were extended and revised so they would be more appropriate for Australian society. This revised set of goals maintained a high test-retest reliability during a 5-week interval (rank order correlation of .96). The findings of this study indicate that couples whose role expectations are incongruent (traditional husband and equalitarian wife) experience significantly lower levels of goal-value consensus after several months of marriage.

KDS-15 Questionnaire

The KDS-15 is a 15-page self-report that covers many aspects of a person's marital relationship: individual development, parental family situation, psychosocial history, courtship, current marital relationship, current living situation, premarital and marital sexual activity, the impact of children on the marriage, work and social activities, the use of leisure time, medical history, and attitudes about role behavior in marriage (Frank, Anderson, & Rubinstein, 1980). In a study of internal consistency, significant correlations ($p <$ .001) were found for all pairs of repeated or similar items (Frank, Anderson, & Rubinstein, 1979).

One section of the instrument contains questions in eight areas concerning marital role ideals and behaviors: (1) caring for the home, cooking, and shopping; (2) making major family decisions; (3) having a career; (4) being sexually faithful; (5) having responsibility for care of children; (6) being sexually aggressive; (7) having interests and activities that do not include spouse; and (8) determining how money is spent. In a study designed to examine the relationship between marital role tensions and sexual satisfaction and to look at the specific role areas in which distressed couples experienced problems, Frank et al. (1979) used only this subscale and the subscale designed to assess sexual difficulties between spouses. Subjects were 80 nonclinical couples, 50 clinical couples, and 50 couples undergoing sex therapy for which role strain scores (discrepancy between one's ideals of marital role behavior and the perception of the actual behaviors in the marriage) and sexual dissatisfaction scores were calculated. The findings of this study showed that higher role strain is correlated with increased sexual dissatisfaction for all three groups. Nonclinical couples had lower levels of role strain than either of the clinical groups.

Using the data gathered in the 1979 study, Frank et al. (1980) examined the discrepancies between each husband's and each wife's ideals and between each husband's and each wife's perceptions of their mate's actual behaviors. Significant differences were found among the three groups with respect to the amount of intraindividual role strain experienced. Significant differences were also found for discrepancies between the husband-wife pairs in actual role assignments. Husband-wife discrepancy for perceived role assignments was greatest for marital therapy couples and lowest for the nonclinical group.

In another study, Frank and Kupfer (1976) administered several sections of the KDS-15 to 20 clinical couples and 20 sex therapy couples to investigate whether significant differences existed in how the husbands and wives viewed selected aspects of their marriages. Mean discrepancy scores for both groups were compared. A high discrepancy score on expectations was noted for both groups, but there was no significant difference between the two.

The finding underscores the failure of both groups to be explicit about their role expectations. No significant difference was found in the couples' ability to agree on whether they were experiencing sexual difficulties.

The KDS-15 was used by Frank et al. (1981) to assess the marital adjustment of couples in which one spouse suffered from manic-depressive illness. The sample comprised 16 patient couples and 16 "normal" couples. Approximately 100 items were analyzed in order to assess the differences and similarities between the two groups. Frank et al. found patient couples achieved an adjustment level similar to that of couples without any psychiatric illness when the patient-spouse is stable.

Marital Roles Inventory

The Marital Roles Inventory was devised by Hurvitz (1960a, 1960b, 1965a, 1965b) for the measurement of marital adjustment within the theoretical framework of role theory. Its theoretical premise is the institutional approach of family sociology. Each spouse's roles are recurring units of conduct that constitute a role set with two aspects: each spouse's performance on his or her role-set and each spouse's expectations of how the other will perform his or her role-set (Hurvitz, 1960b). The compatibility of role performance and role expectations is one aspect of marital adjustment; differences between performance and expectations result in marital strain. The inventory has also been used as a measure of marital success (Hurvitz, 1965b), marital strain (Hurvitz, 1960b, 1965a), and marital satisfaction.

The Marital Roles Inventory consists of two 11-item lists containing the role-set of the husband and the role-set of the wife. Spouses are asked to rank order each list in terms of current role performance. Next, spouses are asked to make ideal rankings. Indices of Role Strain, Deviation of Role Performances, and Deviation of Role Expectations can be calculated. Modal scores for all three rankings have been developed for both middle-class couples and working-class families (Hurvitz, 1965a).

The Marital Roles Inventory and Index of Strain were originally devised for the study of marital roles and adjustment in marriage in a random sample of 104 middle-class couples (Hurvitz, 1960b). In this sample, the wives had a significantly lower Index of Strain (husbands = 6.09, wives = 5.26, $t = 3.46$, $p < .001$), which suggests a clearer definition of the wives' rank order of marital roles, and that the wives' performances of these roles are more in accord with their husbands' expectations. A significant positive correlation was found for the distribution of the Indexes of Strain for the husbands and wives ($r = .20$, $p < .05$), which indicates a tendency for both spouses to have either high or low Indexes of Strain. This suggests the tendency for couples who agree about the rank order of the role-set of one spouse to agree about the rank order of the role-set of the other spouse. Significant correlations were found between the Index of Strain for each spouse and their Index of Deviation of Performance roles (husbands $r = .31$; wives $r = .34$; $p < .05$), which suggests that spouses experience increasing strain in their relationship the more they perform their roles differently from the modal rank order of role performance in their subculture.

A significant correlation was found between the wives' Index of Strain and the husbands' Index of Deviation of Performance roles ($r = .39$, $p < .05$), but none was found for the husbands' Index of Strain and the wives' Index of Deviation of Performance roles. Although the wives' strain increased as the husbands performed their roles differently from other husbands, the husbands' strain seemed independent in this regard. Correlations were found between one spouse's Index of Strain and the other spouse's Index of Deviation of Expectation roles ($r = .28$, husbands; and $r = .50$, wives), indicating that marital strain increased the more the spouse's expectations of role-set differed from the other spouse's modal rank ordering of expectations.

These subjects also completed the Locke-Wallace Short Marital Adjustment Test (Locke & Wallace, 1959). Significant inverse correlations were found between the husbands' Index of Strain and the adjustment scores of the husbands ($r = -.22$) and the wives ($r = -.23$), but none were found between the wives' Index of Strain and the marital adjustment scores of the husbands and wives ($r = -.07$ and $r = -.08$, respectively). These findings indicate that husbands who express less strain in their relationships are happier than those who express more. The fact that a similar association was not found for the wives was explained by the possible inadequacies of both the MRI and the LWMAT as well as the special characteristics of the sample. As a result of this study, the Marital Roles Inventory was modified to its present form by adding two roles to the wife's role-set and one to the husband's.

Hurvitz (1965b) proposed that marital role strain is "the sociological variable in measuring marital success" (p. 39) and stated that although scales such as the Locke-Wallace are capable of differentiating between happy and unhappy married persons, the sociological value of this differentiation is questionable. The sociological significance of studying happiness in marriage is to locate personal and social strain points, and Hurvitz proposed the Marital Roles Inventory as a method of measuring marital strain.

Marriage Role Questionnaire (MRQ)

The MRQ was constructed by Tharp (1963a, 1963b), who factor-analyzed 48 variables that were the responses to 98 items on a questionnaire treating 48 units of marital behavior concerned with role expectations and role enactments. The factor analysis resulted in 12 factors or dimensions of marriage roles. In addition to describing these dimensions, the purpose of this study was to "judge the equivalence or nonequivalence of these dimensions for men and women" (1963a, p. 390). Therefore, each set of variables was factored separately for men, for women, and for men and women together. From the separate analyses, 12 factors emerged for each of the three groups for the dimensions of expectations; for role enactments, 10 factors emerged for the men and for the women, 11 for the combined group.

From the factor analysis, the 98 items were eventually reduced to 22 factors. These factors can be grouped into five classes, each describing a main marriage function: (1) internal instrumentality (adequacy and performance); (2) division of responsibility (social influence versus role sharing); (3) solidarity (intimacy, integration); (4) external relations (social activity); (5) sexuality (fidelity, gratification).

The MRQ was later expanded and revised to contain 71 item sets for women and 78 item sets for men (Crago & Tharp, 1968). Every statement concerning a role expectation has a matching question concerning the same role enactment. Role discrepancy is measured by the difference on the 5-point rating scale score for each expectation/enactment set.

When partners differ in their role definitions in any of the five functional areas, conflict and discord may arise. At that point, treatment should be oriented toward helping the couple negotiate and reorganize the allocation of roles to allow maximum role satisfaction for husband and for wife. Crago and Tharp (1968) administered the MRQ to 35 psychiatric patients and their spouses in order to test the notion that individual psychopathology is symptomatic of social system disorder characterized by disturbances in family roles. They found that the patient/spouse populations were experiencing greater marital role disturbance than were their nonclinical counterparts.

The MRQ has been used in numerous validation studies and has been shown to be a reliable measure. We believe that the MRQ shows promise as a clinical assessment tool.

Yale Marital Interaction Battery

The Yale Marital Interaction Battery, a questionnaire devised by Buerkle and Badgley (1959) to measure interaction patterns, is composed of two sections. The first section of the original version consists of 40 behavior sequences in which the husband and wife are faced with hypothetical conflicting roles in marriage and the family. The two separate forms for the husband and wife are the same except that the sex referents are reversed. The spouses are asked to resolve the dilemma by choosing one of four solutions, either taking the role of the other or not. Each of the four replies represents a different order of response along the role-taking dimension. The partners are asked to choose the alternative most closely approximating their normal solution to such a problem.

Of the four alternatives, one indicates that no role taking has occurred.

By choosing this alternative, the respondent terminates the behavior sequence without taking the other spouse's attitude into account. The second alternative represents a position where the other spouse's attitude is recognized, or the role of the other is taken, but the respondent decides in favor of his or her own attitudinal set. By choosing the third alternative, the respondent weighs his or her attitude set against the spouse's and decides in favor of the spouse. The fourth alternative indicates that the respondent takes the role of the spouse immediately and chooses in the spouse's favor.

In a later study (Buerkle, Anderson, & Badgley, 1961), the responses of both the husband and the wife were scored for each sequence and combined to form a couple score. If one spouse takes the role of the other and the other spouse does not, the couple has agreed on a frame of reference or course of action, even though one spouse is a low role-taker. If both spouses take the role of the other, the couple has responded with reciprocal role taking. In both instances, the response patterns received high scores in the final weighing for a Guttman scale analysis.

Using the couple's raw score, the Reciprocal Dyad Scale of 14 items was devised that received a .90 coefficient of reproducibility. Couples with a high scale score are characterized by either a high degree of reciprocal role taking and reciprocal sympathy or by a high agreement on a frame of reference. Couples who score low are characterized by a low amount of role taking, low sympathy, and an inability to agree on a course of action.

This battery was used to discover whether 36 couples receiving marriage counseling would display interaction patterns different from 186 couples who stated that their marriages were "not in trouble." The scale was found to be capable of distinguishing the interactive patterns of these two groups: The members of the group receiving counseling were significantly lower role-takers. The authors suggested that this battery be used as an independent measure of marital interaction but that it should not be regarded as a substitute for thorough clinical probing.

Buerkle et al. (1961) questioned the usefulness of conceptualizing sympathy and adaptability as "general" factors of adjusted individuals in marriage, as had been concluded by other researchers. In this study, sympathy and adaptability were treated as "situation" variables that were linked with specified roles in adjusted marital interaction and were combined as a measure of altruism, or "the tendency to favor the other." Adjusted marital interactions are characterized by mutual altruism and agreement on a frame of reference. For this study, the 17 items of the revised battery were factor-analyzed; the data had been obtained from the sample of an earlier study (Buerkle & Badgley, 1959). The hypothesis that altruism is a general factor associated with adjusted interaction in marriage was rejected, although altruism was positively associated with marital adjustment. It was stated that altruism "must be interpreted in light of those situational norms dictating sex role prerogatives" (Buerkle et al., 1961, p. 26).

MARITAL SATISFACTION

Marital satisfaction incorporates a number of virtually interchangeable terms (Lewis & Spanier, 1979): *happiness, adjustment*, and *integration*. Although marital satisfaction is often assumed to be synonymous with marital quality and marital stability, such an assumption is erroneous. Empirically, theorists do suggest a strong correlation between satisfaction and quality. However, to suggest that these two concepts are one and the same is to discount the fact that couples can be very satisfied with marriages of very low quality or can be very dissatisfied with marriages of high quality. Satisfaction may be considered one's subjective evaluation of one's marriage. Marital stability, however, is completely separate from quality or satisfaction (Hicks & Platt, 1970).

In their review of husband-wife interaction and marital satisfaction, Gray-Little and Burks (1983) criticized both self-report and observational measures of marital power interactions for their tendency to include overly simplistic conceptualizations of power processes and for limitations in the measurement of marital power and satisfaction. In spite of these criticisms, most studies have consistently indicated that marriages in which the wife seems to be dominant are the most likely to be unhappy and that the highest levels of satisfaction are found in egalitarian couples. Marital dissatisfaction may also be related to the use of coercive control techniques. These reviewers concluded that additional expanded theoretical frameworks and substantive empirical contributions are needed to more adequately understand power and satisfaction in marriage.

Another definition of marital quality was studied by Rettig and Bubolz (1983), who tested Foa and Foa's (1974) resource exchange theory in predicting marital satisfaction. They studied 224 couples who provided information concerning their feelings about the perceived quality of the marriage, resources received from the spouse, and shared time. They found significant support for the relationship between resources received and marital satisfaction.

A number of measures of marital satisfaction are available (Spanier, 1976). Two of these—the Marital Adjustment Test, or LWMAT (Locke & Wallace, 1959), and the Dyadic Adjustment Scale (Spanier, 1976)—were discussed in the preceding chapter. This section focuses on other measures of marital satisfaction. With one exception, all the measures reviewed have demonstrated some degree of reliability and validity. The one exception—the Index of Marital Quality—has at least demonstrated its reliability.

Marital Satisfaction Inventory (MSI)

The MSI (Snyder, 1979, 1981, 1982, 1983) consists of 280 items making up 11 scales: (1) conventionalization, (2) global distress—overall dissatisfaction with the marriage, (3) affective communication, (4) problem-solving communication, (5) time together, (6) disagreement about finances, (7) sexual dissatisfaction, (8) role orientation, (9) family history of distress, (10) dissatisfaction with children, and (11) conflicts about child rearing.

The test was designed so that Scales 1-9 may be given to couples who have no children. Test-retest reliability on each of the scales yielded an average score of .89. Tests for validity were made by comparing MSI and LWMAT with the Global Distress subscale of the measure itself. All but one of the subscales correlated significantly with the concurrent criterion ($p > .01$).

In another study (Snyder, Wills, & Keiser, 1981), couples who were in therapy and couples who were not in therapy completed the MSI. Correlations were all significant ($p > .001$). The results suggest that the MSI is capable of differentiating distressed from nondistressed couples. The design of the scales permits diagnostic application.

In conclusion, the MSI seems to be a well-constructed instrument, with some evidence for validity. The attention to diagnostic detail is worthy of further investigation.

Marital Satisfaction Questionnaire (MSQ)

The MSQ (Madden & Janoff-Bulman, 1976) was designed to assess 12 areas of marital functioning. The respondent indicates to what degree his or her mate is thought to agree with him or her on each of the 36 items.

Test-retest reliability was tested by Cronbach's alpha and yielded alpha = .95. A rather crude test of validity was performed: The interviewer coded her perceptions of the respondent's marital satisfaction, immediately following the intake interview, in one of three categories—less happy than average, average happiness, and happier than average. Using this questionable procedure, interviewers' scores were significantly correlated with the MSQ ($p < .001$).

Madden and Janoff-Bulman (1976) used the MSQ to investigate attributions of control and blame for marital conflict. All subjects were asked to discuss two standard conflict situations in their marriages. The results supported the hypothesis that blaming one's spouse for problems in the marriage would be negatively associated with marital satisfaction. On the other hand, perceived personal control over problems in the marriage was positively correlated with marital satisfaction.

MARITAL TRUST

Various measures have been developed to assess trust in marital relationships. Some of the most commonly used measures are reviewed below.

Dyadic Trust Scale

The Dyadic Trust Scale (Larzelere & Huston, 1980) contains 57 items borrowed or adapted from other scales that measure trust—for example, Dion and Dion's Romantic Love Questionnaire (1975), the Feelings Questionnaire of Driscoll, Davis, and Lipetz (1972), and Rotter's Interpersonal Trust Scale (1967). A factor analysis was performed on this item pool. Items were selected on the basis of (1) item-total correlations and correlations between the items and social desirability, (2) distribution of responses to each of the items, (3) repetitiveness of items' contents, and (4) the direction of wording. These criteria were to maximize reliability and minimize social desirability, skewness, and repetitiveness in the final form of the scale. Eight items were selected for the final form, five of which are reverse-scored.

The item-total correlations of these items range from .72 to .89. Using a third of the sample of 195 dating persons and 127 married or previously married persons who had not been used in the item selection, the researchers established reliability of .93 (coefficient alpha). Nonsignificant correlations with social desirability were found. Couples' trust scores were found to be positively correlated with love scores ($r = .55$, $p < .001$), depth of self-disclosure ($r = .40$ for married couples, $p < .01$), and relationship status, offering some support for concurrent validity.

Dyadic trust was also found to be positively correlated with love and self-disclosure.

Cavanaugh and Guerney (1985) designed a comprehensive two-part scale, the View Sharing Inventory (VSI), for use with couples involved in premarital problem-prevention programs. The first part assesses the respondents' views in 10 relationship areas: leisure/vacations, job/community, finances, friends/relatives, sex, children, housekeeping/grooming, religion, communication, and roles/division of labor. The second part deals with spouses' views of how they interact with each other. Attitudes and behaviors that affect the relationship are also assessed.

Its high reliability (.90 and .79 for the two parts) was established with single undergraduates, and its user confidence was established by questioning 10 lay leaders in a Catholic Family Life Center. This instrument did discriminate between 50 "relating" and 50 "nonrelating" couples. Comprehensiveness and an easy-to-administer format make this a promising instrument.

Feelings Questionnaire

On the 14-item Feelings Questionnaire (Driscoll et al., 1972), spouses use a 6-point scale to rate their feelings toward their mates. They are also asked to rate how they believe their mates feel about them. Thirty-six aspects of a relationship are tapped to make three scales: Love, Criticalness, and Trust. In a sample of 49 unmarried couples, scale reliabilities using Cronbach's alpha were .88 on Love, .74 on Criticalness, and .80 on Trust. In a sample of 91 married couples, the reliabilities on Love, Criticalness, and Trust were .90, .84, and .89 respectively.

Driscoll, Davis, and Lipetz (1972) distinguished between romantic and conjugal love: Conjugal love between mature adults evolves out of satisfying interaction and increasing confidence in the relationship; romantic love is associated with uncertainty and one's need for reassurance about the partner's love. The association of love and trust is considered important in distinguishing the two types of love.

It was hypothesized that "feelings of love become more highly correlated with trust and acceptance as relationships develop through time" (p. 1). To test this hypothesis, 140 couples were administered the Feelings Questionnaire twice, at intervals ranging from 6 to 10 months. Love was found to be more highly correlated with trust for married couples (.76) than for unmarried couples (.34), a difference that was significant ($p < .02$). For unmarried couples, love was more highly correlated with trust on the second administration of Feelings Questionnaire. The difference between these two correlations was significant ($r = .45$ and $r = .69$, $p < .10$). These findings supported the authors' expectation that feelings of love and trust would be more highly correlated with length of association.

Interpersonal Trust Scale

The Interpersonal Trust Scale (Rotter, 1967) was constructed by first administering an experimental form, along with the Marlowe-Crowne Social Desirability Scale, to 248 male and 299 female psychology students. Items were included in the final scale (1) if they correlated significantly with the total item score; (2) if they had relatively low correlations with the Marlowe-Crowne Social Desirability Scale Score; and (3) if endorsement of the item showed a reasonable spread over the five Likert categories used as response alternatives.

The final version included all but three items from the initial experimental version. It is made up of 25 items. Half are scored in reverse, and 15 filler items were added to disguise the purpose of the scale. The higher the score, the more trust that person is said to have of others. Interpersonal trust was defined in this study as "an expectancy held by an individual or a group that the word, promise, verbal or written statement of another individual or group can be relied upon" (p. 651).

The ITS has been shown to have acceptable internal consistency. Split-half reliability using the Spearman-Brown formula was .76 ($p < .001$). Test-retest reliability for two different groups was .56 ($p < .01$) and .68 ($p < .01$). Testing intervals were 7 months and 3 months respectively. The overall correlation with the social desirability scale was .29, which is statistically significant.

Validity was assessed through a field study. Subjects from two fraternities and two sororities were asked to rate members of their groups on interpersonal trust, dependency, gullibility, trustworthiness, and various other control variables. Subjects also rated themselves on trust using a 4-point scale. The intercorrelations for the variables indicated an overall correlation of .37, which is not very impressive.

A NOTE ON CONVENTIONALISM

Response sets that accord with social mores and norms are one of the many confounding variables that affect the results of self-report measures as well as couple/family interaction testing. Depending upon the instrument or procedure, the testing context, and the skill of the tester, a spouse or family member's tendency to respond in a socially desirable or conventional way may be more or less important. In any respect, it is our belief that social desirability must be taken into account during any assessment process. This is especially true in marital and family work where the "correct" responses are obvious (e.g., Murray Straus's Conflict Tactics Scale) and subject to faking on so many of the instruments we reviewed. We suggest that a measure of marital conventionalism be included as a standard test included in a family psychological battery.

Edmonds (1967) developed a measure of conventionalization, The Edmonds Marital Conventionalism Scale (MCS), in which a respondent has the opportunity to select behaviorally improbable responses—for example, "There is never a moment that I do not feel 'head over heels in love' with my mate" (Item 9). A spouse who answers "true" is said to be giving a socially desirable response.

The MCS, containing 50 true/false items of marital adjustment and conventionality, has consistently demonstrated its acceptable reliability. Content and concurrent validity have also been established. These criteria have likewise been met by the shorter, 15-item version (Schumm, Hess, Bollman, & Jurich, 1981). The MCS has been used in a number of studies (Jorgensen & Gaudy, 1980; Snyder & Regts, 1982).

CONCLUSION

Perhaps the simplest and yet most important conclusion is that much more research is necessary to validate the majority of assessment instruments reviewed in this chapter. There is no doubt that some of these instruments are useful; but some are of questionable value, especially for clinicians.

We believe that there is a surfeit of instruments that are not theoretically or conceptually tied to any recognizable theory of marital/family development, behavior, or functioning. Such measures are of little practical value to the family psychologist and family therapist. We also believe that the time has come to call a halt to the development and proliferation of measures that are not conceptually anchored in theory. We strongly suggest that family psychologists and family clinical researchers devote their valuable time to improving the validity and reliability of existing instruments that are theoretically grounded and that have demonstrated their usefulness in research as well as in clinical assessment and practice.

Recently, Bagarozzi (1989) suggested that family psychologists begin to offer family psychological testing as a clinical service to marital/family therapists and other professionals who work closely with couples and family systems. In family psychological testing, the psychologist does not use tests that were developed to assess the functioning of individuals since these tests offer no information or insight into how couples and families function as systems. Rather, the family psychologist uses instruments, tests, and procedures that have been developed specifically to assess and evaluate critical areas of marital/family functioning (e.g., marital/family cohesion and/or structure; power, satisfaction, stability, coping mechanisms; communication patterns, conflict negotiation styles, problem-solving skills; intergenerational influences; and adaptability patterns). Bagarozzi (1989) concluded that recommendations concerning treatment, intervention, child placement, custodial arrangements, and so forth can then be made to the referral agent based upon test findings. These findings are presented in the form of a family diagnostic psychological profile report. A prototype of such a report is offered by Bagarozzi (1989).

REFERENCES

Bagarozzi, D. A. (1989). Family diagnostic testing: A neglected area of expertise for the family psychologist. *American Journal of Family Therapy, 17*, 257–272.

Baugh, C. W., Avery, A. W., & Sheets-Haworth, K. L. (1982). Marital Problem-Solving Scale: A measure to assess relationship conflict negotiation ability. *Family Therapy, 9*, 43–51.

Beach, S. R. H., & Arias, I. (1983). Assessment of perceptual discrepancy: Utility of the Primary Communication Inventory. *Family Process, 22*, 309–316.

Bienvenu, M. J. (1970). Measurement of marital communication. *Family Coordinator, 19,* 26–31.

Bienvenu, M. J., & Stewart, W. W. (1976). Dimensions of interpersonal communication. *Journal of Psychology, 93,* 105–111.

Brown, C. T., & Keller, P. W. (1979). *Monologue to dialogue* (2nd ed.). Englewood Cliffs, NJ: Prentice Hall.

Brown, C. T., Yelsma, P. L., & Keller, P. W. (1979). *Communication conflict instrument.* Kalamazoo, MI: Western Michigan University.

Bryson, C. (1978). Personality differentiation and communication (Doctoral dissertation, Georgia State University, 1978). *Dissertation Abstracts International, 40,* 442B.

Buerkle, J. V., Anderson, T. R., & Badgley, R. F. (1961). Altruism, role conflict, and marital adjustment: A factor analysis of marital interaction. *Marriage and Family Living, 23,* 20–26.

Buerkle, J. V., & Badgley, R. F. (1959). Couple role-taking: The Yale marital interaction battery. *Marriage and Family Living, 21,* 53–58.

Cavanaugh, J., & Guerney, B., Jr. (1985). The View Sharing Inventory for couples. In P. E. Keller & L. G. Ritt (Eds.), *Innovations in clinical practice: Vol. 4. A source book* (pp. 285–304). Sarasota, FL: Professional Resource Exchange.

Cohen, J. (1975). *Sex differences in differentiation.* Unpublished master's thesis, Georgia State University, Atlanta.

Craddock, A. E. (1980). The effect of incongruent marital role expectations upon couples' degree of goal-value consensus in the first year of marriage. *Australian Journal of Psychology, 32,* 117–125.

Crago, M., & Tharp, R. G. (1968). Psychopathology and marital role disturbance: A test of the Tharp-Otis descriptive hypothesis. *Journal of Consulting and Clinical Psychology, 32,* 338–341.

Crain, A. J., Sussman, M. B., & Weil, W. B. (1966). Effects of a diabetic child on marital integration and related measures of family functioning. *Journal of Health and Social Behavior, 7,* 122–127.

Del Monte, R. (1976). *Locus of control and conceptual systems in personality differentiation.* Unpublished master's thesis, Georgia State University, Atlanta.

Dion, K. K., & Dion, K. L. (1975). Self-esteem and romantic love. *Journal of Personality, 43,* 39–57.

Driscoll, R., Davis, K. E., & Lipetz, M. E. (1972). Parental interference and romantic love: The Romeo and Juliet effect. *Journal of Personality and Social Psychology, 24,* 1–10.

Edmonds, V. H. (1967). Marital conventionalization: Definition and measurement. *Journal of Marriage and the Family, 29,* 681–688.

Farber, B. (1957). An index of marital integration. *Sociometry, 20,* 117–134.

Farber, B. (1959). Effects of a severely mentally retarded child on family integration. *Monographs of the Society for Research in Child Development, 24*(1).

Farber, B. (1960). Family organization and crisis: Maintenance of integration in families with a severely mentally retarded child. *Monographs of the Society for Research in Child Development, 25* (Serial No. 75).

Farber, B., & McHale, J. L. (1959). Marital integration and parents' agreement on satisfaction with their child's behavior. *Marriage and Family Living, 21,* 65–69.

Foa, U. G., & Foa, E. B. (1974). *Societal structures of the mind.* Springfield, IL: Thomas.

Fowle, C. M. (1969). The effect of the severely mentally retarded child on his family. *American Journal of Mental Deficiency, 73,* 468–473.

Frank, E., Anderson, C., & Rubinstein, D. (1979). Marital role strain and sexual satisfaction. *Journal of Consulting and Clinical Psychology, 47,* 1096–1103.

Frank, E., Anderson, C., & Rubinstein, D. (1980). Marital role ideals and perceptions of marital role behavior in distressed and non-distressed couples. *Journal of Marital and Family Therapy, 6,* 55–63.

Frank, E., & Kupfer, D. J. (1976). In every marriage there are two marriages. *Journal of Sex and Marital Therapy, 2,* 137–143.

Frank, E., Targum, S. D., Gershon, E. S., Anderson, D., Stewart, B. D., Davenport, Y., Ketchum, K. L., & Kupfer, D. J. (1981). A comparison of nonpatient and bipolar patient–well spouse couples. *American Journal of Psychiatry, 138,* 764–768.

Gray-Little, B., & Burks, N. (1983). Power and satisfaction in marriage: A review and a critique. *Psychological Bulletin, 93,* 513-538.

Hicks, M. W., & Platt, M. (1970). Marital happiness and stability: A review of the research in the sixties. *Journal of Marriage and the Family, 32,* 553–574.

Hurvitz, N. (1960a). The marital roles inventory and the measurement of marital adjustment. *Journal of Clinical Psychology, 16,* 377–380.

Hurvitz, N. (1960b). The measurement of marital strain. *American Journal of Sociology, 65,* 610–615.

Hurvitz, N. (1965a). Control roles, marital strain, role deviation, and marital adjustment. *Journal of Marriage and the Family, 27,* 29–31.

Hurvitz, N. (1965b). Marital roles strain as a sociological variable. *Family Life Coordinator, 14,* 39–42.

Hutton, S. P. (1974). Self-esteem, values and self-differentiation in pre-marital dyads. (Doctoral dissertation, Georgia State University, 1974). *Dissertation Abstracts International, 36,* 888B.

Jessee, E. (1978). *Separation and differentiation in the college individual.* Unpublished master's thesis, Georgia State University, Atlanta.

Jorgensen, S. R., & Gaudy, J. C. (1980). Self-disclosure and satisfaction in marriage: The relation examined. *Family Relations, 29,* 281–287.

Kahn, M. (1970). Nonverbal communication and marital satisfaction. *Family Process, 9,* 449–456.

Kerckhoff, A. C., & Bean, F. D. (1967). Role-related factors in person perception among engaged couples. *Sociometry, 30,* 176–186

Kerckhoff, A. C., & Davis, K. (1962). Value consensus and need complementarity in mate selection. *American Sociological Review, 27,* 295–303.

Kirkpatrick, S. W. (1978). Adjustment to parenthood: A structural model. *Genetic Psychology Monographs, 98,* 51–82.

Krause, H. D. (1977). *Family law in a nutshell.* St. Paul, MN: West.

L'Abate, L. (1976). *Understanding and helping the individual in the family.* New York: Grune & Stratton.

L'Abate, L. (1977). *Enrichment: Structured interventions with couples, families, and groups.* Washington, DC: University Press of America.

L'Abate, L. (1983). Intimacy is sharing hurt feelings: A reply to David Mace. In L. L'Abate (Ed.), *Family psychology: Theory, therapy and training* (pp. 101–122). Washington, DC: University Press of America. (Reprinted from *Journal of Marriage and Family Counseling, 1977, 3,* 13–16.)

L'Abate, L. (1986). *Systematic family therapy.* New York: Brunner/Mazel.

L'Abate, L. (1993). *A theory of personality development.* (Submitted for publication).

L'Abate, L., & Goodrich, M. (1980). Marital adjustment. In R. Woody (Ed.), *Encyclopedia of clinical evaluation* (pp. 60–73). San Francisco: Jossey-Bass.

L'Abate, L., & Wagner, V. (1985). Theory-derived, family-oriented test batteries. In L. L'Abate (Ed.), *The handbook of family psychology and therapy* (Vol. 2, pp. 1006–1031). Pacific Grove, CA: Brooks/Cole.

L'Abate, L., & Wagner, V. (1988). Testing a theory of developmental competence in the family. *American Journal of Family Therapy, 16,* 23–35.

Larzelere, R. E., & Huston, R. L. (1980). The dyadic trust scale: Toward understanding interpersonal trust in close relationships. *Journal of Marriage and the Family, 42,* 595–604.

Lewis, R. A., & Spanier, G. B. (1979). Theorizing about the quality and stability of marriage. In W. R. Burr, R. Hill, F. I. Nye, & I. L. Reiss (Eds.), *Contemporary theories about the family: General theories/theoretical orientations* (Vol. 1, pp. 268–294). New York: Free Press.

Locke, H. J., Sabagh, G., & Thomas, M. (1956). Correlates of primary communication and empathy. *Research Studies of the State College of Washington, 24,* 116–124.

Locke, H. J., & Wallace, K. M. (1959). Short marital-adjustment and prediction tests. Their reliability and validity. *Marriage and Family Living, 21,* 251–255.

Madden, M. E., & Janoff-Bulman, R. (1976). Blame, control, and marital satisfaction: Wives' attributions for conflict in marriage. *Journal of Marriage and the Family, 38,* 301–309.

Minuchin, S. (1974). *Families and family therapy.* Cambridge, MA: Harvard University Press.

Murphy, D. C., & Mendelson, L. (1973). Use of the observational method in the study of live marital communication. *Journal of Marriage and the Family, 35,* 256–263.

Murstein, B. I., Cerreto, M., & MacDonald, M. (1977). A theory and investigation of the effect of exchange-orientation on marriage and friendship. *Journal of Marriage and the Family, 39,* 543–549.

Navran, L. (1967). Communication and adjustment in marriage. *Family Process, 6,* 173–184.

Olson, D. H., & Ryder, R. G. (1970). Inventory of Marital Conflicts (IMC): An experimental interaction procedure. *Journal of Marriage and the Family, 32,* 443–448.

Rettig, K. D., & Bubolz, M. M. (1983). Interpersonal resource exchanges as indicators of quality of marriage. *Journal of Marriage and the Family, 45,* 497–509.

Rotter, J. B. (1967). A new scale for the measurement of interpersonal trust. *Journal of Personality, 34,* 651–665.

Satir, V. (1972). *Peoplemaking.* Palo Alto, CA: Science and Behavior Books.

Scanzoni, J. (1975). Sex roles, economic factors, and marital solidarity in black and white marriages. *Journal of Marriage and the Family, 37,* 130–144.

Schumm, W. R., Figley, C.R., & Jurich, A.P. (1979). Dimensionality of Marital Communication Inventory: A preliminary factor analytic study. *Psychological Reports, 45,*123–128.

Schumm, W. R., Hess, J. L., Bollman, S. R., & Jurich, A. P. (1981). Marital conventionalization revisited. *Psychological Reports, 49,* 607–615.

Snyder, D. K. (1979). Multidimensional assessment of marital satisfaction. *Journal of Marriage and the Family, 41,* 813–823.

Snyder, D. K. (1981). *Marital Satisfaction Inventory manual.* Los Angeles: Western Psychological Services.

Snyder, D. K. (1982). Advances in marital assessment: Behavioral, communications, and psychometric approaches. In C. D. Spielberger & J. N. Butcher (Eds.), *Advances in personality assessment* (Vol. 1, pp. 169–202). Hillsdale, NJ: Erlbaum.

Snyder, D. K. (1983). Clinical and researach applications of the Marital Satisfaction Inventory. In E. E. Filsinger (Ed.), *Marriage and family assessment: A sourcebook for family therapy* (pp. 169–189). Beverly Hills: Sage.

Snyder, D. K., & Regts, J. M. (1982). Factor scales for assessing marital disharmony and disaffection. *Journal of Consulting and Clinical Psychology, 50,* 736–743.

Snyder, D. K., Wills, R. M., & Keiser, T. W. (1981). Empirical validation of the Marital Satisfacation Inventory: An actuarial approach. *Journal of Consulting and Clinical Psychology, 49,* 262–268.

Spanier, G. B. (1976). Measuring dyadic adjustment: New scales for assessing the quality of marriage and similar dyads. *Journal of Marriage and the Family, 38,* 15–28.

Steinmann, A. (1975). Studies in male-female sex-role identification. *Psychotherapy: Theories, Research and Practice, 12,* 412–417.

Swenson, C. H., & Fiore, A. (1982). A scale of marriage problems. In P. A. Keller & L. G. Ritt (Eds.), *Innovations in clinical practice: A source book* (pp. 240–256). Sarasota, FL: Professional Resource Exchange.

Tharp, R. G. (1963a). Dimensions of marriage roles. *Marriage and Family Living, 25,* 389–404.

Tharp, R. G. (1963b). Psychological patterning in marriage. *Psychological Bulletin, 60,* 97–117.

Wagner, V. (1980). *Validation of a theory-based marital evaluation battery.* Unpublished doctoral dissertation, Georgia State University, Atlanta.

Wright, L. (1976). *Self differentiation and marital happiness over two stages of the family life cycle.* Unpublished master's thesis, Georgia State University, Atlanta.

Yelsma, P., (1981). Conflict predisposition: Differences between happy and clinical couples. *American Journal of Family Therapy, 9,* 57–63.

SECTION III
Families

8

Self-Report of Family Functioning

We begin our discussion of standardized, objective family assessment techniques with a review of the instruments developed at the University of Minnesota by David Olson and his colleagues from the Department of Family Social Sciences.

In 1982 Olson, et al. published *Family Inventories*, a compendium of nine instruments developed and used by Olson and his colleagues in their national survey of families. The instruments include FACES (Family Adaptability and Cohesion Scale), ENRICH (Enriching and Nurturing Relationship Issues, Communication, and Happiness), FILE (Family Inventory of Life Events and Changes), F-COPES (Family Coping Strategies), Family Strengths, and Quality of Life.

FACES is discussed in depth because it has undergone substantial revision since it was first developed in 1979. After the discussion of FACES, we review the instruments that have been developed specifically for assessing the entire family.

FAMILY ADAPTABILITY AND COHESION SCALE
(FACES I, II, AND III)

The Circumplex Model of Marital and Family Systems focuses upon two aspects of marital/family functioning: *adaptability* and *cohesion*. Olson, Sprenkle, and Russell (1979) completed a comprehensive review of family therapy literature and found that cohesion and adaptability appeared as underlying dimensions of family behavior for a multitude of concepts in the field. These two dimensions were arrived at inductively rather than through empirical testing. The theoretical orientation used by these authors to conceptualize family behavior is based upon general systems theory as explicated by von Bertalanffy (1968) and Buckley (1967).

167

Olson et al. (1979) found at least 40 concepts that were related to the cohesive dimension of family functioning. Their extensive review of six social science fields (psychiatry, family therapy, family sociology, small group theory and group therapy, social psychology, and anthropology) lends strong support to the importance of this dimension of family behavior.

Cohesion is defined as the emotional bonding that members have with one another and the degree of individual autonomy a person experiences in the family system. Their definition of family cohesion has two components: bonding and autonomy. At the extreme of high family cohesion is *enmeshment*, in which overidentification with the family results in extreme bonding or closeness, which limits individual autonomy. At the low end of the cohesion scale is *disengagement*, which is characterized by little bonding and high individual autonomy from the family group.

Olson et al. (1979) hypothesized that a balanced degree of family cohesion is the most conducive to effective family functioning and to optimal individual development. Specific variables used by these researchers to assess the degree of family cohesion are emotional bonding and independence, boundaries, coalitions, time, space, friends, decision making, interests, and recreation.

The second dimension, *adaptability,* is defined as the ability of a marital/family system to change its power structure, role relationships, and relationship rules in response to situational and developmental stresses. The specific variables associated with this dimension are family power structure (assertiveness, control, and discipline), negotiation style, role relationships, relationship rules, and feedback processes (negative and positive). At one extreme of this dimension, we find a rigid family structure that is characterized by closed boundaries and the use of negative feedback to maintain a stable, morphostatic family system. At the other extreme, we find the absence of structure: Chaos reigns. System boundaries and leadership are absent, and positive feedback predominates.

Earlier we described the extremes of the cohesion and adaptability as disengagement-enmeshment and chaos-rigidity, respectively. The more balanced regions of the cohesion continuum include relationship patterns that facilitate intimacy. These are described as separate and connected. The more balanced portions of the adaptability continuum, described as flexible and structured, are thought to represent the simultaneous pushes toward both stability and change.

In sum, the cohesion dimension consists of four distinct levels: disengaged, separated, connected, and enmeshed. The four levels of the adaptability continuum are chaotic, flexible, structured, and rigid.

Olson et al. (1979) identified 16 ideal types of marital and family systems when they combined the four levels of cohesion with those of adaptability. Four of these family types fall into the extremes on both dimensions: chaotically disengaged, chaotically enmeshed, rigidly enmeshed, and rigidly disengaged. Families falling into these quadrants are thought to be severely dysfunctional. Eight types of families are extreme on one dimension and moderate on another. These systems are thought to be relatively closed: flexibly disengaged, chaotically separated, chaotically connected, flexibly enmeshed, structurally enmeshed, rigidly connected, rigidly separated, and structurally disengaged. The final four types, which are moderate or balanced, are believed to be the most functional (i.e., open) family systems: flexibly separated, flexibly connected, structurally connected, and structurally separated.

FACES I

FACES was developed in 1978 in two dissertations by Portner (1980) and Bell (1980), under the supervision of David H. Olson at the University of Minnesota. Using the descriptions of the 16 variables thought to represent the various aspects of cohesion and adaptability, short statements were formulated that described high, balanced, and low levels of family cohesion and adaptability. In developing items, the researchers attempted to cover the range of the concepts with easily understood single-stimulus statements. Initially, 203 statements were developed: 103 tapped levels of cohesion; 100 dealt with family adaptability. A pilot study was conducted on two samples.

To assess clinical validity, 35 marriage and family counselors were presented with the stimulus definitions and asked to rate each item on a 9-point Likert scale that ranged from low cohesion or low adaptability to high cohesion or high adaptability.

A second sample, consisting of 410 undergraduate students from the University of Minnesota and Iowa State University, answered each item on the basis of its applicability to their families of origin. A 4-point scale was used: *true all the time* (4), *true most of the time* (3), *true some of the time* (2), and *true none of the time* (1).

Analysis of both data sets began with a computation of the means, modes, standard deviations, and percentage scores of the items. The student data percentages showed the distribution of response choice for each item. These data were used to select items that had a good distribution of responses. Counselor data showed which portion of the counselors ranked each item low (1–3), moderate (4–6), or high (7–9). These data were used to select items that had high agreement among counselors.

A factor analysis was conducted on the data gathered from the 410 students. The varimax orthogonal rotation method was used. Analysis of the items with each factor revealed that the factors corresponded very closely with the response strength of the items (i.e., chaotic, moderate, and rigid for the adaptability dimension; disengaged, moderate, and enmeshed for cohesion).

The items included in FACES were chosen on the basis of the following criteria: (1) a means-and-mode score that fell within the appropriate range (according to counselor rankings); (2) the lowest possible standard deviation, indicating high consensus among counselors on the item rankings; and (3) the highest factor scores from student data.

The original FACES consisted of 111 items. Six items were used to assess each of the 16 variables related to the Circumplex Model of Marital and Family Systems. A 15-item social desirability scale was also included.

Additional data analyses were done by Portner (1980) and Bell (1980), who used 201 families to determine the relationship between social desirability and the two dimensions of the circumplex model (i.e., adaptability and cohesion). A modified version of The Edmonds Conventionalism Scale was used to obtain a measure of social desirability. Social desirability did not correlate with the total Adaptability subscale score. However, social desirability was highly correlated with the total Cohesion subscale score, $r = .45$.

A factor analysis of both scales, Adaptability and Cohesion, was undertaken again by these two researchers. This second factor analysis replicated the initial formulation of the scales, whose items were written for high, moderate, and low levels of adaptability and cohesion.

Internal consistencies (alpha reliabilities) of the total scores for the Adaptability and Cohesion subscales were $r = .75$ and $r = .83$, respectively. However, split-half reliability for each of the subscales was reported to be "very low." Because of these findings, the researchers suggested the use of total scores on Adaptability and Cohesion rather than separate scores on the two subscales. Olson (1979) suggested that the individual subscales should not be used for research purposes but that they might be used as clinical aids.

FACES II

In 1982 FACES was revised (Olson, Bell, & Portner, 1982). FACES II was developed to overcome weaknesses found by the researchers in the original instrument. They wanted to develop a shorter instrument with simple sentences so that FACES II could be used by children and by adults with limited reading ability. Olson, Bell, and Portner reduced the number of double negatives that had appeared in many of the questions in the original FACES. A 5-point Likert scale replaced the 4-point scale used initially: *almost never* (1), *once in a while* (2), *sometimes* (3), *frequently* (4), and *almost always* (5). The Individual Autonomy scale was deleted from the Cohesion subscale of FACES II.

The researchers' main goal in this second group of studies was "to develop a scale with two empirically reliable, valid and independent dimensions" (p. 9).

During the initial development of FACES II, 464 adults (average age, 30.5 years) responded to 90 items, covering the 15 content areas (6 items in each area) of the Cohesion and the Adaptability scales. On the basis of factor analysis and reliability analysis, the initial scale was reduced to 50 items.

Factor analysis was done separately for the items on the Cohesion and the Adaptability subscales. Olson, Bell, and Portner (1982) reported that these analyses produced 13 factors for the Cohesion subscale and 9 factors for the Adaptability subscale. However, the first 4 factors for each dimension accounted for 75% of the variance. Cronbach's alpha reliabilities were .94 for the Cohesion subscale and .80 for the Adaptability subscale.

This 50-item scale of FACES II was administered to 2,412 individuals in a national survey. Factor analyses and reliability checks were performed, and FACES II was reduced to a 30-item scale. The final version of FACES II includes 14 content areas: 16 items on the Cohesion subscale; 14 on the Adaptability subscale (2 to 3 items for each content area).

Two types of reliability have been reported for FACES II. The total national sample of 2,412 was divided into two equal subgroups to check internal consistency (Cronbach's alpha). The reliabilities for the total sample and both subgroups are quite high, from .78 to .90.

The 50-item version of FACES II was used for test-retest reliability. Retest was done 4 to 5 weeks after the initial testing. Respondents were 124 university and high school students (average age, 19.2 years) who were asked to describe their families of origin. The Pearson correlation for the 50-item FACES II was .84; the Pearson correlations for the Cohesion and the Adaptability subscales were .83 and .80, respectively.

Construct validity is the only type of validity reported by these researchers. It appears that these authors called for a two-factor solution in their final analysis. Items for Cohesion loaded on the first factor, and Adaptability items were reported as loading "primarily on factor II" (Olson, Bell, & Portner, 1982, p. 10). The rotational procedure used is not reported. Factor loadings on Cohesion range from .35 to .61. However, factor loadings on the Adaptability subscale, ranging from .10 to .55, are less impressive. Five of these items fall below .30 (the cutoff point, considered by many factor analysts to be the minimum acceptable level for significant factor loadings). Even though the sample was large (2,412), some of the factor loadings are extremely low (e.g., .10, .19, .22).

We have used FACES and FACES II in our research, teaching, and clinical practice; and we have found FACES II to be a vast improvement over the original instrument. FACES took approximately 35 minutes to administer. Hand-scoring FACES was tedious and boring: It took approximately 10 minutes to score one family member's answer sheet, or approximately 40 minutes of scoring for a family of four. FACES II takes about 10 minutes to complete, and scoring one family member's answer sheet takes approximately 3 minutes. However, there are some limitations. Clients must read at a seventh-grade level to complete FACES II.

Two new features have been added. First, separate questionnaires have been developed for families and for couples. Second, the answer sheet for FACES II was designed so that each family member can respond twice to each question: once for how he or she currently perceives the family, and once for how he or she would like the family to be (i.e., one's ideal family). Olson, Bell, and Portner (1982) said that this procedure makes it possible to assess each family member's level of satisfaction with the current family system. It also is used as an indication of how much change in the system each family member desires. Both the perceived-ideal discrepancy and the amount of change desired by each family member offer the clinician important information for family evaluation and treatment planning.

However, the answer sheet given to clients is poorly constructed. Responses to odd-numbered questions (Cohesion subscale) for both perceived and ideal views of family functioning appear in parallel columns on the left-hand side of the answer sheet. The right-hand side of the answer sheet is similarly arranged for even-numbered responses (Adaptability). Because of this cumbersome arrangement, clients may place their responses in the wrong columns, jeopardizing the accuracy of family evaluation.

FACES III

In 1985, Olson, Portner, and Lavee set out to improve the reliability, validity, and clinical usefulness of FACES II. Specifically, their objectives in revising FACES II were as follows:

(1) to shorten the instrument so that it could be administered under "perceived" and "ideal" conditions (i.e., to offer each family member an opportunity to rate the family as he or she perceives the family to be and to allow each family member to profile the ideal family system—the way he or she would like the family to be);

(2) to develop two statistically independent or orthogonal factors so that FACES III would more closely approximate the theoretical criteria of the circumplex model;

(3) to eliminate all negative items so that FACES III could be scored more easily and be compared with established norms;

(4) to rewrite the ideal version of the instrument so that it could be more easily understood by family members;

(5) to develop items that are relevant for a variety of family forms (e.g., nuclear, blended, single parent) and couples (married, cohabiting) without children;

(6) to develop specific norms for adults across the life cycle, adults and adolescents combined for the adolescent stage, and young couples without children.

To achieve these ends, Olson, Portner, and Lavee (1985) administered the 50-item FACES II questionnaire to a national sample of 2,412 individuals from "nonproblem" families representing all stages of the family life cycle. This sample was then divided into two random and independent subsamples. The first sample ($n = 1,206$) was used as the basis for a factor analysis designed to produce two totally independent factors. After an initial factor analysis, items were selected if they clearly loaded on only one factor. Based upon this factor analysis and the original conceptual subscales, an iterative process of coding, eliminating, and replacing items was used. Following each of these steps, factor analyses were performed to ensure the validity and independence of the scales.

This process resulted in the selection of 20 items: 10 items for Cohesion; 10 items for Adaptability. These 20 items were then factor-analyzed by using data from the second sample. The same factor structure was found with the second sample, and the two dimensions were found to be independent ($r = .03$). Factor loadings for the 10 Cohesion items ranged from .39 to .69. Factor loadings for the Adaptability dimension ranged from .34 to .48. Although the loadings on the Adaptability dimension are statistically significant, they are extremely low. Of the 10 Adaptability items, 8 fell between .34 and .38; the remaining 2 items were .45 and .48.

Reliabilities (Cronbach's alpha) for each subsample were not as high as the earlier version (FACES II) of their scale: .58 for Adaptability to .76 for Cohesion, for the total sample.

Essentially, FACES III is a shortened version of FACES II. The new instrument, consisting of 20 items, is easy to administer and simple to score. Olson and his colleagues have stressed the importance of administering FACES III twice in order to obtain each family member's perceived and ideal description of the marital/family system. They stated that by comparing the perceived-ideal discrepancies for each family member, it is possible to assess each individual's subjective level of family satisfaction with the current family system. However, Olson and his coworkers provided no empirical data to support this assumption. The perceived-ideal discrepancies are believed to be theoretically and clinically useful.

FACES III is a theoretically derived self-report instrument developed to assess two dimensions of family process: cohesion and adaptability. FACES III has gone through considerable refinement. Construct validity has been established, yet internal consistency for the 20-item revision is not impressive. Although FACES III is easy to administer, score, and interpret, how one uses the perceived-ideal discrepancy scores of all family members to devise a coherent family treatment plan is unclear.

In reviewing a FACES III family profile, a number of critical questions arise:

(1) How is this information used to develop a family treatment plan?

(2) What type of feedback does the therapist give to the family concerning vast ideal-perceived discrepancies?

(3) Because each family member is asked to "describe your family now" and to describe "ideally, how you would like your family to be," family members are not being asked to focus on their relationships with any one particular family member. It is erroneous to assume that each respondent perceives that all relationships with all family members are of the same quality or that the respondent would like to see a change in his or her relationships with every other family member. Therefore, in order to develop a viable, concrete, and behavioral treatment plan, each family member must be asked to specify the changes he or she would like to see in his or her relationship with each family member. If this is the case, why use FACES III? Would it not be easier just to ask each family member to describe the changes he or she would like to see in relationships with all other family members?

(4) If one subscribes to a systems view of family functioning, the identified patient's (IP) symptomatic behavior is believed to maintain a homeostatic family balance; the family's unique process, in turn, is believed to support and maintain the IP's symptomatic behavior. In keeping with this philosophical and theoretical premise, the IP's symptomatic behavior is believed to be a metaphorical representation of a parental conflict. The parents may perceive the family differently and desire vastly different outcomes. Helping the parents learn how to negotiate more satisfactory patterns of leadership, control, rules, and roles and to develop mutually acceptable levels of separateness and connectedness would seem to be a desirable goal.

FACES III scores for both parents, for example, might seem to highlight their conflict and provide the therapist with a concrete reason for focusing on the marital dyad. Helping parents negotiate these differences so that they might become a more effective team to help the IP would be a possible strategy. However, if one subscribes to a systems view, treating the dysfunctional parental subsystem would be a central focus as a matter of course. Reestablishing a more efficient parental coalition would be a foregone conclusion, a sine qua non for achieving a successful treatment outcome.

(5) Finally, how does one use perceived-ideal discrepancies between spouses and family members whose goals for their desired family system run counter to what the therapist knows to be desirable and therapeutic? How does the therapist interpret such findings to family members? How does the therapist justify to the family members any

intervention strategies that are obviously designed to bring about changes in family structure and process that are in opposition to the family's stated goals?

(6) As far as we are concerned, the main theoretical byproduct of this research has been the classification of various ranges of cohesion (disengaged, separate, connected, and enmeshed) and adaptability (chaotic, flexible, structured, and rigid). If these ranges proved to be valid and if they could be assessed validly, a great advance may be made here.

The preceeding underscores only a few of the problems encountered when using FACES III to guide clinical practice. Although FACES III is relatively easy to administer and score, interpretation (for the purposes of giving feedback to families and for treatment planning) is not that simple. The translation of all family members' perceptions into a viable treatment plan requires considerable clinical expertise and judgment. The novice may find this task too much to cope with. Olson and his colleagues must address these issues if FACES III is to be used by a large number of clinicians.

Another serious difficulty with FACES III has to do with the cutoff scores used to discriminate and type families according to the Circumplex Model of Marital and Family Systems. For example, Olson, Portner, and Lavee (1985) provided a table as a guide for typing family members' responses to FACES III. However, this table reveals considerable variability in the ranges for the four dimensions of Cohesion and Adaptability. Especially for the enmeshed dimensions of Cohesion, the probability seems high that family members will obtain extreme scores. This presents a serious problem in interpreting discrepant perceived-ideal scores. For example, none of the family members may describe a balanced ideal. Although this flip-flop (Russell & Olson, 1983) from one extreme to the other may be diagnostic (or even characteristic) of distressed family systems, the clinician is still left with plans that he or she believes to be appropriate but that are in direct conflict with family members' stated outcomes for therapy.

Once again, in our opinion, Olson and his coworkers must address these issues if FACES III is to become a viable tool for clinical practice.

FAMILY SATISFACTION

In their review of instruments dealing with family assessment, Cromwell, Olson, and Fournier (1976) were unable to locate any measure of family satisfaction. Therefore, the Family Satisfaction Scale was developed to fill this conceptual and theoretical void. Olson and his colleagues stressed the importance of evaluating each family member's subjective level of satisfaction, regardless of how a family member rates himself or herself on the Circumplex Model of Marital and Family Systems in terms of his or her levels of adaptability and cohesion and in spite of how the family system is perceived by outsiders.

Cromwell et al. (1976) postulated two ways to assess a person's subjective level of satisfaction: (1) an indirect method built into FACES III, in which people describe both their "perceived" and "ideal" family (the degree of discrepancy between these two evaluations provides an indirect measure); or (2) a more direct assessment, derived from a standardized scale. The Family Satisfaction Scale represents the latter approach.

The Family Satisfaction Scale was developed to measure the major dimensions of the Circumplex Model of Marital and Family Systems and each of the 14 subscales of the model. To obtain one item for each of the 14 subscales of the circumplex model, the researchers developed and tested a 28-item questionnaire, with each area represented by 2 items. These 28 items were then administered to approximately 800 college students. Slightly more than half (433) of the questionnaires were returned.

A factor analysis was then performed, and 1 item was chosen from each pair that represented each subscale. Of the 14 items selected, only 9 items achieved loadings of .40 or more on the first rotated factor. Cronbach's alpha coefficients of .82 and .86 were found for the Cohesion and the Adaptability subscales, respectively. The total-scale Cronbach's alpha was .90.

A final 14-item scale retained 1 item for each of the 8 Cohesion subscales and 1 item for each of the 6 Adaptability subscales. Cronbach's alpha reliabilities for the final scale were .85 for the Cohesion subscale, .84 for Adaptability, and .92 for the 14-item (total) Family Satisfaction Scale. Test-retest reliabilities computed after a 5-week interval were .76 (Cohesion), .67 (Adaptability), and .75 (Family Satisfaction Scale).

Cromwell et al. (1976) stated that their factor analyses clearly indicate that Family Satisfaction is a unidimensional scale and that a total scale score is the most valid method of determining family satisfaction. They suggested that the subscale scores be used primarily for research and clinical practice.

FAMILY INVENTORY OF LIFE EVENTS AND CHANGES
(FILE)

FILE was developed to investigate the impact of life stresses on family well-being (McCubbin, Thompson, Pirner, & McCubbin, 1988). McCubbin et al. were interested in learning more about the cumulative effects of life changes on family behavior across the family life cycle. They accepted the hypothesis that life events can become stressors that require changes in family members' ongoing life patterns and that stress is the organism's physiological and psychological response to these stressors.

McCubbin et al. stated that although all the individual measures of life stresses include some events that pertain to family life, the focus had been on the individual and his or her adaptive reactions to social stresses. No systematic method of inquiry had been undertaken to document quantitatively the impact of family life events and changes on the family and its individual members. However, McCubbin et al. pointed out that a considerable body of stress theory and related research had evolved independently of psychobiological stress research.

Beginning with the early work of Hill (1949), who studied the stressors of war separation and reunion, family scholars have made an effort to understand why families faced with a single stressor event (e.g., a loss, illness, or separation) differ in their ability to adjust. Hill (1958) advanced the ABCX family crisis model, which states that A (the stressor event), interacting with B (the family's crisis meeting resources), interacting with C (the definition the family makes of the event), produces X (the crisis).

Building on the ABCX model, family scholars examined family behavior in response to a vast array of stressor events. McCubbin et al. (1988) characterized this early research as focusing on a single stressor or event. During the 1980s Mederer and Hill (1983) suggested the "pileup" concept as a way of looking at multiple-role complex changes occurring within a short period of time. In 1983, McCubbin and Patterson offered an explanation for why some families may be more vulnerable to a single stressor or may lack the regenerative power to recover from a crisis. If a family's resources (to cope with stressors) are already overtaxed or exhausted because of other life changes (both normative and situational), family members may be unable to adjust further if confronted with additional social stressors. In other words, family life changes are additive and at some point reach a family's limit to adjust to them. At this juncture, one would anticipate some negative consequence in the family system.

McCubbin and Patterson therefore advanced the double ABCX model to more adequately describe family adaptation to stress or crisis. This extension of Hill's ABCX model added a component to each of the factors. This model now includes not only the original stressor but also the pileup of life events experienced by the family at the same time.

FILE assesses the pileup of life events experienced by a family (the A factor of the double ABCX model). It is a 71-item self-report instrument designed to record the normative and nonnormative life events and changes experienced by a family unit during the preceding year. FILE also records certain life events (34 items that are a subset of the 71 items) experienced by a family before the preceding year. These events are those that frequently take longer to adapt to or, by their nature, are chronic, generating a prolonged residue of strain and distress.

As a family life change inventory, all events experienced by any member of the family are recorded: From a family systems perspective, what happens to one member affects the other members to some degree. Families usually are dealing with several stressors simultaneously, and FILE provides an index of a family's vulnerability as a result of this pileup.

The initial selection of items was guided in part by those life changes appearing on other individual life change inventories (Psychiatric Epidemiology Research Interview, PERI, from Dohrenwend, Krasnoff, Askenasy, & Dohrenwend, 1978; Coddington, 1972a, 1972b; Social Readjustment Rating Scale, SRRS, from Holmes & Rahe, 1967). In addition, situational and developmental changes experienced by families at different stages of the life cycle were included. Each item is worded to reflect a change of sufficient magnitude to require some adjustment in the interactional pattern of family members. The emphasis is on change, which may be positive or negative.

The final scale consists of the following nine subscales.

(1) Intra-Family Strains (17 items), comprising two dimensions: conflict and parenting;
(2) Marital Strains (4 items, 2 of which concern stressors arising from sexual or separation issues);
(3) Pregnancy and Childbearing Strains (4 items);
(4) Finance and Business Strains (12 items), comprising two dimensions: family finances and family business (i.e., family-owned business or investments);
(5) Work-Family Transitions and Strains (10 items), comprising two dimensions: work transitions (moving in or out of the work force) and family transitions and work strains (changes occurring at work or moves made by a family member);
(6) Illness and Family "Care" Strains (8 items), comprising three dimensions: illness onset and child care, chronic illness, and dependency (the strain felt by a family member who requires help or care);
(7) Losses (6 items), which may concern death or broken relationships;
(8) Transitions "In and Out" (5 items), reflecting a member's moving out, moving back home, or taking on a major involvement outside the family;
(9) Legal Strains (5 items), focusing on a family member's breaking society's laws.

Construct validity was established through factor analysis. Cronbach's alpha for the entire scale was .82, with subscales ranging from .30 to .73. Such a wide range of reliability coefficients for the nine subscales means that internal consistency is most soundly established for the total scale; the researcher should therefore refrain from using the subscales separately. Clinically, however, the separation of life stressor events seems to be advisable.

FAMILY STRENGTHS

Olson, Larsen, and McCubbin (1982), who reviewed the vast amount of literature and empirical research on family strengths, concluded that the expansive definitions of the concept made it virtually impossible to measure. Thus, these researchers found it necessary to limit the definition in order to operationalize this concept. The research team narrowed its focus, concentrating on three major components of family strengths that were underscored in the empirical literature. The three components are (1) *pride*: family attributes relating to respect, trust, and loyalty within the family; (2) *positive values and beliefs*: optimism and shared values; and (3) *accord*: attributes relating to a family's sense of mastery or competency.

The responses of 119 students on a 25-item Likert-type scale were factor-analyzed. This factor analysis reduced the 25 items to 14. Three factors emerged: (1) Pride and Loyalty, (2) Positive Values and Beliefs, and (3) Accord. These three factors had eigenvalues greater than 1 and an item factor loading greater than or equal to .35. A second factor analysis was performed on a sample of 2,740, split into halves. Final item selection and development were completed with the second sample ($n = 1,410$), which was used to replicate the findings from the first sample ($n = 1,330$).

Factor analyses using varimax rotation were completed on Sample 1. The factor structure was identical to the initial factor analyses, except that the first two factors (Pride and Loyalty and Positive Values and Beliefs) merged into one factor on the second analysis. Therefore, this final factor analysis produced two factors: Pride and Accord. These findings were replicated with Sample 2.

Cronbach's alpha was computed for each factor separately and for the total scale on Sample 1 and Sample 2. The overall alpha reliability is .83 for both samples. Test-retest reliability coefficients were also computed on this final factor structure. The time lapse between the first and the second administration was 4 weeks.

FAMILY COPING STRATEGIES SCALE
(F-COPES)

The F-COPES, developed by McCubbin, Larsen, and Olson (1982), features two general concepts: internal and external coping strategies. These are broken down into five subscales: two for internal coping (reframing and passive appraisal) and three for external coping (acquiring social support, seeking spiritual support, and mobilizing family to acquire and accept help).

A 49-item version of F-COPES was administered to 119 students from the University of Minnesota for factor analysis and reliability assessment; then to 150 students at the same university for a study of test-retest reliability; and finally to a sample of 2,740 families. Another test-retest reliability study was conducted with the final instrument on a group of 116 Minnesota students. Factor analyses were used to establish construct validity. Reliability in terms of internal consistency (lowest alpha = .62) and test-retest reliability (lowest r = .61) have been established.

The instrument is a behavioral self-report measure. It is easily scored by a simple summation of item scores and is easy to administer in less than 30 minutes. The clinical utility of the instrument remains to be established.

THE FAMILY ENVIRONMENT SCALE
(FES)

The FES is a 90-item, true/false, self-report questionnaire developed by Moos (1974) to measure the social-environmental characteristics of families. "It focuses on the measurement and description of the interpersonal relationships among family members, on the directions of personal growth which are emphasized in the family, and on the basic organizational structure of the family" (p. 3).

Moos (1974) assumed that environments can be accurately detailed and measured and that these environments exert a directional influence on behavior. The FES consists of 10 subscales (nine items on each), which assess three underlying dimensions: relationship, personal growth, and system maintenance.

The following is a list of the subscales subsumed under each dimension.

(1) Relationship Dimension (Cohesion, Expressiveness, and Conflicts);
(2) Personal Growth Dimension (Independence, Achievement Orientation, Intellectual-Cultural Orientation, Active-Recreational Orientation, and Moral-Religious Emphasis);
(3) System Maintenance Dimension (Organization and Control).

An initial pool of 200 items was derived from information gathered in unstructured family interviews and from social climate scales developed earlier by Moos (1974). From reading all materials associated with the development of the FES, we were unable to identify any particular conceptual framework or theoretical orientation to family development, process, functioning, or family therapy that served as a guide for the selection of the 200 items in the initial item pool. Moos (1974) said that the exact choice and wording of these items was guided by "a general formulation of environmental press" (p. 3). Each item had to identify characteristics of an environment that would exert a press toward cohesion, achievement, or moral-religious emphasis.

Two forms of the FES were developed: Form A and Form R. The 200-item Form A was administered to a sample of 1,000 individuals (285 families). Data were collected from a wide range of families to ensure that the resulting scale would be applicable to the broadest possible variety of families. Families were recruited from three different church groups through newspaper advertisements and from local high schools. An ethnic minority subsample of Black and Mexican-American families was also included. Finally, a sample of distressed families was recruited from a psychiatric clinic and a correctional facility ($n = 42$).

The data from these samples were used to develop a revised 90-item, 10-subscale R (real) form of the FES. The following psychometric test construction criteria were used to select the 90 items.

(1) The overall item split was to be as close as possible to 50–50 to avoid items characteristic only of extreme families.
(2) Items that correlated more highly with their own rather than with any other subscale were to be selected.
(3) Each of the subscales was to have an approximately equal number of items scored true and items scored false to control for acquiescence response sets.
(4) The final subscales were to show only low-to-moderate intercorrelations.
(5) Each item on each subscale had to show a maximum degree of discrimination among families.

Moos (1974) stated that "basically, each of these psychometric criteria was met in all three subsamples" (p. 5). However, no statistical analyses were reported for Form A. For example, neither the interitem correlations for each subscale nor the correlational matrix for all items was given, and the "low-to-moderate intercorrelations" for the final subscales were not presented. Finally, no discussion was offered of the "maximum degree of discrimination" among families for each of the items on the 10 subscales. Essentially, one is asked to accept the author's statements about the statistical soundness of this research without having access to the figures themselves.

Next, Moos began to collect data for Form R of the FES. Normative data for this second form of the FES were collected from "1,125 normal and 500 distressed families" (p. 4). Included in this second sample were the 285 families used in the first study (i.e., 243 "normal" families and 42 "distressed" families).

Normal families were recruited "from all areas of the country," including "single parent and multigenerational families, families drawn from ethnic minority groups and families of all age groups (newly married student families, families with preschool and adolescent children, families whose children have left home and families composed of older, retired adults" (p. 4).

The sample of normal families also included "a group of 294 families drawn randomly from specific census tracts in the San Francisco area" (p. 4).

In addition to the 42 distressed families included in the first study, distressed families with alcohol abuse as the presenting problem ($n = 220$) and "general psychiatric patients" ($n = 77$) were included in the second study. An additional 161 distressed families with problem children and adolescents were also included in the subsample of distressed families.

The unscientific sampling procedures used in these studies makes it impossible to say that Moos's findings can be considered representative of any particular population. Moos (1981) compared the means and standard deviations for normal and distressed families for each of the 10 subscales of the FES.

In discussing the findings, Moos (1981) stated: "As expected, when compared to normal families, distressed families are lower on cohesion, expressiveness, independence, and intellectual and recreational orientation and higher on conflict and control" (p. 4). However, he offered no theoretical rationale to explain why these differences are to be expected. Assuming that the observed differences are statistically significant (a point not addressed by Moos) and leaving aside the fact that with 10 comparisons one can expect to find at least one statistically significant difference purely by chance, one must question whether the statistically significant differences reflect qualitative and meaningful differences between the two groups of families. For example, what is the significance of the difference between a normal family mean of 4.34 and a distressed family mean of 4.48 on the Control subscale? Similarly, what do the differences in means for Achievement Orientation (normal mean = 5.47; distressed mean = 5.29) and Moral-Religious Emphasis (normal mean = 4.72; distressed mean = 4.45) tell us about the theoretical importance or clinical usefulness of these findings? Moos apparently assumed that higher scores on certain dimensions are preferable to lower scores simply because normal families scored higher than distressed families on these dimensions. For example, family means for Cohesion are reported as 6.61 and 5.03 for normal and for distressed families, respectively. However, it is inappropriate to assume that higher levels of cohesion are always desirable, given the fact that severely dysfunctional psychosomatic family systems are very cohesive (Minuchin, Rosman, & Baker, 1978).

Conversely, Moos intimated that lower levels of overt conflict are desirable because normal families had lower means on this dimension than distressed families did. Again, this quantitative, linear approach to family health and pathology is misleading and ignores both clinical and empirical findings. For example, skewed family systems that are severely dysfunctional showed little, if any, overt conflict (Wynne, Ryckoff, Day, & Hirsch, 1958). Similar observations were made by Beavers and Voeller (1983), who labeled families in which the expression of overt conflict was not permitted "borderline centripetal."

Moos (1981) reported three methods for establishing reliability: internal consistency, test-retest, and profile stability. Internal consistency scores (Cronbach's alpha) for the 10 subscales range from .61 to .78, which Moos described as "an acceptable range." However, considering the sample size, these reliabilities are not impressive. Anderson (1984) suggested that the 2-point, true/false response format of the FES may inflate internal consistency scores with larger samples. Test-retest reliabilities of individual scores for the 10 subscales on a subsample of 47 individuals from nine families who took the test again after an 8-week interval range from .68 to .86. Test-retest reliabilities for family means of two subsamples of families ($n = 35$; $n = 241$) were taken at 4- and 12-month intervals, respectively. Reliabilities for the first group range from .54 to .91. For the second group, reliabilities range from .52 to .89.

In studying the intercorrelational matrix of the 10 subscales for adults ($n = 1,468$) and for children and adolescents ($n = 621$), one is struck by the number of positive correlations. For the adult sample, positive correlations range from .04 to .45. For children and adolescents, the range is approximately the same, .04 to .40. Moos did not specify which correlations are statistically significant. However, of the 45 pairs of possible intercorrelations for each subsample, 18 exceeded .20 in the adult subsample; and 19 intercorrelations of .22 or greater were found in the children and adolescent subsample.

Based upon these data, many of the 10 subscale dimensions are not statistically independent. Therefore, whether these subscales actually measure conceptually distinct factors is questionable.

Finally, profile stability correlations were obtained for 35 families retested after 4 months and for 85 families retested after 12 months. Family means for each subscale were correlated to produce stability scores. Moos (1981) reported his findings as follows:

> The mean 4-month profile stability was .78. Of the 35 stabilities, 29 were .70 or above and 20 were .80 or above. The mean 12-month profile stability was .71. Of the 85 stabilities, 56 were .70 or above and 45 were .80 or above. The form R profiles are therefore quite stable over time intervals of as long as a year, although they also reflect changes that occur in the family milieu. (p. 7)

From this quotation, family stability scores were apparently computed in the following manner. Family means for each of the 10 subscales were computed at two distinct time periods. These means were then correlated to produce stability scores. Essentially, for the subsample of 35 families, 350 correlations (stability scores) were produced. Of these, 49 were greater than .70. For the subsample of 85 families, 850 correlations (stability scores) were calculated. Of these, 101 scores exceeded .70. For the subsample of 35 families, approximately 14% of the correlations (stability scores) exceeded .70. For the subsample of 85 families, approximately 12% of the correlations (stability scores) exceeded .70. These figures are not at all impressive.

Moos's statement that Form R profiles are "quite stable over time intervals of as long as a year" is misleading. As a matter of fact, one would expect family members' perceptions of these 10 dimensions to change throughout the family life cycle. These findings seem to reflect these changing perceptions. The validity of using this procedure to establish profile stability (reliability) is questionable.

Researchers have commonly correlated all 10 subscales with an array of dependent variables in order to determine which of the subscales best "predicts" a given criterion; for example, which subscales correlate significantly with positive therapeutic outcome (Finney, Moos, & Mewborn, 1980). When positive correlations were found, these researchers claimed predictive validity. However, what these studies actually demonstrate is a positive association between certain subscales and select criterion variables.

Studies attempting to establish concurrent validity for the Cohesion subscale have failed to produce significant findings (Oliveri & Reiss, 1984; Russell, 1980). However, Moos and Moos (1981) have reported positive correlations between subscale scores for Moral-Religious Emphasis, Active-Recreational Orientation, Conflict, and Intellectual-Cultural Orientation and self-reports of frequency counts of family members on these dimensions.

As far as we can determine, the validity of this measure remains in question. To date, no factor analyses have been undertaken to offer statistical support for the validity of the FES and its 10 subscales.

The limited amount of time required to administer and score the FES has probably contributed to its clinical use. Respondents simply answer the 90 items in the test booklet on answer sheets. Scoring is a simple clerical task with the answer templates. Items are arranged on the template score sheets so that each column of responses constitutes one of the subscales. The scorer counts the number of X's showing through the template in each column and enters the total raw score in the box at the bottom.

Moos and Moos (1981) recommended calculating an average score for all the members of each family for each subscale. Individual subscale scores or family averages can be converted to standard scores and displayed to produce a family profile or family typology. Families are classified according to their most salient characteristics, considering their personal growth orientation first, their interpersonal-relationship orientation second, and their systems maintenance characteristics last (Billings & Moos, 1982).

The usefulness of average family scores in assessing family dynamics and devising treatment plans is questionable. Because means are highly sensitive to extreme scores, it is quite possible that vastly different family systems, having different hierarchical arrangements and diverse family structures, will present similar profiles. Billings and Moos (1982) claimed that FES typologies are useful in directing interventions, but they did not explain how one uses these profiles to guide interventions.

Finally, Billings and Moos claimed that this instrument provides "a method of evaluating changes in family interaction" (p. 37). It seems that Moos and his colleagues have falsely assumed that family members' perceptions represent valid and reliable portrayals of family behavior.

It is our opinion that the FES, in its present state, suffers from a variety of inadequacies. It is not conceptually grounded in a theory of family process or family development, the methodology used to develop the scale is faulty, ample evidence for validity and reliability have not been offered, and the clinical usefulness of this measure has yet to be demonstrated.

FAMILY OF ORIGIN SCALE
(FOS)

The FOS (Hovestadt, Anderson, Piercy, Cochran, & Fine, 1985) grew out of the initial efforts of Lutz and Anderson to develop a scale that would measure the level of health a person perceives in his or her family of origin (reported in Lee, Gordon, & O'Dell, 1989). Lutz and Anderson began their work on the FOS by drawing from the empirical work of some investigators, the theoretical formulations of a number of therapists, and the clinical observations of pioneering family therapists (e.g., Boszormenyi-Nagy & Spark, 1973; Bowen, 1978; Bowlby, 1969, 1980; Fairbain, 1952; Framo, 1976; Gourevitch, 1978; Lewis, Beavers, Gossett, & Phillips, 1976; Williamson, 1978).

First, two subscales were constructed: Autonomy and Intimacy. Autonomy was conceptualized as including five distinct concepts: clarity of expression, responsibility, respect for others, openness to others, and acceptance of separation and loss. Intimacy was conceptualized as comprising trust, empathy, conflict resolution, range of feelings, and mood and tone.

Next, a pool of 60 items was developed with the assistance of a group of graduate students enrolled in a marital therapy class at East Texas State University. The researchers then wrote to 10 experts, asking them to rate each of the 60 items on a Likert scale, indicating the degree to which the item measured the particular concept it was intended to measure. Of the 10 experts, 6 agreed to judge the items.

After the judges completed this task, the researchers selected the two positive items and the two negative items that received the highest ratings for each of the 10 concepts. The resulting 40 items were used to construct a Likert-type FOS.

Only content validity was claimed. No other type of validity was presented in this initial study. Test-retest reliability of the 40-item scale was calculated on a sample of 41 psychology graduate students after a 2-week interval. Reliability for the entire scale was reported as .97. Autonomy and Intimacy test-retest reliabilities were .94 and .96, respectively.

In 1985 Hovestadt et al. reported the findings of a 1980 study conducted by Lutz and Anderson. The FOS was administered to 278 graduate students, of whom 39 were Black Americans, at East Texas State University. No significant differences were found in how the two racial groups responded to the FOS.

Hovestadt et al. (1985) cited three studies that offer some support for the validity of the FOS. Holter (1982) found the FOS to discriminate between alcoholic-distressed marriages and nonalcoholic-distressed marriages in terms of the husbands' perceptions of their families of origin. Fine and Hovestadt (1984) found that individuals who perceived their families of origin as higher in overall health had more positive perceptions of marriage than did those who perceived their families of origin as low in overall family health. Finally, Canfield (1983) reported a positive correlation between the FOS scores and scores on the Healthy Family Functioning Scale (Sennott, 1981). However, the reliability and validity of the measures used in these studies were not reported.

Lee et al. (1989) applied the FOS, along with the 16PF scale and a scale of authoritarianism, to 100 adults in psychotherapy, 100 adults who were not in psychotherapy, 32 adults who had sought treatment, and 41 college students. They found that the FOS differentiated between patients and nonpatients, but it measured only one general factor and delivered little information.

The theoretical base of the FOS was drawn from the works of Lewis et al. (1976), specifically the Beavers-Timberlawn Family Evaluation Scales (BTFES). The theoretical soundness and validity of these scales are discussed in Chapter 9. Given the inadequacies of the BTFES, one can argue that the FOS is built upon a very shaky theoretical foundation. Construct validity has not been convincingly established. At this time, the best that can be said for the FOS is that much more research needs to be done to establish it as a valid instrument.

THE FAMILY CONCEPT TEST

The Family Concept Test (van der Veen, 1965, 1969, 1979; van der Veen & Olson, 1983) is an instrument for measuring the interrelated perceptions and attitudes regarding a family. Here, the family concept is analogous to self-concept on an individual level. In the Family Concept Test, social and emotional aspects of family life are described by 80 one-sentence statements that apply to the entire family unit. The test has two forms: the Family Concept Q Sort and the Family Concept Inventory.

The final 80 items used in the development of the Family Concept Test were selected from a larger pool of 138 items developed by van der Veen and his associates. These were rated by an unspecified number of mental health workers for clarity and for their relevance to family functioning (van der Veen & Olson, 1983). Each item was constructed to apply to the family unit, not to particular family positions or relationships. Each item is believed to assess a person's view of the family as an "affective-cognitive unit." It is assumed that a family member rates an item according to what is most salient in his or her perception of the family.

Initially, eight content dimensions of the Family Concept Test were derived through factor analysis. These eight factors showed no overlap of items and accounted for approximately 30% of the item variance. However, a correlational analysis of all items with factor scores revealed a group of eight items that correlated significantly with four of the factors but that had not been omitted because of numerous cross-loadings across factors. These were combined into a separate item set and treated as a ninth factor. The eight factors are labeled Consideration versus Conflict, Family Actualization versus Inadequacy, Open Communication, Community Sociability, Family Ambition, Familial versus External Focus of Control, Togetherness versus Separateness, and Family Loyalty. The ninth factor is labeled Closeness versus Estrangement.

A number of studies reporting convergent validity findings were also cited by van der Veen and Olson (1983). Test-retest reliabilities for the Q Sort procedure were reported for fairly small samples (e.g., $n = 10, 12, 15, 16, 18, 25, 26, 37$). Test-retest periods ranged from 2 weeks to 17 months. Reliabilities range from .54 to .71. Reliability for the inventory was reported as .80. Test-retest reliabilities when the same samples responded to items according to their "ideal" families were .64 to .80 for the Q Sort and .87 for the Inventory form of the Family Concept Test.

In their *Manual and Handbook for the Family Concept Assessment Method,* van der Veen and Olson (1983) summarized 51 studies in which the Family Concept Test was used to test various hypotheses and to evaluate the effects of interventions. However, how one uses the Family Concept Test as an assessment device to plan treatments and evaluate therapeutic outcome was not discussed.

FAMILY FUNCTIONING INDEX

The Family Functioning Index (Pless & Satterwhite, 1973) was developed as part of a semistructured interview used in a study of the adjustment of children with chronic physical illnesses. The index was administered to the parents of 399 school-aged children, all of whom were part of a 1% random sample of families. Of these children, 209 had chronic disorders at the time of the study; the remainder were healthy.

The original index was based on 16 questions chosen to reflect the multidimensional nature of the construct being assessed. The choice was eclectic and was based on both theoretical and empirical considerations.

Responses to these questionnaires were factor-analyzed. Pless and Satterwhite (1973) reported five main factors: Communication, Togetherness, Closeness, Decision Making, and Child Orientation. However, they did not report the factor matrix, making it impossible to determine whether there were any cross-loadings of items across factors. Similarly, eigenvalues and the amount of variance accounted for by each factor were not reported.

Essentially, no reliability data were reported. However, Pless and Satterwhite (1973) did report the correlations of husbands' and wives' scores on the Family Functioning Index as .72.

FAMILY ASSESSMENT DEVICE
(FAD)

Based upon the McMaster Model of Family Functioning, the FAD (Epstein, Baldwin, & Bishop, 1983) was designed as a screening instrument to identify family problems in "the most simple and efficient fashion" (p. 171). The FAD was constructed to collect information on a variety of dimensions originally outlined by Epstein, Sigal, and Rakoff (1962) and by Westley and Epstein (1969). This model identifies six dimensions of family functioning drawn from the fields of family sociology, family studies, and family therapy. This problem-focused approach to family assessment *identities* is made up of seven scales: a general functioning scale used to assess the "overall health/ pathology of the family" and the six dimensions of family functioning considered important by the scale developers. These are (1) Problem Solving, (2) Communication, (3) Roles, (4) Affective Responsiveness, (5) Affective Involvement, and (6) Behavior Control.

A pool of 240 items was developed. These items were determined by the researchers to be representative of the six dimensions of family functioning in the McMaster model. For each of the six dimensions, 40 items were selected.

The 240 items were administered to two extremely different, nonrepresentative samples. The first group consisted of 294 individuals from 112 families (e.g., psychiatric day-hospital-patient families, $n = 4$; stroke-patient families, $n = 6$; students in advanced psychology courses, $n = 9$; and psychiatric inpatients and their families, $n = 93$). The second group consisted of 209 students enrolled in an introductory psychology course.

The format of the 240-item questionnaire was not described. Responses to the questionnaire were subjected to tests of internal consistency. However, the entire questionnaire was not subjected to any test of internal consistency. Only the items that had been grouped into the six dimensions of family functioning were subjected to six separate tests of internal consistency by the use of Cronbach's procedures. Items that did not correlate highly were discarded from each of the six subscales.

The reliabilities from this first attempt to construct six subscales range from .83 to .90. However, the researchers reported that these initial subscales were highly intercorrelated. As a result, Epstein et al. (1983) pooled all items that "correlated highly with all six scale scores" and "selected the most highly intercorrelated subset of these items to make a General Functioning Scale" (p. 175). The statistical procedures used to accomplish this last task were not described by the researchers.

Epstein et al. (1983) then returned to the original 240 items and used a number of a priori procedures to regroup items into the six subscales. As far as we can determine from their discussion of this process, each time items were added or subtracted from each of the six subscales, the researchers performed tests of internal consistency. This procedure was continued until "the scale reliability was over a minimum (alpha = .70) and either there were no items to add which would increase scale reliability or any item which might increase the scale reliability would also increase the correlation of that scale with one of the other scales" (p. 175). This procedure resulted in a 53-item scale.

In an attempt to establish predictive or criterion-related validity, the researchers returned to their original sample and compared clinical families with nonclinical families. Data from only one person in each family were used. On the basis of family status, clinical or nonclinical, the scores from these two groups were compared. Having attempted to predict family status from the FAD scores, the authors stated that they were able to predict family status for "sixty-seven percent of the nonclinical group and sixty-four percent of the clinical group" (p. 177). They went on to state that "in every case the nonclinical group mean was lower (more healthy) than the mean for the clinically present group" (p. 177).

In another attempt to establish concurrent validity, Epstein et al. (1983) correlated the FAD with the Locke-Wallace Marital Satisfaction Scale. They claimed that the FAD accounted for 28% of the variance (for husbands and wives) in the Locke-Wallace. This should not be surprising when one considers that items from the Locke-Wallace served as a model for items included in the FAD. Given this fact, an $r = .53$ correlation between these two measures is understandable.

As far as we can tell from the procedures outlined by Epstein et al. (1983), this study represents one of the most poorly conceived and executed research attempts that we have come across in our review of published assessment instruments. The FAD does not rest firmly on any recognizable theory of family process or family structure. In terms of the domains of family functioning that this instrument is designed to assess, the coverage is, at best, incomplete. The samples used for instrument development are not at all representative of some larger population or universe. In addition, test administration procedures were not standardized, and data collection was poorly organized. The procedures used to establish reliability and validity are so methodologically flawed that we must say that we cannot determine what the FAD actually measures or how reliably it measures it.

STRUCTURAL FAMILY INTERACTION SCALE

Perosa, Hansen, and Perosa (1981) used Minuchin's (1974) and Minuchin, Montalvo, Guerney, Rosman, & Schumer (1967) structural model of family functioning to develop an instrument to assess perceived interaction patterns in families.

The authors wrote 200 items in an attempt to operationalize 13 concepts: enmeshment, disengagement, neglect, overprotection, rigidity, flexibility, parent conflict avoidance, parent conflict without resolution, parent conflict resolution, parent management, triangulation, parent-child coalition, and detouring. The 200 items, along with a description of each of the 13 concepts, were given to six family therapists who were asked to categorize each statement and to rate the degree of fit. Items were retained if at least four of the six judges agreed upon item fit. For each item, interjudge agreement ranged from .81 to .100. The overall interjudge agreement for the 95 retained items was .95. These 95 items were divided into 13 scales corresponding to the 13 structural concepts listed earlier.

The volunteer participants in the pilot study were 50 white Anglo-Saxon, Protestant and Catholic, college-educated, middle-class families from New York City and its suburbs. The format of the Structural Family Interaction Scale administered to these families was not described, but the authors stated that internal consistencies for the subscales "ranged from substantial to high" (Perosa et al., 1981, p. 80).

Data from the pilot study were used to construct a 65-item Structural Family Interaction Scale. The authors added 20 new items "to make items more accurately portray specific family interaction patterns" (p. 81). These 20 items were used to construct 10 two-item "secondary subscales" (p. 81) (e.g., Mother Overprotection, Father Overprotection, Mother Neglect, Father Neglect, Parent Conflict Avoidance, Parents-Children Conflict Avoidance, Parent Conflict Expression Without Resolution, Parents-Children Conflict Expression Without Resolution, Parent Conflict Resolution, and Parents-Children Conflict Resolution).

The Structural Family Interaction Scale was then given to two samples of 25 families (*N* = 50 families). One group consisted of families with learning-disabled children; the second group had no child as an identified patient. Internal consistencies of the primary scales range from .25 (neglect) to .74 (parent-child coalition). Secondary scale correlations range from −.08 (parent conflict avoidance) to .56 (father neglect).

The items making up the 25 subscales were not identified. However, internal consistencies are quite low, so reliability is suspect. The authors attempted to make a case for the scale's validity by proposing that the inter-correlations of the 25 subscales "follow a pattern predicted by Minuchin's model" (p. 86). This is not an accepted measure of construct validity. As a matter of fact, the high intercorrelations of a number of subscales suggest that they are not really independent constructs.

Essentially, the Structural Family Interaction Scale does not stand up to tests of reliability, and validity has yet to be demonstrated.

FAMILY PROCESS SCALE

The Family Process Scale (Barbarin, 1982) was intended to be "a screening device to provide a summary appraisal of families along dimensions drawn from systems theories, to generate hypotheses about family process which could be tested through subsequent observation and to identify issues that could be scrutinized in subsequent interviews with families" (p. 6). The instrument was developed with the goal of helping clinicians and research-ers learn more about the family as a system and to understand the individual family member's perception of that system.

The selection of items for the Family Process Scale was "guided by the major assumptions of family systems theory regarding circular causality, nonsummativity, equifinality, homeostasis and morphogenesis" (pp. 6–7). These assumptions emphasize (1) the interdependence of family members, (2) the ability of the family to adapt flexibly to change in the external and internal environments, and (3) the capacity to foster the healthy growth and development of family members. The following were conceptual guidelines for the selection of specific items: differentiation, enmeshment, dependence, control, support, flexibility, satisfaction, and problem solving.

For each concept identified, a group of items was developed according to procedures used in Thurstone scaling. Graduate and undergraduate psy-chology students served as judges, rating each item on a 7-point scale.

The items were then administered to two groups of families: nonproblem families who volunteered to participate in a research-training program for parents interested in learning about child development and families in which an adolescent had been hospitalized for a psychiatric condition (*N* = 48). Approximately 124 respondents were used in the initial test to deter-mine internal consistency according to the Kuder-Richardson formula, KR-20. Barbarin did not specify which family members (in either group) served as subjects. Barbarin (1982) stated that "the initial KR-20 estimates of internal consistency were computed for a priori scales and found to be highly acceptable. They range from .88 to .94" (p. 13).

Items without high item-total correlations were deleted, and additional items were added to the initial group. The original true/false format was replaced by a 4-point Likert-type scale.

A nonspecified sample of 535 persons completed the revised version, and the responses were factor-analyzed. This procedure resulted in 20 factors whose eigenvalues were greater than 1. Each factor, or scale, was then tested for internal consistency. Scales whose internal consistency fell below .74 were dropped. Only seven scales were retained, for which reliabilities range from .46 to .92. However, only three of the seven scales (Support, Mutuality, and Family Satisfaction) were reported as having acceptable reliabilities of .86 or greater (Barbarin, 1982).

A multitrait-multimethod procedure was used to establish concurrent and discriminant validity. Among the instruments used to assess the degree of concurrent validity were FACES I (Olson, Bell, & Portner, 1982), and the FES (Moos, 1974). The Rosenberg Self-Esteem Scale (Rosenberg, 1965) was used to determine discriminant validity.

Although many of the correlations between the three dimensions of the Family Process Scale are in the expected direction for concurrent validity, the three subscales are also highly intercorrelated (e.g., Support and Mutuality, $r = .62$; Support and Family Satisfaction, $r = .71$; and Mutuality and Family Satisfaction, $r = .72$). In addition, Family Satisfaction, as measured by the Family Process Scale, correlated at .66 with social desirability as measured by FACES I. Although Barbarin (1982) stated that his purpose in developing the Family Process Scale was to construct a screening device to appraise families along certain systems dimensions and to help clinicians/ researchers learn more about how a family is perceived by its members, he concluded his discussion of the scale by saying that this instrument can be used to assess "basic family processes, stressful transitions, family coping styles and coping outcomes" (p. 19). In our opinion, no data have been presented by Barbarin to support such claims. The three basic concepts that were shown to have some construct validity are Support, Mutuality, and Family Satisfaction. These three constructs were also highly intercorrelated, suggesting that they are part of some larger, more encompassing construct, such as family togetherness.

This 66-item self-report questionnaire does not tap family processes, nor does it give us any information about how families go through stressful transitions or what their coping styles are. McCubbin et al.'s (1982) F-COPES is a much more valid and reliable instrument for these purposes.

VERBAL PROBLEM CHECKLIST
(VPC)

Thomas, Walter, and O'Flaherty (1974) developed the VPC, a checklist of verbal behavior, in an attempt to have a tool for fast and efficient "response specification," which they considered necessary to accurately select behavior for modification. Each family member is rated on 49 categories of verbal response. The amount of each response is rated on a 4-point scale; whether or not the behavior presents a problem is rated on a 3-point scale.

The 49 categories include 10 that deal with vocal characteristics, such as speed and volume. Others deal with "referent representation," such as overgeneralization and presumptive attribution; and still others with the amount of information given (too much, too little, redundant). Six response categories measure aspects of content irregularities, such as content avoidance, shifting, persistence, detached utterance, and over-and underresponsiveness. Control and direction of the conversation are measured by excessive question asking, obtrusions, and excessive cuing. The remaining 15 categories deal with the content itself (e.g., pedantry, dogmatic statements, positive and negative talk). Each of the 49 categories is intended to be as concrete as possible and to require a minimum of inference by the observer.

Nine couples were scored by two raters using the checklist. The couples were asked to discuss four topics involving marital expectations, decision making, and marital problems. The raters independently scored the couples for the amount as well as the extent of the problem in each category. The amount and problem ratings correlated very highly across the categories, rho = .95 for husbands, .96 for wives.

On a 4-point scale, the median rating was 1.44 for husbands and 1.35 for wives. The amount of each verbal response category thus tended to be low both for husbands and for wives. Nearly all individual category scores were very similar for husbands and wives, except "overtalk" rated higher for wives and "quiet talk" and "unaffective talk" rated higher for husbands.

The data were examined to determine whether the VPC successfully narrowed the problem behavior. Approximately seven categories were rated 4 by at least one rater, and three fourths of the categories were rated 1 by at least one rater. This suggested to Thomas et al. that the checklist can in fact specify a focal response area for modification.

The VPC data were tested for interrater reliability by use of the Kruskal-Goodman gamma, for which the authors considered a value of .5 to show moderate reliability. They found that 78% of the ratings for the husbands exceeded this rating, as did 83% of those for the wives.

When individual category reliability was examined, the reliability for the lower response categories was overinflated because of the truncated lower range of the amounts of response. The categories receiving higher ratings were less highly related over the four discussion sessions.

Validity was tested for the most clearly quantifiable behavior—overtalk and undertalk. The timed amount of talking was highly related to the ratings of undertalk and overtalk.

In spite of the reliability problems with frequent response classes, the

VPC is successful in specifying a clearly defined problem area. The authors suggested further validation studies with other objective criteria.

REPERTORY GRID

Ryle (1975) developed a grid technique for clarifying constructs and elements in an individual's experience that can be applied to a person's view of family members and dyadic relationships within the family. The approach is based on Kelly's (1955) theory of personal constructs. Kelly attempted to delineate a system of determining an individual's representations or models of the world as viewed in the form of bipolar descriptive constructs.

The basic process of grid construction involves first the determining of *elements* in the area of experience to be examined (e.g., the members of the subject's family). In the next step, the *constructs* are elicited from the subject by choosing any two of the elements and asking the subject to name qualities in which the two elements are similar and qualities in which they differ. This procedure can be repeated until the investigator is satisfied that the most distinct and emotionally laden constructs have been elicited. Next, the subject is asked to rate on a 5- or a 7-point scale (*not at all* to *very true*) the extent to which each construct describes each element.

Having rated each element by each construct, the investigator is prepared to analyze the relationship between elements and the relationship between constructs. Elements can be compared according to whether both are rated high (or low) on the same scales. Opposite elements tend to be rated differently on most constructs. Conversely, constructs are analyzed according to how they tend to compare with other constructs when the same elements are rated. That is, constructs are related positively when most elements receive identical ratings.

When the ratings of elements on one construct are opposite to their ratings on another construct, these constructs are negatively related and may be seen to represent polar categorizations of the subject's experience. In other words, elements are highly correlated across positively related constructs and negatively correlated across negatively related constructs.

The next step is to identify bipolar components consisting of two constructs or two sets of highly correlated constructs that are negatively correlated. For example, suppose "sexually attractive" and "passive" occur highly as powerful descriptors of the same people. If "ruthless" and "dominating" are very low in their description of these same people, these two sets of constructs would compose a bipolar component. The *principal component* is the component that accounts for the greatest variance. According to Ryle, this amounts to 30% to 50% of the total variance for most grids. The *secondary component* is the bipolar component that accounts for the next greatest total variance, 10% to 25% for most samples.

The graphing technique proposed by the author is to plot an orthogonal Cartesian graph. The principal and the secondary components are placed on the horizontal and vertical axes, respectively. The various descriptive constructs are then located at the periphery of the grid at a point that maps their conceptual relationships to the primary and the secondary components. For example, constructs correlated with the lower construct of the secondary component and with the right-hand construct of the primary component would be placed at the periphery of the lower right quadrant. The elements would then be plotted at their location in reference to the primary and secondary components. The grid technique provides a virtual map of the subject's conceptual framework.

Variations on the basic grid method allow the plotting of the real and the ideal aspects of elements, including the self, and of the elements in different roles and situations, such as the self at work, the self at home, the self as husband, the self as father. In addition, the grid can be used effectively when elements are rated at different times, such as self before therapy and self after therapy.

Another variation is the plotting of a dyadic grid, in which the constructs are interactional descriptors such as "indifferent to" or "guilty about." The pairs of elements are thus a subject and an object for each descriptor. They are connected by lines on the graph. Role reciprocity in relationships is thus evidenced when the dyad extends beyond one quadrant, and role sameness is evidenced when the elements are proximal to each other. Note also that the slopes of the lines are diagnostic. If all dyads for a subject have the same slope, the subject may have a fairly undifferentiated perception of relationships and roles, viewing all of them in terms of one dichotomous set of descriptors.

A final elaboration of grid technique is the *double dyad grid*. In this approach, both partners produce grids for themselves and for predicting their mate's responses. The similarities and differences of these four graphs yield information about distortions and projections and the specific areas in which they occur.

The grid technique seems to be an effective assessment of the conceptual structure of interpersonal feelings and attitudes, mapped clearly enough to be useful. In a case example of a 10-year-old boy, Ravenette (1975) concluded that the test is suitable for children 8 years and older, that administration and statistical analysis are fast and effective, and that the technique has the advantage of allowing the child to look at his or her own perception of the self and others.

PERSONAL AUTHORITY IN THE FAMILY
SYSTEMS (PAFS) QUESTIONNAIRE

The PAFS Questionnaire was developed by Bray, Williamson, and Malone (1984) in an attempt to operationalize key concepts postulated by transgenerational theorists (e.g., Boszormenyi-Nagy & Spark, 1973; Bowen, 1978; Framo, 1981; Paul & Paul, 1975).

Williamson (1982) defined "personal authority" as an ability to:

(1) Order and direct one's own thoughts and opinions;
(2) Choose to express or not express one's thoughts and opinions regardless of social pressures to do so;
(3) Make and respect one's personal judgments to the point of regarding these as justifications for action;
(4) Take responsibility for the totality of one's experiences in life;
(5) Initiate or receive as well as decline intimacy voluntarily, in conjunction with the ability to establish clear boundaries to the self;
(6) Experience and relate to all other persons without exception, including viewing parents as peers in the experience of being human.

Achievement of PAFS is seen as both an individual and a systemic, biopsychosocial developmental task that usually occurs "during the fourth or early fifth decade of life" (Bray et al., 1984, p. 168). The development of PAFS results from a reciprocal and coevolutionary renegotiation process established between the first and the second generations in the three-generational family life cycle. PAFS is viewed as a continuum, with personal authority at one end of the pole and intergenerational intimidation at the other end. PAFS implies the patterns of behavior characteristic of an integrated and differentiated self as well as a resolution of the vocational, achievement, and intimacy conflicts generated by transgenerational mandates and loyalties. Finally, it includes one's reconnection and sense of belonging to the family of origin while one acts from a differentiated position within the family of origin.

Bray et al. (1984) hypothesized that the absence of PAFS in an adult in the fourth or fifth decade of life and afterward implies a dysfunctional intergenerational hierarchy. This results in continuing fusion and triangulation with parents and a parental marriage on the part of the adult in the second generation. It also implies the continuation of covert loyalty commitments to previous generations, the continuation of distorted parental introjects, and the extension of unresolved mourning from previous generations. The absence of PAFS works against a differentiated self within the family of origin. The authors hypothesized that this pattern of intergenerational relationships, if continued long enough, is likely to result in the transmission of these pathological patterns and structures to the next generation.

The central concepts and behavioral patterns that the PAFS is concerned with are individuation, fusion, triangulation, intimacy, personal authority, and intergenerational intimidation.

Items were written to measure the following seven constructs: (1) spousal fusion/individuation, (2) intergenerational fusion/individuation, (3) spousal intimacy, (4) intergenerational intimacy, (5) nuclear family triangulation, (6) intergenerational triangulation, and (7) intergenerational intimidation.

The number of items in the initial questionnaire was not specified by Bray et al. (1984). The items were judged appropriate in terms of content and clarity by nine graduate students in psychology and nine experienced mental health professionals. On the basis of the judges' evaluations, items were reworded, deleted, or placed in different subscales. A third group of judges then assessed the items for content and clarity, resulting in the final 181-item version of Likert-type questions.

The 181-item questionnaire was administered twice to volunteers from a local medical center/university community (Bray et al., 1984), along with the Dyadic Adjustment Scale (DAS) (Spanier, 1976) and FACES II (Olson, Bell, & Portner, 1982). Coefficient alpha (Cronbach, 1951) analyses were calculated at both times of testing. Test-retest reliabilities for the seven subscales range from .55 for Intergenerational Fusion/Individuation to .95 for Nuclear Family Triangulation. Internal consistencies for the seven subscales completed after a 2-week interval range from .82 to .95 during the first testing and .80 to .95 during the second.

Although a multitrait-multimethod procedure was not undertaken, Bray et al. (1984) did report low-level concurrent validity coefficients for subscale scores for Cohesion when they used FACES I and PAFS Spousal Intimacy and Intergenerational Intimacy (.33 and .22, respectively). Correlations with the Social Desirability scale in FACES I for the seven PAFS subscales range from −.18 to .42. Spousal Intimacy and the DAS have the highest correlations produced in this research, $r = .69$.

A more robust study to establish construct validity was undertaken. Four hundred volunteers from the same medical center/university community were administered the revised PAFS Questionnaire, consisting of 123 items retained from the first study and 18 items developed for a new subscale labeled Personal Authority. The responses to this 141-item questionnaire were factor-analyzed. After preliminary analysis, a seven-factor solution was called for. Only items loading .35 or more were retained. However, items that cross-loaded on two or more factors were retained and were allocated to the factor on which they received the highest loading. Internal consistency correlations (Cronbach's alpha) range from .74 to .96 for the eight factors.

The final scale (Williamson, Bray, & Malone, 1984) contains 132 questions. Williamson et al. have not reported any procedure for transforming raw subscale scores into standard scores, which represents a limitation for both clinicians and researchers. In their 1984 publication, Williamson et al. presented data describing the means and ranges of subscale scores computed for their validation samples. They suggested that these scores be used as normative scores against which other sample scores can be compared.

The PAFS is a well-thought-out scale that has solid theoretical roots in transgenerational theories of family therapy, and it seems to be highly reliable. However, the researchers did not report the number of items that crossloaded on two or more factors or the degree to which any of the subscales intercorrelated. Thus, construct validity may not be as strong as it seems at first glance. Replicating these findings with a larger, more representative sample, reporting the factor matrix, correlating all eight subscales, and providing tables that can be used to transform raw scores into standard scores would greatly improve the validity and interpretability of the PAFS scale.

A more detailed discussion of how the therapist uses the information gleaned from the PAFS scale to make family assessments and formulate treatment plans is also needed. However, the PAFS scale shows much promise and has the potential to become a valuable tool for family assessment and outcome evaluation.

CONCLUSION

The field of marriage and family evaluation does not lack measures to evaluate dyadic and multipersonal relationships. These measures, separate from overt behavior, provide another way to learn about how people feel about or see themselves in intimate contexts. We realize now that they may not need to be related to overt, observable behaviors but do need to show some degree of validity to them or to other internal, individual states or traits. Consequently, the task of the future will be to find a nomological network of individual and family correlates.

REFERENCES

Anderson, S. A. (1984). The Family Environment Scale (FES): A review and critique. *American Journal of Family Therapy, 12,* 59–62.

Barbarin, O. A. (1982). *Family Process Scale manual.* Unpublished manuscript, University of Michigan, Ann Arbor.

Beavers, W. R., & Voeller, M. N. (1983). Comparing and contrasting the Olson circumplex model with the Beavers systems model. *Family Process, 22,* 85–97.

Bell, R. (1980). *Adolescent runaways and family interaction.* Unpublished doctoral dissertation, University of Minnesota, Minneapolis.

Billings, A. G., & Moos, R. H. (1982). Family environments and adaptation: A clinically applicable typology. *American Journal of Family Therapy, 10,* 26–38.

Boszormenyi-Nagy, I., & Spark, G. M. (1973). *Invisible loyalties.* New York: Harper & Row. (Reprinted 1984 by Brunner/Mazel, New York.)

Bowen, M. (1978). *Family therapy in clinical practice.* Northvale, NJ: Jason Aronson.

Bowlby, J. (1969). *Attachment and loss: Vol. 1. Attachment.* New York: Basic Books.

Bowlby, J. (1980). *Attachment and loss: Vol. 3. Loss, sadness and depression.* New York: Basic Books.

Bray, J. H., Williamson, D. S., & Malone, P. E. (1984). Personal authority in the family system: Development of a questionnaire to measure personal authoritiy in intergenerational processes. *Journal of Marital and Family Therapy, 10,* 167–178.

Buckley, W. (1967). *Sociology and modern systems theory.* Englewood Cliffs, NJ: Prentice Hall.

Canfield, B. S. (1983). *Family-of-origin experiences and selected demographic factors as predictors of current family functioning.* Unpublished doctoral dissertation, East Texas State University, Commerce.

Coddington, R. D. (1972a). The significance of life events as etiologic factors in the diseases of children: 1. A survey of professional workers. *Journal of Psychosomatic Research, 16,* 7–18.

Coddington, R. D. (1972b). The significance of life events as etiologic factors in the diseases of children: 2. A study of a normal population. *Journal of Psychosomatic Research, 16,* 205–213.

Cromwell, R. E., Olson, D. K. A., & Fournier, D. G. (1976). Tools and techniques for diagnosis and evaluation in marital and family therapy. *Family Process, 15,* 1–49.

Cronbach, L. J. (1951). Coefficient alpha and the internal structure of tests. *Psychometrika, 16,* 297–334.

Dohrenwend, B. S., Krasnoff, L., Askenasy, A. R., & Dohrenwend, B. P. (1978). Exemplification of a method of scaling events: The PERI life events scale. *Journal of Health and Social Behavior, 19,* 205–229.

Epstein, N. B., Baldwin, L. M., & Bishop, D. S. (1983). The McMaster Family Assessment Device. *Journal of Marital and Family Therapy, 9,* 171–180.

Epstein, N. B., Bishop, D. S., & Levin, S. (1978). The McMaster model of family functioning. *Journal of Marriage and Family Counseling, 4,* 19–31.

Epstein, N. B., Sigal, J. J., & Rakoff, V. (1962). *Family categories schema.* Unpublished manuscript, Department of Psychiatry, Jewish General Hospital, in collaboration with McGill Human Development Study, Montreal.

Fairbain, W. R. D. (1952). *Psychoanalytic studies of the personality.* London: Tavistock.

Fine, M., & Hovestadt, A. J. (1984). Perceptions of marriage and reliabilility by levels of perceived health in the family of origin. *Journal of Marital and Family Therapy, 10,* 193–195.

Finney, J.W., Moos, R.H., & Mewborn, C.R. (1980). Post-treatment experiences and treatment outcome of alcoholic patients six months and two years after hospitalization. *Journal of Counseltative & Clinical Psychiatry, 48,* 17–29.

Framo, J. L. (1976). Family of origin as a therapeutic resource for adults in marital and family therapy: You can and should go home again. *Family Process, 15,* 193–210.

Framo, J. L. (1981). The integration of marital therapy with sessions with family of origin. In A. S. Gurman & D. P. Kniskern (Eds.), *Handbook of family therapy* (pp. 133–158). New York: Brunner/Mazel.

Gourevitch, A. (1978). Origins: The impact of parental background. *Contemporary Psychoanalysis, 14,* 226–245.

Hill, R. (1949). *Families under stress.* New York: Harper & Row.

Hill, R. (1958). Generic features of families under stress. *Social Casework, 49,* 139–150.

Holmes, T. H., & Rahe, R. (1967). The Social Readjustment Rating Scale. *Journal of Psychosomatic Research, 11,* 213–218.

Holter, J. (1982). *A comparison of selected family-of-origin perceptions within the alcohol-distressed marital dyad and the non-alcohol-distressed marital dyad.* Unpublished doctoral dissertation, East Texas State University, Commerce.

Hovestadt, A. J., Anderson, W. T., Piercy, F. P., Cochran, S. W., & Fine, M. (1985). A family-of-origin scale. *Journal of Marriage and Family Therapy, 11,* 287–297.

Kelly, G. A. (1955). *The psychology of personal constructs.* New York: Norton.

Lee, R. E., Gordon, N. G., & O'Dell, J. W. (1989). The validity and use of the family-of-origin scale. *Journal of Marital and Family Therapy, 15,* 19–27.

Lewis, J. M., Beavers, W. R., Gossett, J. T., & Phillips, V. A. (1976). *No single thread: Psychological health in family systems.* New York: Brunner/Mazel.

McCubbin, H. I., Larsen, A., & Olson, D.H. (1982). F-COPES: Family coping strategies. In D.H. Olson, H. I. McCubbin, H. Barnes, A. Larsen, M. Maxen, & M. Wilson (Eds.), *Family inventories: Inventories used in a national survey of families across the family life cycle* (pp. 101–120). St. Paul: University of Minnesota.

McCubbin, H. I., & Patterson, J. (1983). The family stress process: The double ABCX model of adjustment and adaptation. *Marriage and Family Review, 6,* 7–37.

McCubbin, H. I., Thompson, A. I., Pirner, P. A., & McCubbin, M. A. (1988). *Family types and strengths: A life cycle and ecological perspective.* Edina, MN: Burgess.

Mederer, H., & Hill, R. (1983). Critical transitions over the family life span: Theory and research. In H. I. McCubbin, M. B. Sussman, & M. Patterson (Eds.), *Social stress and the family: Advances and developments in family stress theory and research* (pp. 39–60). New York: Harvest.

Minuchin, S. (1974). *Families and family therapy.* Cambridge, MA: Harvard University Press.

Minuchin, S., Rosman, B. L., & Baker, L. (1978). *Psychosomatic families.* Cambridge, MA: Harvard University Press.

Minuchin, S., Montalvo, B., Guerney, B., Jr., Rosman, B., & Schumer, F. (1967). *Families of the slums: An exploration of their structure and treatment.* New York: Basic Books.

Moos, R. H. (1974). *Family Environment Scale (Form R).* Palo Alto, CA: Consulting Psychologists Press.

Moos, R. H. (1981). *Work Environment Scale manual.* Palo Alto, CA: Consulting Psychologists Press.

Moos, R. H., & Moos, B. S. (1981). *Family Environment Scale Manual.* Palo Alto, CA: Consulting Psychologists Press.

Oliveri, M. E., & Reiss, D. (1984). Family concepts and measurement: Things are seldom what they seem. *Family Process, 23,* 33–48.

Olson, D. H. (1979). *Inventory of marriage and family literature, Vol 5, 1977-1978.* Beverly Hills: Sage.

Olson, D. H., Bell, R., & Portner, J. (1982). *FACES II: Family adaptability and cohesion evaluation scales.* St. Paul: University of Minnesota, Family Social Science.

Olson, D. H., Larsen, A. S., & McCubbin, H. I. (1982). Family strengths. In D. H. Olson, H. I. McCubbin, H. Barnes, A. Larsen, M. Maxen, & M. Wilson (Eds.), *Family inventories: Inventories used in a national survey of families across the life cycle* (pp. 121–132). St. Paul: University of Minnesota.

Olson, D. H., McCubbin, H. I., Barnes, H., Larsen, A., Maxen, M., & Wilson, M. (Eds.). (1982). *Family inventories: Inventories used in a national survey of families across the life cycle.* St. Paul: University of Minnesota.

Olson, D. H., Portner, J., & Lavee, Y. (1985). *FACES III.* St. Paul: University of Minnesota, Family Social Science.

Olson, D. H., & Ryder, R. G. (1978). *Marital and family interaction coding system.*

Olson, D. H., Sprenkle, D. H., & Russell, C. S. (1979). Circumplex model of marital and family systems: I. Cohesion and adaptability dimensions, family types, and clinical applications. *Family Process, 18,* 3–28.

Paul, N. L., & Paul, B. B. (1975). *Marital Puzzle*. New York: Norton.

Perosa, C., Hansen, J., and Perosa, S. (1981). Development of the structural family interaction scale. *Family Therapy, 8*, 77–90.

Pless, I., & Satterwhite, B. (1973). A measure of family functioning and its application. *Social Science and Medicine, 7*, 613–621.

Portner, J. (1980). *Family therapy and parent-adolescent interaction*. Unpublished doctoral dissertation, University of Minnesota, St. Paul.

Premo, B. E., & Stiles, W. B. (1983). Familiarity in verbal interactions of married couples versus strangers. *Journal of Social and Clinical Psychology, 1*, 209–230.

Ravenette, A. T. (1975). Grid techniques for children. *Journal of Child Psychology and Psychiatric and Allied Disciplines, 16*, 79–83.

Rosenberg, M. (1965). *Society and the adolescent self-image*. Princeton, NJ: Princeton University Press.

Russell, C. S. (1980). A methodological study of family cohesion and adaptability. *Journal of Marital and Family Therapy, 6*, 459–470.

Russell, C. S., & Olson, D. H. (1983). Circumplex model of marital and family systems: Review of empirical support and elaborations of therapeutic process. In D. A. Bagarozzi, A. P. Jurich, & R. W. Jackson (Eds.), *Marital and family therapy: New perspectives in theory, research, and practice*. New York: Human Sciences.

Ryle, A. (1975). *Frames and cages*. New York: International Universities Press.

Sennott, J. S. (1981). *Healthy family functioning scale: Family member's perceptions of cohesion, adaptability, and communication*. Unpublished doctoral dissertation, Purdue University, West Lafayette, IN.

Spanier, G. B. (1976). Measuring dyadic adjustment: New scales for assessing the quality of marriage and similar dyads. *Journal of Marriage and the Family, 38*, 15–28.

Thomas, E. J., Walter, C. L., & O'Flaherty, K. (1974). A verbal problem checklist for use in assessing family verbal behavior. *Behavior Therapy, 5*, 235–246.

van der Veen, F. (1965). The parents' concept of the family unit and child adjustment. *Journal of Counseling Psychology, 12*, 196–200.

van der Veen, F. (1969). *Family psychotherapy and a person's concept of family: Some clinical and research formulations*. Unpublished manuscript, Institute for Juvenile Research, Chicago.

van der Veen, F. (1976). Family concept test. In O. G. Johnson (Ed.), *Tests and measurements in child development: Handbook II* (pp. 776–777). San Francisco: Jossey-Bass.

van der Veen, F. (1979). Content dimensions of the family concept and their relation to disturbance, generation, and gender. In J. Howells (Ed.), *Advances in family psychiatry* (pp. 171–190). New York: International Universities Press.

van der Veen, F., and Olson, R. E. (1983). *Manual and handbook for the family concept assessment method*. (Available from F. van der Veen, P. O. Box 73, Encinitas, CA.)

von Bertalanffy, L. (1968). *General systems theory: Foundations, developments, applications*. New York: Braziller.

Westley, W. A., & Epstein, N. B. (1969). *The silent majority*. San Francisco: Jossey-Bass.

Williamson, D. S. (1978). New life at the graveyard: A method of therapy for individuation from a dead former parent. *Journal of Marriage and Family Counseling, 4*, 93–102.

Williamson, D. S. (1982). Personal authority in family experience via termination of the intergeneration hierarchical boundary: Part III. Personal authority defined, and the power of play in change process. *Journal of Marital and Family Therapy, 8*, 309–333.

Williamson, D. S., Bray, J. H., & Malone, P. E. (1984). PAFS: Personal Authority in the Family System Questionnaire. Houston: Houston Family Institute.

Wynne, L. C., Ryckoff, I. M., Day, J., & Hirsch, S. I. (1958). Pseudo-mutuality in the family relations of schizophrenics. *Psychiatry, 21*, 205–220.

9

Atheoretical and Eclectic Approaches

In this chapter we continue the review of the most commonly used and more promising nonbehavioral measures. These particular measures are free of theoretical orientation and are eclectic in nature.

ASSESSMENT TOOLS OF WARREN KINSTON AND THE FAMILY STUDIES GROUP

The work of Kinston and his colleagues developed from their desire for objective assessment. The group's intent was to combine objective descriptions with subjective reports and historical details.

The first instrument developed by this group was the Family Interaction Summary Format (FISF), which was intended to be a systematic, comprehensive, atheoretical rating system. The FISF groups items into conceptual categories, such as: atmosphere, communication, affective status, boundaries, separateness, family operations, alliances, parental function, and relation to environment. No validity or reliability data have been published for the FISF. In our opinion, it is of questionable value.

In 1979 Kinston, Loader, and Stratford developed the 30-item, 5-point Likert-type Family Health Scales (FHS). Pilot studies with the FHS produced poor interrater agreement. As a result of these initial failures, the research group began work on developing scales that would be clinically meaningful and would enable clinicians to make comparisons of interaction across families (Bingley, Loader, & Kinston, 1984; Loader, Burck, Stratford, Kinston, & Bentovim, 1981). The ratings themselves were designed to conform to clinical logic (Kinston et al., 1979). This means that the rater should be allowed to use clinical judgment to recognize defensive behavior; to give additional weight to pathological interactions; and to take into account family context, size, and ages of children as an integral part of the rating process. Consequently, the scales are highly subjective.

Structural Characteristics of the Family Health Scales

The Family Health Scales are designed to yield a single figure of overall family health. The FHS consists of a number of dimensions, similar to those found in the FISF—Affective Status, Communication, Boundaries, Alliances, Family Competence, Adaptability, and Stability.

The FHS is not intended to produce a profile of scores on a variety of dimensions. Each dimension is thought of as a way of assessing the family as a whole rather than as a way of measuring the particular dimension (Kinston et al., 1979).

The anchor descriptions for concepts that make up each subscale are not meant to be behavioral operationalizations of a theoretical construct. On the contrary, the researchers used abstract phrases to convey the idea of continuum for each subscale.

Reliability

Reliability was measured in a number of studies during and after the development of the instrument. Two types of reliability were used: test-retest and interrater agreement. Mean scores were used in these analyses, but the authors did not state whether these were subscale means or total scale means. Test-retest correlations for three studies range from .59 to .90. Interrater agreement in six studies ranges from .37 to .95.

Validity

The researchers reported discriminant validity and content (i.e., face) validity. We concentrate on discriminant validity because face validity is not actually a measure of validity. In their discussion of discriminant validity, Kinston, Loader, and Miller (1987) stated:

For the scale to be valid it must, first of all, be able to discriminate between groups of families whose levels of functioning are intuitively known to be different. We predicted that the FHS means and standard deviations would be similar for groups obtained through some form of psychiatric referral and similar for groups generated by a nonlabelled or physically ill member, but that these two types of families would be discriminated. Table 5 bears this out, with psychiatrically labelled families having mean scores between 3 and 4, and nonlabelled families having mean scores between 4 and 5. Statistical calculations have not been provided in this case because first, no deliberate study of discriminative validity was performed, second, the raters were not always blind to the group, and third, the methods of obtaining FHS scores are not comparable. Despite the evidence for discrimination, examination of the standard deviations suggests that there is a considerable degree of overlap. (p. 59)

Taking these comments into consideration, we can say that the research team has not offered any scientifically acceptable evidence for construct validity.

Discussion

In sum, the Family Health Scales are not based upon a recognizable theory of family structure, process, or development. The theoretical and clinical relevance of the concepts under consideration has not been clearly explained. The sampling procedures used to select the families who participated in these studies were poor, and the methodological procedures used to establish validity were seriously flawed.

Although the FHS are easily used by the busy practitioner, they encourage the therapist to be subjective and interpretive. There seems to be no logical or theoretical rationale for the manner in which these researchers grouped the adjectives used to describe and anchor the gradations on many of the subscales. The researchers' encouragement to the observer to be "intuitive" not only adds to the subjective nature of the instrument but compromises reliability. Like the FISF, the FHS is of questionable value.

Related Measures

Although this volume is devoted to the critical review of instruments and procedures that have been developed expressly for the evaluation of marital/family relationships, observational procedures that were initially developed for the analysis of group process have been adopted for the study of family interaction: the Hill Interaction Matrix (HIM) (Hill, 1971) and the Interaction Process Analysis of Bales (1950a, 1950b). Both procedures can be considered macroanalytic rating systems that require varying degrees of subjective judgment and interpretation on the part of the observers.

The Hill Interaction Matrix (HIM)

The HIM asks the observer to judge participants' communication styles and subject content (the two dimensions that make up the HIM). Miller (1971) modified the HIM so that it could be used to evaluate communication patterns in marriages. This revised model was used to evaluate the relative merits of two marital enrichment programs (Russell, Bagarozzi, Atilano, & Morris, 1984). Five interaction styles and four content dimensions were identified.

Styles.

(1) Conventional: sociable, playful, simple reporting of factual information, storytelling.
(2) Closed: directive, persuasive, evaluative, and manipulative.
(3) Speculative: intellectual, searching, tentative.
(4) Open: self-revealing, supportive, attentive.
(5) Mixed: Style 2 containing 1, 3, or 4.

Content dimensions.

(1) Topic-focused: people, things, and events outside the couple's relationship.
(2) Testing-situation-focused: observers, recording equipment, or experimental procedure.
(3) Personally focused: thoughts or feelings about the self or other.
(4) Relationship-focused: thoughts or feelings about the couple/family together as a group, their communication patterns, their disagreement.

The most desirable style of communication is thought to be relationship-focused and open (i.e., a metacommunicative way of interacting and relating). The least desirable styles are (1) conventional and topic-focused or testing-situation-focused; and (2) closed and topic-focused or testing-situation-focused. Speculative styles that are personal or relationship-oriented are considered more functional than the conventional style or the closed style.

The HIM is well suited for assessing communication in families and dyads. It is directly related to communication approaches to family systems functioning as conceptualized by pioneering marital/family therapists such as Satir. The HIM is the only rating system that takes into account the context in which the couple/family is being assessed (i.e., research, therapy). However, the content dimensions do not seem to be all-inclusive. For example, no consideration is given to off-topic communications, defensive communications, disqualifications, or disconfirmations, which are a central part of communication pragmatics (Watzlawick, Beavin, & Jackson, 1967).

The continued development of Hill's matrix to reflect more accurately family systems conceptions of functional communication would be a significant contribution to the field.

Interaction Process Analysis (IPA)

Bales's Interaction Process Analysis (IPA) (1950a; 1950b) was originally developed for use with small groups. This coding schema has 12 categories for scoring behavior; the coder scores an individual's behavior as it is perceived to influence the recipient. The selected unit of analysis is usually the sentence; nonverbal behavior is also scored at 1-minute intervals.

Bales's system does not allow for the recording of nonverbal acts per se. Rather, the scoring of verbal and nonverbal acts requires a great deal of interpretation on the part of the observer. For example, one of his categories, which is an example of "social-emotional area positive" within the interaction issue of "problems of reintegration," is stated as "shows solidarity, raises other's status, gives help, reward." The opposing category, "social-emotional area negative" within the "problems of reintegration" scale, is stated as "shows antagonism, deflates other's status, defends or asserts self." From these examples, it is clear that such categories require considerable interpretation.

In 1970 Bales revised the IPA. The revised system is still based on 12 categories of behavior, which can be grouped into four modes, and includes a tabulation of who speaks to whom. The categories in the revised IPA are designed to reflect more affective interactions, and the definitions for all categories are more inclusive to capture any action that shows the slightest amount of affect. By increasing the number of scores in the affect categories, the stability and range of those categories increase, leading to more accurate and reliable predictions based on norms for those categories within and across groups.

Groups are diagnosed according to the roles played by individuals in the group (group process as a whole is not assessed). In diagnosing groups, one creates a profile of group roles. Group role is first determined through a member's rate of initiation into each of the 12 categories. Depending on one's rate, one is assigned a certain vector within the typology of the group. These directions are forward versus backward, up versus down, and positive versus negative. They refer to group task, status, and affect. The same analysis is done for acts received.

Two types of leadership patterns are identified: task leader and social-emotional leader. The social-emotional leader is one whose behaviors are grouped into categories of friendly, agreeing, and dramatic comments. This person usually has the second-highest score on initiations and receptions of communication. The task leader tends to have a predominance in Categories 4 through 9, dealing with information, opinions, and suggestions.

The second means of analyzing one's role in the group is through the number of initiations and receptions. The group leader is defined as the one who initiates and receives the most group communication, receiving more than initiating.

One of the major drawbacks to using the IPA is shown in the following list of the four modes: Each sentence, phrase, and clause must be assigned to 1 of the 12 categories, regardless of whether what is said actually corresponds to 1 of the 12 categories.

Social-emotional area: Positive and mixed (re)action
  (1) Seems friendly
  (2) Dramatizes
  (3) Agrees
Test area: Attempted answers
  (4) Gives suggestion
  (5) Gives opinion
  (6) Gives information
Task area: Questions
  (7) Asks for information
  (8) Asks for opinion
  (9) Asks for suggestion
Social-emotional area: negative and mixed (re)action
  (10) Disagrees
  (11) Shows tension
  (12) Seems unfriendly

Friesen's Structural-Strategic Family Assessment Scale

Friesen (1985) put together a training manual/workbook entitled *Structural-Strategic Marriage and Family Therapy*. It was designed to give beginning practitioners a very brief overview and thumbnail sketch of structural-strategic theories and clinical practices. The cookbook format of this 167-page paperback may prove very appealing to novices who have little interest in clinical theory or the empirical status of a given treatment approach.

Friesen outlined what he called the Structural-Strategic Family Assessment Scale, which is an a priori scale consisting of eight dimensions, or subscales, that the author believes represent "important dimensions of family dynamics" (p. 125). The eight subscales are as follows: (1) Family Developmental Stages, (2) Family Life Context, (3) Family Structure, (4) Family System Resonance, (5) Family Communication Process, (6) Marital System Dynamic, (7) Family Flexibility, and (8) Individual Dynamics and Pathology. Each of the eight subscales comprises a number of subconcepts. A subscale may have as many as 14 subcomponents (e.g., Family Communication Process) or as few as 1 (e.g., Family Developmental Stages).

Friesen's Structural-Strategic Family Assessment Scale is questionably constructed. Although the author claimed that the scale is based upon family systems theory, the relationship between scale items and family systems concepts is frequently unclear (i.e., concepts are poorly operationalized).

Many concepts are not well defined, which encourages idiosyncratic interpretation, bias, subjectivity, and unwarranted inferences. Some scales are
bipolar (e.g., boundaries are described as rigid-permeable) and represent
logical opposites: the negative polarity represented by (1), the positive
extreme by (5). However, the majority of the scales and subscales are not
semantically bipolar (e.g., Patterns and Sequences = Competing-Warm and
Agreeable, Disengagement = Distant-Autonomous, Differentiated). This
lack of consistency is confusing.

A number of subscales use the same adjective to denote an intended
polarity. For example, the adjective *rigid* is used as a descriptor for boundaries, rules, and roles. Affects such as anger, frustration, depression, and
anxiety are conceptualized as negative and placed at the negative, or undesirable, end of the Likert continuum. Other feelings (e.g., warmth, joy, happiness, empathy) are located at the positive pole. The author failed to see
that affects, in and of themselves, are neither positive nor negative but are
simply responses to one's perceptions of one's experiences. The issue for evaluation is not whether one expresses "good" or "bad" feelings but whether
the affective response is appropriate, given the stimulus and the context.

The items are by no means exhaustive, and there is considerable overlap
and confusion. No data on reliability or validity have been reported, and
the procedures for using these scales have not been specified. Although
Friesen claimed that each subscale is scored on a 5-point Likert scale, each
subscale, in fact, has only 3 points.

In sum, the Structural Strategic Family Assessment Scale is conceptually
weak and methodologically questionable.

MACROANALYTIC PROCEDURES

In this section we turn to more global measures of family interaction. Two
theory-based rating systems that have had considerable impact on family
evaluation are reviewed in substantial detail: the Beavers-Timberlawn Family
Evaluation Scales (Lewis, Beavers, Gossett, & Phillips, 1976) and the Clinical
Rating Scale for the Circumplex Model of Marital and Family Systems (Olson
& Killorin, 1985).

Beavers-Timberlawn Family Evaluation Scales

Variables Measured and Concepts Treated

The Beavers-Timberlawn Family Evaluation Scales focus on five discrete
concepts dealing with specific aspects of family process and structure. These
five concepts are loosely derived from family systems theory:

Subscale I: Structure of the Family—overt power, parental coalition, and closeness

Subscale II: Mythology

Subscale III: Goal-Directed Negotiation

Subscale IV: Autonomy—clarity of expression, responsibility, invasiveness, permeability

Subscale V: Family Affect—range of feelings, mood and tone, unresolvable conflict, empathy

Subscale VI: Global Health-Pathology

(The rater is asked to give a global impression of the family's overall healthy or pathology.)

Lewis and his colleagues put forth their theoretical premise in *No Single Thread: Psychological Health in Family Systems* (1976). In Chapter 3, Beavers briefly outlined the aspects of general systems theory on which the scales were based. Three theoretical papers on cybernetic theory are cited: Beckett (1970), Brillouin (1968), and Speer (1970).

A central concept of cybernetics theory—entropy—is the focus of the theoretical discussion. For Beavers, family systems can be categorized according to the degree of structural organization they demonstrate. Family systems are conceptualized as moving on a continuum of organization from chaos, through rigidity of structure with some differentiation of component parts, toward a greater flexibility and further evolution of coherent structure.

Feedback is another systems concept that Beavers mentioned but did not treat systematically. Basically, he recognized the need for positive and negative feedback processes in family systems. However, he did not explore in any depth the relationship of these processes to family structure and organization.

Following this brief theoretical introduction to entropy and feedback, Beavers typed families. Three "ideal types" have been described: seriously disturbed or chaotic families, midrange families, and healthy families. Seriously disturbed families, believed to be the most entropic, are thought to use negative feedback as their primary mode of processing information. Beavers believes that schizophrenic offspring are most typically reared in such families. Midrange families, believed to be more negentropic than are severely disturbed families, are said to have children that are "sane but limited." Their structure is thought to be "clear but rigid." Midrange families that are centrifugal (i.e., allow members to leave the system) will most likely "produce behavior disorders" and "reactive psychotics." In centripetal families, who hold family members close, separation is difficult, as is autonomy. Such families "produce offspring labeled neurotic." Structure is clear and flexible but is carried lightly. Healthy families use both negative and positive feedback appropriately.

Beavers identified five family qualities that he considers important in the development of capable, adaptive, healthy individuals: (1) family power structure, (2) degree of family individuation, (3) acceptance of separation and loss, (4) perception of reality, and (5) affect. Four of these qualities have conceptual counterparts. For example, acceptance of separation and loss seems to be related to the concept of autonomy; goal-directed negotiation and unresolvable conflict seem to be related to an unspecified concept having to do with family process. However, Beavers did not specifically equate any concept or subcomponents with particular family qualities.

The connection between the central concepts and family qualities remains unclear. Family power can be considered equivalent to overt power and parental coalition. Degree of family individuation can be considered equivalent to autonomy and its subcomponents—clarity of expression, responsibility, invasiveness, and permeability of boundaries. Perception of reality has its counterpart in family mythology. Family affect is directly correlated with affect and three of its subcomponents—range of feelings, mood and tone, and empathy.

Reliability

In a pilot study described in *No Single Thread* (Lewis et al., 1976), 23 families (11 control families and 12 families containing a recently admitted adolescent inpatient) were rated by a panel of 12 judges. The 10-point Likert-type Global Health-Pathology subscale of the Beavers-Timberlawn Family Evaluation Scales was used to gain initial estimates of reliability for this subscale.

Five interrater agreement scores were reported, ranging from .65 to .90 for five distinct family interaction tasks. Two of these five observations were made by the same rater (i.e., Raters A and B, and Raters E and B), and a third represents the test-retest reliability of Rater B after a 3-month interval. The remaining two pairs of raters, (F and G, H and I) showed unimpressively low rates of agreement—.65 and .78, respectively.

Of the 12 judges, 10 were mental health professionals; Raters F and G were wives of the investigators. Rater B was the only judge who was an experienced family therapist.

The family systems rating scales were developed by the research group under the leadership of Beavers. "After much preliminary scale design, the group used each evolving scale to rate segments of the videotaped interactional testing of the 23 families who participated in the pilot study" (Lewis et al., 1976, p. 83). The subscales were continually revised until the group's reliability in the use of the scales reached acceptable levels.

Pearson product moment correlation coefficients were used to estimate interrater agreement. Raters A and B rated 36 families, including 12 "healthy" families, 12 families who had a child with a learning disability, and 12 families who had an adolescent child who was a psychiatric inpatient.

Reliabilities for each of the subscales for Raters A and B range from -.17 (permeability) to .69 (goal-directed negotiation). Reliability coefficients for Raters C and D, who observed only healthy families, range from .17 (clarity of expression) to .82 (mood and tone). Both rating teams produced three nonsignificant reliabilities. Raters A and B showed nonsignificant agreements for parental coalition, invasiveness, and permeability. Raters C and D showed nonsignificant agreements for clarity of expression, responsibility, and expressiveness.

Essentially, interrater agreements for the subscales are unimpressive. Of the 13 subscales, 6 showed nonsignificant correlations, and the correlations of the remaining 7 subscales are low.

Validity

In our estimation, the validity of the Beavers-Timberlawn Family Evaluation Scales has yet to be established. None of the 13 subscales seems to operationalize the two central concepts identified by the authors in their theoretical discussion—entropy (negentropy) and feedback (positive and negative). In addition, the five concepts and the subcomponents identified by Beavers and his colleagues cannot be said to represent comprehensive coverage of major family systems concepts. Neither can they be considered a representative sample of items in the conceptual domain under consideration.

The sole source of validity claimed by these researchers is one that can be loosely considered concurrent validity. Using the Global Health-Pathology subscale, six raters were asked to evaluate the relative health-pathology of the 23 pilot study families. The research question asked by the authors (Lewis et al. 1976) was: "Can raters distinguish between these families containing a patient and control families?" (p. 33). All six raters were experienced mental health professionals. Not surprisingly, they were able to discriminate between families with an IP and healthy families in all instances. However, such discrimination should not be seen as a validation of the Global Health-Pathology subscale. It simply means that experienced mental health professionals were able to identify families containing an IP.

Later, two experienced clinicians who had been trained in the use of the Beavers-Timberlawn Family Evaluation Scales and the Global Health-Pathology subscale were asked to rate a total of 107 families. Of these families, 70 had an IP; 33 were "healthy" families with no IP. Interrater agreements for each of the 13 subscales with the Global Health-Pathology subscale range from .30 (invasiveness) to .79 (mythology).

Experimenter bias in the forms of observer expectancy, halo effects, and Hawthorne effects plague this research. Neither the Global Health-Pathology scale nor the 13 subscales of the Beavers-Timberlawn Family Evaluation Scales were correlated with a measure of group, family, or individual functioning. In a sense, the researchers functioned as a closed system. No external criteria were used to establish validity, and the nonsignificant reliabilities for 6 of the 13 subscales were ignored and retained in the final version of the Beavers-Timberlawn Family Evaluation Scales.

Administration and Scoring

Typically, a family is assigned an interaction task. Tasks frequently used for this purpose include (1) the revealed difference technique (Strodtbeck, 1951); (2) the plan-something-together task (Riskin & Faunce, 1970a; 1970b); or (3) a task in which family members discuss "What is strong about your family?" (Lewis et al., 1976). Family interactions are recorded on videotape. Usually, a 10-minute segment is sampled for assessment.

Training raters to use the Beavers-Timberlawn Family Evaluation Scales is time-consuming. One-day training seminars are offered periodically by Lewis and Beavers, and a 2-hour training tape can be purchased.

Discussion

The Beavers-Timberlawn Family Evaluation Scales suffer from a number of conceptual, theoretical, and methodological inadequacies.

First, the 13 subscales that make up the Beavers-Timberlawn Family Evaluation Scales do not seem to represent a valid operationalization of the central theoretical concepts outlined and discussed by the authors. As a result, the validity of the scale comes into question. In addition, no empirical studies have demonstrated any significant degree of criterion-related validity (e.g., convergent or discriminant validity). As a matter of fact, attempts to correlate the Beavers-Timberlawn Family Evaluation Scales with FACES II (Green, Kolevzon, & Vosler, 1985) have shown a "minimal degree of empirical convergence" (p. 396) between the two instruments.

Second, the research study in which the Beavers-Timberlawn Family Evaluation Scales were developed was severely flawed. Reliability and interrater agreement were seriously compromised by experimenter effects. The six subscales that did not receive respectable levels of interrater agreement were nevertheless retained in the final version of the scales (i.e., coalition, clarity, responsibility, invasiveness, permeability, and expressiveness).

Third, some of the subscales are conceptually unsound and poorly constructed. For example, Beavers assumed that each of the 13 variables can be thought of as existing on a linear, bipolar continuum, an assumption that led to the construction of Likert-type rating scales. However, in some instances, the extremes of the scales do not represent logical opposites. For example, the overt power dimension of the Structure of the Family subscale has two extremes—chaos and egalitarian. For this dimension to be conceptually sound, *chaotic* (having no discernable structure of order) and *ordered* (having a rigid, invariant, hierarchical structure) should be the polar opposites. This would not only make this dimension conceptually sound but would also more accurately operationalize the central systems concepts of entropy and negentropy.

The closeness dimension, as conceptualized by Beavers, includes two distinct concepts. The first involves intimacy; the second deals with subsystem or ego boundaries. However, these two concepts are treated as if they were one and the same. For example, at the negative end of the closeness continuum, one finds "amorphous, vague, and indistinct boundaries among members." The midpoint of this subscale reads "isolating and distancing." The positive extreme is "closeness with distinct boundaries among members." A more conceptually clear and accurate alternative would be to have two subscales—one for closeness (i.e., intimacy) and one for subsystem or ego boundaries—because it is possible (and probably desirable) to have a close and intimate relationship while maintaining distinct subsystem boundaries and ego integrity. Similarly, the Parental Coalitions subscale might be broken into two separate dimensions, for example, strength of parental coalition and degree of parent-child coalition.

Under Family Affect, the component called mood and tone suffers from a number of flaws. First, several distinct concepts that are grouped at the positive end of the scale probably should be treated as separate and distinct. Second, the bipolar dimensions are not totally accurate. For example, the opposite of warmth is usually considered hostility, and the opposite of humorousness is usually thought of as sadness or depression.

Finally, some of the subscales portray a definite sociocultural bias. For example, the positive end of the Structure of the Family continuum is considered an egalitarian power structure. This reflects a certain white middle-class bias. Some subcultural, religious, and ethnic groups that function extremely well with one spouse in a more senior position in the family's hierarchical structure would be seen as less effective and more pathological than the white middle-class families who tend to more closely approximate this ideal. A similar criticism applies to Family Affect, which includes mood and tone and range of feelings. In some subcultural, religious, and ethnic groups, restraint in the expression of feelings is an important value and the direct expression of negative feelings (especially to adults and grandparents) is strictly forbidden.

It seems odd that the authors, given their systems orientation, failed to consider the sociocultural contexts in which families exist. This imposition of the researchers' value system upon the families under consideration can be seen as an additional source of experimenter bias.

Although these criticisms reduce the utility of the Beavers-Timberlawn Family Evaluation Scales as a research tool, we have found this instrument to be a very useful clinical aid in the training and supervision of beginning family therapists. The Beavers-Timberlawn Family Evaluation Scales force the novice to conceptualize the family as a system of interacting components. This is particularly helpful (and difficult) for those students whose only theoretical orientation to human behavior is based upon individual models of human development and personality formation. These scales force the student to focus on family structure and process, to identify structural deficits, and to recognize redundant cyclical behavior patterns. Once the beginner is able to identify structural flaws and process difficulties, he or she can begin to formulate pragmatic treatment goals.

The Beavers-Timberlawn Family Evaluation Scales can be said to be loosely tied to family systems theory. Central concepts are poorly conceptualized and operationalized. Construct validity has yet to be demonstrated. The Beavers-Timberlawn Family Evaluation Scales are easy to use but require would-be raters to undergo a moderate degree of training. A considerable amount of clinical expertise and experience as a family therapist, coupled with a solid understanding of family systems theory, is required to translate scale ratings into viable treatment plans and intervention strategies.

Clinical Rating Scales for the Circumplex Model of Marital and Family Systems

Variables Measured and Concepts Treated

The Clinical Rating Scale is the therapist's version of FACES III. It focuses on the two dimensions of the Circumplex Model of Marital and Family Systems—Adaptability and Cohesion. (For a thorough discussion and critical evaluation of FACES II and III, see Chapter 8.)

Administration and Scoring

In their instructions for use of the Clinical Rating Scale, Olson and Killorin (1985) suggested that in doing a clinical assessment of a family, the therapist should evaluate the family in terms of each of the concepts that make up the two dimensions of the model. For example, the Cohesion dimension consists of six broad concepts: (1) emotional bonding, (2) family involvement, (3) marital relationship, (4) parent-child coalitions, (5) internal boundaries, (6) external boundaries. The last two concepts—internal boundaries and external boundaries—consist of three additional subcomponents (i.e., internal boundaries include subconcepts of time, space, and decision making; external boundaries include friends, interests, and recreation).

The Adaptability dimension consists of five broad concepts: (1) leadership (control), (2) discipline, (3) negotiation, (4) roles, (5) rules.

Olson and Killorin (1985) suggested that the therapist use a semistructured family interview to elicit information germane to the two dimensions, the concepts, and the subconcepts. No specific technique or format was recommended. However, the authors stated that they have found it useful to encourage the family members "to dialogue with each other regarding how they handle these general issues, i.e., time, space, discipline, etc. Asking the family to describe what a typical week is like and how they handle their daily routines, decision making and conflict is often illuminating" (p. 38).

Upon completion of the semistructured interview, the therapist is to read carefully the descriptions for each concept in the Clinical Rating Scale manual and to select a value on an 8-point Likert scale that he or she believes to be most relevant for the family under consideration. Olson and Killorin stressed that even though some individuals or dyads might be classified in different ways, the therapist should remember that the final classification should be based upon how the family "functions as a group." They also advised that if one or two persons function differently from the rest of the family, a separate description of that person might be included in the final assessment.

The instructions for each family specify that only a global rating be made for each separate dimension so that the family can be classified into one of the four levels of Cohesion and Adaptability.

Validity

Olson and Killorin (1985) offered no empirical data to support the validity of the rating scale. Furthermore, several questions arise concerning the equivalence of the Clinical Rating Scale and FACES III. When one compares the two instruments, certain discrepancies, described below, can be observed.

FACES III has five categories for the Cohesion dimension: emotional bonding, supportiveness, family boundaries, time and friends, and interest in recreation. The Clinical Rating Scale, on the other hand, has six categories: emotional bonding, family involvement, marital relationship, parent-child coalitions, internal boundaries (time, space, and decision making) and external boundaries (friends, interests, and recreation).

FACES III has four categories for the Adaptability dimension: leadership, control, discipline, and roles and rules. The Clinical Rating Scale has five categories for this dimension: leadership, discipline, negotiation, roles, and rules.

At first, the discrepancies between the numbers of categories for both dimensions may seem insignificant. However, upon closer examination, one finds that two of the concepts included in the Cohesion dimension of the Clinical Rating Scale (marital relationship and parent-child coalitions) have no counterpart in the empirically derived Cohesion factor of FACES III. Similarly, FACES III has no counterpart for the negotiation category on the Adaptability dimension of the Clinical Rating Scale.

A close examination of these two instruments reveals that the definitions of the concepts that make up the two dimensions of Cohesion and Adaptability are not conceptually identical for both measures. In FACES III, family members are asked to rate the degree to which the following statements (concerning leadership) describe their family: "Different persons act as leaders in our family" and "It is hard to identify who the leader is in our family." However, on the Clinical Rating Scale, the observer is asked to rate leadership patterns according to the following scale definitions: *rigid* (authoritarian, parents highly controlling), rated 1–2 (very low); *structured* (primarily authoritarian but some equalitarian leadership), rated 3–4 (low to moderate); *flexible* (equalitarian leadership with fluid changes, rated 5–6 (moderate to high); and *chaotic* (limited or erratic leadership, parental control unsuccessful or rebuffed), rated 7–8 (very high).

The difference between how family leadership is defined for family members using FACES III and the way in which family therapists are asked to conceptualize family leadership on the Clinical Rating Scale makes it impossible to compare the ratings of family members with those of expert judges (such as therapists). This same criticism applies to most of the concepts that are included in both instruments.

In our opinion, the Clinical Rating Scale should not be considered a valid representation of an outsider's view of the two dimensions of Cohesion and Adaptability, as defined by Olson and his colleagues in the Circumplex Model of Marital and Family Systems. What the Clinical Rating Scale actually measures remains in question. To determine the true dimensions of the Clinical Rating Scale, one should subject this instrument to the same methodological rigor that was used in the development, refinement, and standardization of FACES III.

At the time we began writing this volume, no published reports concerning the practical uses of the Clinical Rating Scale were available. Nevertheless, we have used the Clinical Rating Scales in our work with distressed family systems. Our experience with this instrument underscores what we believe to be an inherent flaw in global rating scales; that is, although they give a thumbnail sketch of the way a particular family is perceived to function, it is difficult to formulate a specific treatment plan or to devise a particular intervention strategy based upon such a description. When global ratings are made, valuable information is lost concerning the precise nature of the family's structural problems, dysfunctional interaction sequences, and redundant cycles. In addition, global ratings shed no light on the unique relationships between and among family members.

Global ratings do have one advantage. They force the therapist to think of interventions that will bring about changes in the way the family unit functions as a self-contained system. Interventions fashioned with this goal in mind are designed to bring about changes in the dysfunctional family rules that maintain the family's homeostatic equilibrium. In this respect, the Clinical Rating Scale moves the therapist one step closer to thinking about family systems intervention.

The Cambridge Model

Kantor and Lehr (1975) developed a theory of family process and behavior based upon distance regulation among the members. A comprehensive discussion of their theoretical thinking can be found in *Inside the Family*. This study is based upon the authors' clinical experiences and naturalistic observations of 10 "normal" and 9 "pathological" families matched on specific demographic and sociological variables (e.g., socioeconomic status, ethnic background, family composition, neighborhood). From their work, these researchers developed what has come to be known as the Cambridge model of family functioning (White, 1978). Kantor and Lehr stressed the organizational complexity of family systems, the adaptability of families (open systems), as well as the reciprocal nature of family life, in which interchanges continually occur between family members and between the family system and the external environment.

Kantor and Lehr discussed at length what they described as the goals or targets of all family behavior. They contended that the family's behavior can best be understood in terms of striving to meet goals such as power, affect, and meaning. Similarly, all families find themselves in a position of negotiating these dimensions. The inevitable clash that occurs at the interface of the various family subsystems or the interface between the family unit and the external environment determines how smoothly the family will function. The authors noted that the goals are regulated by family members' conceptualizations of space, time, and energy. The way the family is able to meet its necessary goals for power, affect, and meaning within the confines of individualistic conceptualizations of space, time, and energy provides valuable information about the process orientation of the family.

Using the concepts of power, affect, and meaning (goals), and the regulation of them according to space, time, and energy, the authors conceptualized family types, representing ideals that are thought to show the interrelatedness of the six components. Specifically, the ideal family types are open, closed, and random, each of which deals with issues of power, affect, and meaning in its own characteristic fashion. Open families have as their central themes adaptability and flexibility. Closed families tend to focus more on stable relationships. Random families show "random exploration" (i.e., the focus of family life is neither stability nor adaptability, but a tendency to operate at a middle ground between these two polarities).

The authors described the behavior of individuals within each family type. Individuals can be categorized according to how they attempt to meet goals: as movers or opposers of others' opinions or goals, followers of others, or bystanders who maintain a middle ground.

The authors' work began with identification of structures in a family system and the determination of which structures work and which do not. To observe structures, one needs a vocabulary to name and classify elements and functions of structures. The four broad frameworks for understanding structures describe what is observed empirically and what is experienced phenomenologically in the family: (1) *interfaces*, (2) *dimensions*, and (3) *player parts*.

Interfaces

Families are conceptualized as open systems. Interchanges between and among family members and between the family and other systems in the environment constitute an interface. Meetings of the various systems or subsystems at interface cause each unit to shape and reshape its space and to regulate traffic into and out of this space.

The family system is composed of three subsystems that interact with each other as well as with the world outside: the *family-unit subsystem*, the *interpersonal subsystem*, and the *personal subsystem*. Each is set apart by boundaries. Because families have an infinite variety of ways in which to organize themselves from subsystem to subsystem, each family should be studied in its entirety rather than in its separate parts. Families also have a variety of ways to regulate their interfaces.

Dimensions

The dimensions of family have to do with the family's goals in terms of *power, affect*, and *meaning* (target dimensions) and the ways a family uses *time, space*, and *energy* (access dimensions) to achieve its goals. Determining the type of family informs the observer about that family's goals or targets. Knowing the characteristic strategies a family uses to reach its target will help the observer learn about the ways in which the family uses the access dimensions to reach those targets.

No matter how goals are achieved, each subsystem seeks certain goals that fall within three broad categories: (1) affect—a sense of intimacy and nurturance; (2) power—the freedom to try to obtain what is wanted in terms of money, goods, or skills; a sense of efficacy; and (3) meaning—a sense of identity, a philosophical framework.

How families access their target dimensions is determined by how families use space, time, and energy. Space deals with the ways a family develops, maintains, and defends its system and subsystem territories and the way it regulates distance among its own members.

Time deals with how families arrange their lives in time. Entire families and each of their subunits must make constant decisions about when work and play events will take place. They must see to it that the various subsystems in a family are "in phase" with one another through the maintenance of harmonious rhythms.

Energy is concerned with how families store and expend their resources for action. Energy that is expended must eventually be replenished, and families have different means of fueling and refueling.

Player Parts and Critical Identity Images.

Kantor (1980) added the concept of critical identity images to his and Lehr's theory of family process. These images concern an individual's concept of self in relation to others. Critical images are the impetus for player roles. To implement one's critical images, an individual must play one of four roles: (1) mover, the person who initiates an action; (2) opposer, the person who takes action against the mover; (3) follower, the person who supports the action of the mover; or (4) bystander, the person who witnesses, neither supporting nor opposing the mover.

Discussion

Kantor and Lehr's work suffers from some serious theoretical flaws and methodological inadequacies. Their conception of ideal family types is simplistic, and no standardized or reliable methods have been presented to establish whether these ideal types have empirically verifiable counterparts in the real world (i.e., validity is a grave concern). Sampling is another serious problem, as are observer effects (i.e., both researchers know the families; and the families, both "normal" and "pathological," could probably guess the researchers' hypotheses).

The relationship between theory and the central concepts used by the authors to describe family process is hazy. The authors do not seem to have adequately operationalized central concepts such as feedback and homeostasis.

No clear instructions have been offered concerning how one is to go about typing families (diagnosing/assessing/evaluating); nor are clear procedures available for observing, recording, coding, or rating family interaction. Therefore, interrater agreement cannot be established. The entire research project was highly subjective and poorly conceptualized. It would be extremely difficult to teach this assessment system to another clinician in a reasonable amount of time.

NATURALISTIC OBSERVATION

The physical environment of the home can be seen as a product of family process and structure, a reflection or metaphysical representation of family dynamics. It also can be seen as a powerful context that has considerable influence upon how family members interact within specific settings. In this section, we survey some procedures that have been devised specifically for observation in the home.

Observing families in their own homes is considered important because it is in the home that one can see how families erect and maintain informational boundaries between the family system and external systems. To some degree, family patterns are modified in the outside world, especially if the outside setting is contrived. Although not without its drawbacks (e.g., observer biases and affects, lack of rigorous control, time considerations, costs), naturalistic observation in the home is an invaluable adjunct to family assessment and therapy. We decided to include in this volume a section on observational procedures, even though most observational measures we came across were loosely tied to theory and offered little in the way of reliability and validity.

The Psychological Ecology of Barker

A pioneering effort in naturalistic family observation was initiated by Barker (1968), who was interested in studying the psychological habitat. Although Barker believed that behavior flowed in *streams*, he chose to look at discrete units called *episodes*. These episodes were seen as being aimed at, directed toward, or converging upon a behavioral result (goal). It can be said that his research is the forerunner of behavioral coding systems and the functional school of family therapy (Gurman & Kniskern, 1981).

The categories used were divided into matrix factors (interactive), action modes (kind of behavior), action attributes (behavior qualities), interplay variables (congruence), subject constants (demography), and associate constants (other's demography). Categories included in the matrix factors relate to the following:

- associate complexity or how many people are in the subject's psychological habitat (simple = one, compound = group);
- sociality of the episode—social (associate), potentially social (another present), or unsocial (subject alone);
- the action circuit—either open (A acts to B; B does not act) or closed (A acts to B; B acts to A);

- social field potency—degree to which behavior is transacted in relation to social behavior objects;
- action sequence—order and complexity;
- relative power—ability of A as perceived by B to change the behavior of B, expressed as a ratio;
- strength and centrality of motivation;
- episode weight—potency of a target episode (isolated or overlapping with others).

Action modes are scored 0 (absent), 1 (lower range), 2 (middle range), or 3 (upper range), depending on the inferred strength of the mode. In dominance, A rules B by exerting social pressure in an arbitrary way. Resistance occurs when A "holds out against" dominance, aggression, appeal, or action of any kind in which B exerts pressure. The episode is scored as aggression if A attacks and tries to injure B or any object forming a unit with B. The category of submission is employed if A "gives in to" dominance, aggression, appeal, or action in which B exerts social pressure. In the action mode of nurturance, A extends himself or herself to benefit B; in appeal, A solicits a benefit from B. Finally, in avoidance, A increases or maintains distance from B in the face of aggression or a negative feature of B's behavior.

Each mode has in turn an action attribute in one of four categories. Pressure is actualized social power or ability to change the behavior of the other. Affection entails A's momentary feeling toward B as a social habitat object. This can be scored as positive, negative, or neutral. This same scoring is used for mood, which is defined as the state in A that exists without any special reference to B as an object. The fourth category, A's evaluation or critical assessment of B, can be scored as disapproving, not judging, or approving.

The interplay variables express the degree of agreement between A and B in the following categories: conflict (incompatible and mutually opposed), disjunction (incompatible), unfriendly rivalry (incompatible and competitive), cooperation (compatible and mutually supporting), conjunction (compatible), friendly rivalry (compatible but competitive), juxtaposition (divergent), and accord (degree of harmony or disharmony). The last category can be scored as negative (at odds), neutral (neither at odds nor at one), or positive (at one).

Demographic variables (age, sex, social group) and the associate-role classifications (mother, father, brother) are included under subject and associate constants.

Observational Procedures

The observer records all episodes and then assigns the data to appropriate categories. Training observers is a long and complex process because much inference is involved. Categories are not mutually exclusive and there is considerable overlap. In addition, ways to standardize inferences are not discussed. Techniques for handling data are not specified. Items have not been completely defined, although some are more specific than others. This possible defect could contribute significantly to observer confusion and error.

Barker's reliability and validity procedures indicate that observers can and do agree at acceptable levels. Nevertheless, one wonders whether the time and effort required for training and the cost involved make this procedure practical. Although Barker's system is deficient in several key respects, it represents a significant contribution to the field and is considered valuable in this respect.

Coding Systems

Early work in the development of coding techniques for naturalistic observation was undertaken by Behrens and Goldfarb (1958), who studied schizophrenic children and their families. These researchers introduced the practice of observing the family during meal time, which became part of family therapy folklore. To analyze their data, Behrens and Galdfarb (1958) developed 47 scales: 41 related to family interaction, 4 focused on investment of the self in the home, and 2 measured pleasure and decisiveness.

Each item was rated on a 5-point scale ranging from *absence of the behavior* (1) to *presence of the behavior* (5). Absence of a behavior was related to poor functioning; presence was related to healthier functioning. An example of one scale follows:

Mutual support and cooperation

(1) absence of mutual support: hostility toward each other, frequent conflict, lack of cooperation
(2)
(3) occasional support
(4)
(5) mutual support among all: interest and respect for the other, absence of conflict

Items 1, 3, and 5 in this example serve as anchoring points and guidelines for the observer.

In 1969, Behrens, Meyers, Goldfarb, Goldfarb, and Fieldsteel revised and refined these scales, calling them the Henry Ittleson Center Family Interaction Scales. The scales were amended so that they would be applicable in comparing emotionally disturbed children (various diagnoses) with normal children and in determining the nature of changes in family functioning over time. The scales could now be used to assign appropriate weights to different aspects of family interaction, enabling quantification of judgments of these interactions. The scale content was changed to allow for coding dyadic interaction as well as the entire family system. The 41 scales devoted to family interactions are grouped into seven categories: (1) family investment of selves in the home; (2) family group patterns of interactions; (3) interaction of husband and wife as marital partners; (4) interaction of husband and wife as parents; (5) parent-child interaction; child-parent interaction; and (6) child-child interaction.

The rating range was expanded from 5 to 7 points, each scale now having four anchoring descriptions of behavior for scores 1, 3, 5, 7: 1–3 points = poor functioning, 5 = average functioning, 7 = very good functioning. Instead of rating the presence or absence of behavior, optimal ratings could now be given to moderate behaviors in order to create a curvilinear distribution for each behavior. Family interactions are rated according to (1) organization and structure of the family (differentiation), (2) affect (congruence), and (3) reality orientation (priorities). Detailed procedures for conducting home observation are given.

Behrens et al. identified three family types that present problems for the observer. The "as if" family is a family characterized by a lack of genuineness in expressing feeling and pretense; behaviors are thought to be contrived, inconsistent, and incongruent. The "disorganized family" is depicted as chaotic, haphazard, and disorderly, having a structure that does not meet the family members' basic needs. The third type, or "rigid family," often misleading the observer by apparently functioning at a high level, uses an oversimplified, superficial set of rules, applying them inflexibly and in an extreme manner.

This is one of the few observational systems where validity and reliability are well documented. However, this system still requires observers to make a substantial degree of inference.

Home Observation Assessment Method (HOAM)

In 1979 Steinglass described a coding system designed to study family interactions over extended periods. The Home Observation Assessment Method (HOAM) is a computer-compatible coding system that "permits on-line data reduction of interactional variables emphasizing contextual and structural dimensions of family behavior" (p. 337).

Designed to collect behavioral information as it unfolds over time, HOAM has five principal characteristics:

(1) It is designed to collect data in a real-time framework.
(2) It attempts to preserve the natural relation between behavioral events and meaningful contextual variables.

(3) Coding categories emphasize objective-structural variables rather than subjective-process variables.
(4) The coding system is capable of generating sequential data.
(5) Content coding of verbal interaction is kept to a minimum.

Coding is done by a two-person team and coding sessions are structured in the following manner. The overall time block (2 to 4 hours) is subdivided into active coding periods and rest periods. The two observers synchronously code up to four 40-minute time blocks, followed by 15-minute breaks. Each 40-minute coding session is further subdivided into 20 two-minute time segments. Each observer uses an electronic timer that emits an audible signal every 2 minutes to indicate the start of a new coding segment.

During each 2-minute sampling period, two types of coding decisions are made. The first verbal interaction that occurs between the observer's subject and any other person currently in the household is labeled the Initial Interactional Sequence, and the coder makes a series of coding decisions about this interaction (including some decisions about the content of the interaction). Because of the way they are defined, these interactions usually do not occupy an entire 2-minute time segment, but the observer makes a series of objective coding decisions and records them in the precise sequence in which they occur. All coding decisions are recorded on a coding sheet.

Within each 2-minute time block, four basic types of coding decisions are made: (1) context codes (location, persons in the field, interactional distance), (2) behavioral characteristics codes, (3) who-to-whom speech codes, and (4) interaction codes (subjective judgments about the task orientation, affective level, and outcome of the Initial Interactional Sequence).

CONCLUSION

If we were asked to rate the evaluative procedures in this volume, we would probably reply that the ones in this chapter seem to be the most promising. In spite of their shortcomings, such as weak links with theory and poor psychometric constructions, these observational procedures represent the best that the field has to offer. Perhaps the best is not good enough. Yet the best remains promising.

These measures indicate that families can be observed and evaluated in the natural environment and that some reliable and valid procedures can be developed. We hope that clinical researchers will devote more time and effort to refining these procedures and strengthening their theoretical underpinnings.

REFERENCES

Bales, R. F. (1950a). *Interaction process analysis: A method for the study of small groups*. Cambridge, MA: Addison-Wesley.

Bales, R. F. (1950b). A set of categories for the analysis of small group interaction. *American Sociological Review, 15,* 257–263.

Bales, R. F. (1970). *Personality and interpersonal behavior*. New York: Holt, Rinehart & Winston.

Barker, R. (1968). *Ecological psychology*. Stanford, CA: Stanford University Press.

Beavers, W. R., & Hampson, R. B. (1990). *Successful families: Assessment and intervention*. New York: Norton.

Beckett, J. A. (1970). General systems theory, psychiatry and psychotherapy. *International Journal of Group Psychotherapy, 23,* 292–305.

Behrens, M. L., & Goldfarb, W. A. (1958). A study of patterns of interaction of families of schizophrenic children in residential treatment. *American Journal of Orthopsychiatry, 28,* 300–312.

Behrens, M. L., Meyers, D. I., Goldfarb, W., Goldfarb, N., & Fieldsteel, N. D. (1969). The Henry Ittleson Center family interaction scales. *Genetic Psychology Monographs, 80,* 203–295.

Bingley, L., Loader, P., & Kinston, W. (1984). Research report: Further developments of a format for family description. *Australian Journal of Family Therapy, 5,* 215–218.

Brillouin, S. (1968). Life, thermodynamics and cybernetics. In W. Buckley (Ed.), *Modern systems research for the behavioral scientist* (pp. 147–156). Chicago: Aldine.

Dreyer, C. A., & Dreyer, A. S. (1973). Family dinner time as a unique behavior habitat. *Family Process, 12,* 291–301.

Friesen, J. D. (1985). *Structural-strategic marriage and family therapy*. New York: Gardner.

Green, R. G., & Kolevzon, M. F. (1983). The correlates of healthy family functioning: The role of consensus and conflict in the practice of family therapy. *Journal of Marital and Family Therapy, 12,* 75–84.

Green, R. G., Kolevzon, M., & Vosler, N. (1985). The Beavers-Timberlawn model of family competence and the circumplex model of family adaptability and cohesion: Separate but equal? *Family Process, 24,* 385–397.

Gurman, A. S., & Kniskern, D. P. (Eds.).(1981). *Handbook of family therapy*. New York: Brunner/Mazel.

Hill, W. F. (1971). The Hill Interaction Matrix. *Personnel and Guidance Journal, 49,* 619–623.

Ittleson, W. H., Prushansky, H. M., & Rivlin, L. G. (1970). A study of bedroom use on two psychiatric wards. *Hospital & Community Psychiatry, 21*(6), 177–180.

Kantor, D. (1980). Critical identity image: A concept linking individual, couple, and family development. In J.K. Pearce & L.J. Friedman, (Eds.). *Family therapy: Combining psychodynomic and systems approaches,* pp. 137–167. New York: Grune & Stratton.

Kantor, D., & Lehr, W. (1975). *Inside the family: Toward a theory of family process*. San Francisco: Jossey-Bass.

Kinston, W., Loader, P., & Miller, L. (1987). Quantifying the clinical assessment of family health. *Journal of Marital and Family Therapy, 13,* 49–67.

Kinston, W., Loader, P., & Stratford, J. (1979). Clinical assessment of family interaction: A reliability study. *Journal of Family Therapy, 1,* 291–312.

Lewis, J. M., Beavers, W. R., Gossett, J. T., & Phillips, V. A. (1976). *No single thread: Psychological health in family systems*. New York: Brunner/Mazel.

Loader, P., Burck, C., Stratford, J., Kinston, W., & Bentovim, W. (1981). A method for organizing the clinical description of family interaction: The "Family Interaction Summary Format." *Australian Journal of Family Therapy, 2,* 131–141.

Miller, S. (1971). *The effects of communication training in small groups upon self-disclosure and openness in engaged couples' system of interaction: A field experiment.* Unpublished doctoral dissertation, University of Minnesota Family Social Science, St. Paul.

Olson, D. H., & Killorin, E. A. (1985). *Clinical rating scale (CRS) for the circumplex model.* St. Paul: University of Minnesota Family Social Science.

Riskin, J., & Faunce, E. E. (1970a). Family interaction scales: 1. Theoretical framework and method. *Archives of General Psychiatry, 22,* 526–537.

Riskin, J., & Faunce, E. E. (1970b). Family interaction scales: 3. Discussion of methodology and substantive findings. *Archives of General Psychiatry, 22,* 526–537.

Riskin, J.,& Faunce, E. E. (1972). Evaluative review of family interaction research. *Family Process, 11,* 365–455.

Russell, C. S., Bagarozzi, D. A., Atilano, R. B., & Morris, J. E. (1984). A comparison of two approaches to marital enrichment and conjugal skills training: Minnesota Couples Communication Program and Structural Behavioral Exchange Contracting. *American Journal of Family Therapy, 12,* 13–25.

Scheflen, A. E. (1971). Living space in a urban ghetto. *Family Process, 10,* 429–450.

Speer, D. C. (1970). Family systems: Morphogenesis and morphostasis, or is homeostasis enough? *Family Process, 9,* 259–278.

Steinglass, P. (1979). The Home Observation Assessment Method (HOAM): Real time naturalistic observation of families in their homes. *Family Process, 18,* 337–354.

Strodbeck, F. L. (1951). Husband-wife interaction over revealed differences. *American Sociological Review, 16,* 468–473.

Watzlawick, P. A., Beavin, J. H., & Jackson, D. D. (1967). *Pragmatics of human communication.* New York: Norton.

White, P. (1978). The dual-career couple: Constraints and supports. *Family Coordinator, 27,* 253–259.

10
Projective Techniques

Anastasi (1982) wrote that the distinguishing feature of projective techniques is the assignment of a relatively "unstructured task" (p. 565) that permits an almost unlimited variety of responses. To allow free play to the subject's fantasy, the therapist gives only brief and general instructions. Similarly, test stimuli are often vague or ambiguous. The underlying hypothesis is that the way in which a subject perceives and interprets test materials and the manner in which the subject structures the testing situation reflect fundamental aspects of psychological functioning. Test materials serve as a screen onto which subjects project their characteristic thoughts, needs, motives, anxieties, themes, conflicts.

Projective instruments represent a disguised testing procedure because the subjects are not aware of the types of psychological interpretations of their responses that will be made. Projective techniques are characterized by a global approach. Attention is drawn to a composite picture of the subject's whole personality rather than to the assessment of a separate personality trait or a group of traits.

Projective procedures are thought to be very effective in revealing covert, latent, and unconscious aspects of personality and relationship dynamics. The more unstructured the test, the more sensitive it is thought to be in revealing unconscious processes. Most projective tests offer an effective means for establishing rapport with subjects. They tend to divert the respondent's attention away from the self and the family, reducing anxiety and embarrassment as well as defensiveness.

In general, projective techniques are less susceptible to faking than are other self-report procedures. Subjects tend to become absorbed in the task and are therefore less likely to modify their responses. For these reasons, projective techniques can be used as stimuli for creating family interaction that may be subject to less conscious modification than are problem-solving tasks, decision-making tasks, conflict-resolution tasks, and naturalistic tasks. However, it cannot be assumed that projective techniques are completely immune to faking (Davids & Pildner, 1958; Masling, 1960).

227

Unfortunately, most projective techniques suffer from poor methods of standardization in administration. Even subtle differences in the phrasing of verbal instructions and in the relationship established between the tester and the subjects have been shown to alter subjects' performance (Baughman, 1951; Hamilton & Robertson, 1966; Herron, 1964; Klinger, 1966; Klopfer & Taulbee, 1976).

Another serious problem with projective tests is the lack of objectivity in scoring. Usually, the scoring and interpretation of test protocols are dependent upon the examiner's clinical expertise, acumen, and theoretical orientation, even when objective scoring systems have been developed for a particular instrument (Anastasi, 1982). Such a situation makes it difficult to achieve acceptable levels of interrater agreement.

Another difficulty encountered with the use of projective techniques is that, in many instances, normative data are absent, inadequate, or based upon poorly defined populations. In the absence of such norms, the clinician must rely upon clinical experience, intuition, speculations, hypotheses, and hunches, to interpret clients' responses. In the end, one is dealing with extremely subjective interpretations. Even the classic studies of families with schizophrenic members, in which projective techniques were used to measure communication deviance (Singer & Wynne, 1963, 1965a, 1965b), could not be replicated (Hirsch & Leff, 1971; Wender, Rosenthal, Zahn, & Kety, 1971).

Obviously, reliability of interpretation is a serious concern. Internal consistency is characteristically low (Anastasi, 1982). Split-half reliability cannot be computed because different TAT or Rorschach cards are not comparable. Test-retest reliability is of little use because testing over long intervals of time may show low correlations due to changes in the subject's unconscious dynamics. Retesting subjects after short time intervals may reflect only the tester's ability to recall the earlier interpretations.

Concerning the validity of projective tests, Anastasi wrote:

> When experienced clinicians are given an opportunity to examine and interpret in their own ways examinee's protocols from such projective tests as the Rorschach and TAT, their evaluations of the examinees' personalities tend to match independent case history evaluations significantly better than chance. Insofar as can be ascertained, however, the obtained relations are low. Moreover, the relationship appears to be a function of a particular clinician and examinee, a number of individual matches being no better than chance. There is also little agreement among evaluations based on different projective techniques or among different clinicians using the same technique. (1982, p. 588)

Finally, there is no empirical evidence to support the projective hypothesis. Marked changes in subjects' responses over time are common; subjects' responses have been shown to be significantly influenced by temporary states (e.g., anxiety, frustration, hunger, sleep deprivation); and response variability has been shown to be associated with slight changes in test stimuli and the testing situation. In her final comments about the empirical status of projective techniques, Anastasi concluded that "there is ample evidence that alternative explanations may account as well as or better for the individual's responses to unstructured test stimuli" (p. 589).

With these comments in mind, we now offer a brief overview of how projective techniques have been used to gain some understanding of family members' perceptions of family structure and dynamics. Next we discuss the projective techniques that have been developed specifically for use with families. Let us stress, from the outset, that the majority of these techniques do not hold up under empirical scrutiny. For the most part, data on reliability, validity, and standardization are absent. However, the instruments and procedures reviewed are considered valuable clinical tools and assessment aids. They provide the therapist with a totally different type of data, offering the clinician a variety of strategies for exploring the individual's symbolic representations of his or her family life and providing a rare glimpse of the family's unique symbol system.

HISTORICAL OVERVIEW

The projective tests most frequently used with families have been the Rorschach and TAT. Usually, investigators have applied content analysis methods to the responses of individual members, focusing on their individual psychodynamics and attempting to reconstruct relationships with significant others (Fisher & Mendell, 1956; Prout & White, 1950).

Evidence of the degree to which individually administered projective tests can offer limited, yet clinically useful information about family functioning and dynamics is presented in the pioneering studies of Goldstein, Rodnick, Judd, and Gould (1970); Kadushin, Waxenberg, and Sager (1971); Sohler, Holzberg, Fleck, Cornelison, and Lidz (1957); Winter and Ferriera (1970); Winter, Ferriera, and Olson (1965, 1966).

The Rorschach is the most commonly reported projective method and accordingly has received more family interest. Two groups of clinicians independently developed interaction or consensus applications of the Rorschach in family evaluation (Levy & Epstein, 1964; Loveland, Wynne, & Singer, 1963). The approaches used were relatively similar in most respects, as were their findings. The Rorschach was first administered individually to each family member; then the family got together and a consensus administration was given. In this session the family members discussed each plate and decided upon consensus responses. The discussions were recorded, and family interactions and communications patterns were noted.

In the Levy and Epstein study, family equilibrium, individual areas of difficulty, and family pathological areas were examined. Loveland et al.

added other dimensions. Some of their families, rather than taking the traditional individual Rorschach, performed a solo administration in which each member, in a separate room, wrote down responses to each card prior to the group administration. As a further interaction check, during the family Rorschach, each member wrote down his or her idea of what the family had decided upon as the consensus response.

Loveland et al. reported the following advantages of the family Rorschach: standard procedure, rich and broad interaction, clear exposition of transactions and communication styles, and noninvolvement of the experimenter. As disadvantages, they listed the overwhelming richness of interaction, the subjectivity of interpretation, and time consumption.

In 1967 Loveland devised an objective scoring system for conjointly administered Rorschachs. Using projective techniques in their assessment of family interaction, Roman and Bauman (1960) introduced a method they called Interaction Testing. Testing is done separately on each member of a family, using the Wechsler-Bellevue, the Rorschach, and the TAT. Then these tests are readministered to the whole group to get consensual responses. Both intellectual and personality characteristics changed dramatically as a result of this interaction. Roman and Bauman used these data to support their thesis that a group is a unique entity that cannot be understood or defined as the sum of the characteristics of its members.

Although conventional TAT cards have been used most frequently in conjoint family research, (e.g., Alkire & Brunse, 1974), a few studies have used specially designed TAT-type stimuli portraying family scenes. Elbert, Rosman, Minuchin, and Guerney (1964) developed the Family Interaction Apperception Test (FIAT). Friedman and Friedman (1970) developed a similar test, which they called the Adult Family Scene.

Howells and Lickorish (1973) also developed a picture-projective method, the Family Relations Indicator. However, this test is administered only to children. More recently, Sotile, Julian, Henry, and Sotile (1988) developed the Family Apperception Test.

Probably one of the most innovative projective approaches to conjoint assessment is offered by the Marbles Test, developed by Usandivaras, Grimson, Hammond, and Issaharoff (1967). Each family member chooses a bag of 20 marbles, each bag containing marbles of one color so that each family member has a different color. The family is presented with a square board with holes and asked to make something, working together. The results can be quantitatively, as well as qualitatively, assessed. In addition, observations can be made about family communication and rule making.

EVALUATION INSTRUMENTS

The Chronological Chart

The Chronological Chart was developed over a 20-year period by Duhl (1981) at the Boston Family Institute. Its purpose is twofold: (1) to help clinicians integrate individual and family histories and (2) to help clinicians integrate information gained from the three levels of systems functioning—intrapsychic, interactional, and transactional. The chart facilitates the collection, organization, and integration of personal and family histories as family members tell their own stories to the therapist. It also allows the therapist to explore the impact that the events described in these stories have had on other family members. This is one method Duhl uses to help family members develop multicentricity.

The chart is a simple grid with a time dimension along its vertical axis. In one column, the dates of all significant events are listed in chronological order. Family members are listed in the vertical column, used to record the impact of a particular experience on that individual. The ages of each member at the time of the events are also recorded.

The second large column on the chart, labeled "Wider Context," offers the interviewer an opportunity to record historical events in the community, the nation, and the world that have had an impact on one or more family members. The next column, "Family Context," is used to record events that affected everyone in the family (no one family member is the focus). The next set of columns provides spaces to record the stories of individual family members, significant others, and extended family members.

Duhl has offered two simple rules for using the chart: (1) One must always inquire into the impact of any event upon all family members, and (2) One should never consider an empty space in the chart of no value. An empty space highlights an area with "no information," offering an opportunity for the therapist to fill in the gaps.

Family Evaluation Battery

The Family Evaluation Battery, developed by L'Abate and Wagner (1985), consists of four separate nonverbal tests that can be administered to families with children as young as six years old. Consisting of pictures on cards, it can be administered to families regardless of socioeconomic status.

The first test in the battery is the Bell-Fagan Symbols Test, made up of 52 nonsense symbols associated with anxiety, anger, sadness, love, happiness, and calmness. Instructions are to divide the cards into as many piles as there are family members present. Individual answer sheets are reduced to the six emotions. These are then combined with those from the other members, yielding a family rating of each member along the six emotions.

Description of Feelings in the Family, the second test in the battery, has 72 pictures of six family members (two parents, two adolescents, two children), depicting the four feelings underlying the orthogonal version of the Satirian model—anger, sadness, distraction, and smugness. Each family member picks the cards that show the family, and individual scoring sheets are again reduced to family scores.

The Family Situations Picture Series consists of 262 cards of the possible combinations of the four Satirian stances in a six-member family. Members pick the cards that apply to their family, and individual answers are reduced to family scores.

The final test of the battery, the Animal Concepts Picture Series, consists of 90 cards of pictures of animals, with instructions for each member to pick one card for each family member. This is done twice for the family as it is (actual) and twice for what each family member would like it to be (ideal). These scores are then translated into 10 dimensions, such as good-bad, helpful-helpless, small-large, pleasant-unpleasant.

The Family Evaluation Battery thus taps phenotypical and genotypical family behavior as well as the more presentational type of behavior usually tapped by verbal tests of family functioning. The battery has been the subject of a validation study (Golden, 1974), and an attempt has been made to distinguish the IP in disturbed families as opposed to test profiles of normal families (Gallope, 1979). Test-retest reliability, along with a discussion of the use of each test in the battery and its usefulness, can be found in L'Abate (1977, 1983).

One drawback of the Family Evaluation Battery is its lack of standard scores. This means that profiles from one family can be compared only descriptively with those of another family. However, it is one of the few instruments in objective familial measures that provides and combines individual and family data.

The Family Behavioral Snapshot

Meyerstein (1979) developed the Family Behavioral Snapshot to help beginning family therapists focus on key areas of family structure, development, and problem solving as conceptualized by ecological family systems theorists (Auerswald, 1968).

As an interviewing guide, the Snapshot leads the beginner through a structured interview that is organized sequentially into five sections (general information about family lifestyles, presenting problem, developmental issues and aspects of family adaptation, family interaction, the therapist-family contract).

Team Family Evaluation (TFE)

In a 1981 paper, Manosevitz and Stedman presented their ideas for a practical set of guidelines that could be used to train beginning family therapists in family assessment. Their assessment approach is based upon Multiple Impact Therapy (MacGregor, Ritchie, Serrano, and Shuster, 1964). Manosevitz and Stedman modified this model to include some of the ideas and concepts from Minuchin's work. Having completed the assessment procedure, therapists are expected to formulate specific treatment goals related to family structure, developmental stage, generational boundary lines, collusions, family hierarchies, family secrets and myths, the marital subsystem, multigenerational problems, special stimuli and response patterns, significant concerns related to a child or adolescent, adult's psychopathology, and resistances.

Assessing Stepfamilies

Based upon the first author's doctoral work, Katz and Stein (1983) developed a model for understanding the unique qualities of blended, reconstituted, remarried, or "stepfamilies." They identified three sets of issues that must be taken into account in any attempt to understand the dynamics of stepfamilies: (1) issues related to the previous marriages and family units, (2) issues related to the divorce and the single-parenting experience, and (3) issues related to the remarriage.

Another important group of considerations has to do with the development of stepfamily systems. They conceptualized the stepfamily developmental process as passing through six hierarchically ordered stages. Each stage has its own unique developmental tasks that are to be mastered.

In Stage 1, the single-parent-headed household, the tasks are to relinquish investment in the previous family unit, renegotiate the relationships altered by the dissolution of that family unit, and establish a single-parent-headed household. In Stage 2, the remarriage, the tasks are to relinquish the exclusive gratifications received in the single-parent family and establish clear family boundaries and roles. In Stage 3, when the first child is born into the stepfamily, the tasks are to further develop and enhance the relationships established in Stage 2 and to develop new roles as parents to the biological child and as half-siblings to that child.

In Stage 4, when individuation takes place in the stepfamily, the main task is to allow appropriate individuation despite potential interferences caused by earlier family dissolution and the work of forming a new family. In Stage 5 the children depart; the task is to allow children to depart from two households and to appropriately leave the biological parents and the stepparents. In Stage 6 losses are integrated. The tasks here are to resolve any losses.

When stepfamilies present themselves for therapy, Katz and Stein attempt to form hypotheses about the connection in the presenting problem, the family's structural patterns, and the family's ability to resolve the particular developmental tasks at hand. Data collection for assessment revolves around two pragmatic questions: (1) What is the reality of your family situation? and (2) How well have you adapted to this reality? To assess functioning, Katz and Stein ask a series of diagnostic questions related to each developmental stage of the stepfamily life cycle.

ART TECHNIQUES

The use of art methods in evaluating families was built upon a foundation of art procedures designed to evaluate children (Buck, 1948; Goodenough, 1926; Machover, 1949). The most frequently used techniques are outlined below.

Kinetic Family Drawings

Burns and Kaufman (1970) believe that the action orientation of the Kinetic Family Drawings increases its value as an assessment procedure. The characteristics of K-F-D involve both the style of the drawings and the actions taking place.

Although these clinicians offered no empirical data to support their interpretations, certain recurrent themes emerged in the drawings of the children tested. Only three empirical studies of Kinetic Family Drawings have been reported; all deal with children's responses (McPhee & Wegner, 1976; Myers, 1978; O'Brian & Patton, 1974).

Family Art Therapy

Kwiatkowska (1978) developed the most comprehensive and empirically based art evaluation procedure available to date. During a 2-hour session, the family is asked to draw: (1) a free-style picture, (2) a picture of the family, (3) an abstract portrait of the family, (4) a picture developed from a scribble,

(5) a joint family mural, and (6) a freestyle scribble. A 25-page scoring manual is used to score each picture.

Family art therapy was introduced by Kwiatkowska at the National Institute of Mental Health (NIMH) during the late 1950s and early 1960s in research conducted with families having a schizophrenic member. Later, Kwiatkowska developed a series of six pictures for family art evaluations.

At about the same time as Kwiatkowska's early work, Zierer and his colleagues began practicing family creative analysis and therapy. Their techniques were highly structured and focused more on the healing aspect of the task than on correcting the family process (Zierer, Sternberg, Finn, & Farmer, 1966a & b). Wadeson (1972, 1976), also at NIMH and known for her work on depression, suicide, and manic-depressive illness, developed her own method of conjoint marital art therapy. In 1970, at the Philadelphia Child Guidance Center, Rubin introduced family art therapy (Rubin & Magnussen, 1974). She developed her own family art evaluation techniques and in her subsequent work focused predominantly on family subgroups (Rubin, 1974, 1978; Rubin, Ragins, Schachter, & Wimberly, 1979). Although Zierer, Wadeson, and Rubin are recognized among the founders of family art therapy, Kwiatkowska is given the widest recognition. Therefore her work has had the greatest impact on the field.

Sherr and Hicks (1973) developed their own variation of Kwiatkowska's evaluation of family themes, added background music, and programmed the environment for maximum relaxation to enhance family participation. Harriss and Landgarten (1973) found family art therapy especially beneficial for brain-damaged adults and their families. Willmuth and Boedy (1979) extended this evaluation procedure, having found that the art media gave children a voice through which to express their views of the family.

Several art therapists have used family art therapy techniques in group formats with whole families and subgroups (e.g., Landgarten, 1975; Rubin, 1974; Rubin & Magnussen, 1974; Wadeson, 1972).

Family Sculpting

Family sculpting is another projective technique similar to psychodrama (Moreno, 1946) in its origin and procedure. However, there are some distinct differences. The purpose of sculpting is to portray family system processes symbolically, not to "re-live" an affective experience or a significant event. Sculpting attempts to remove the respondent from situational events, foster greater objectivity, and encourage insight into the family's interactional patterns.

Kantor and Lehr (1975) stressed the concept of *space* as a key dimension in family systems. Space is also a central interest in family sculpting. Early contributors include Papp, Silverstein, and Carter (1973) and Satir (1972).

Sculpting has been used with a variety of populations, including "well" families (Papp et al., 1973) and families having schizophrenic members (Julius, 1978). Another important use of sculpting is in professional training (Ferber & Mendelsohn, 1969; Satir, 1972; Simon, 1972). Although the more obvious goal of family sculpting is to promote insight into systems relationships, it also points out the impact that any one member may have on the system when he or she is making a real, observable, behavioral change. Because of the many uses and styles of family sculpting, it is not feasible to review all the techniques that have been used.

Family sculpting is a creative, flexible, and revealing approach to exploring family process, including the dimension of space and the quality of interactions. The family is portrayed in a visual, symbolic representation of the sculptor's perceptions of the system. The clinician may test his or her own perceptions and hypotheses by sculpting the family and asking for feedback from the family members. Although specific procedures can be found in the literature, the more experienced family clinician may experiment with sculpting in order to be more helpful in assessing particular families and to test specific hypotheses.

In Bagarozzi's work with families (1981), sculpting has been used as a pretest-posttest assessment technique. Each family member is asked to sculpt the family as he or she perceives it to be in the present. Next, each family member is asked to sculpt the family as he or she would like it to be at the end of successful therapy. The family is then instructed to create a final posttherapy family sculpture that all family members can agree upon. The conflicts that develop during this sculpting highlight structural difficulties, coalitions, alliances, triangles, as well as the family's ability to work cooperatively to arrive at an acceptable family goal. Families that are able to agree upon a family sculpture are then asked to devise strategies to negotiate contracts that will help the family achieve its agreed-upon goals.

At the end of treatment, all family members are again asked to sculpt the family as it appears to them at that time. Finally, another group consensus sculpture is constructed. This is compared with the group consensus sculpture in the pretreatment/assessment interview. A comparison between the pretreatment and posttreatment group consensus sculptures is used to assess the degree to which family outcome goals have been achieved. Photographs of pretreatment and posttreatment group consensus sculptures are used to make this comparison.

Family Sculpture Test

The Family Sculpture Test was developed by Kvebaek (1974). The test materials consist of an 8'' × 8'' board containing 64 one-inch squares and a group of abstract figures of three different sizes. The figures represent father, mother, and child. Each family member is asked to do a family sculpture, privately or in the company of the therapist. Next, the family is asked to produce a family group sculpture. Instructions for making the sculpture are simple and straightforward.

The Family Sculpture Test has been used to assess the distance between family members and has served as a dependent behavioral measure of cohesion in validation studies of FACES I (Olson, Bell, & Portner, 1982; Russell, 1979). Statistical techniques have been developed (Fournier, 1977) to calculate distance scores for each dyadic relationship, across individuals, and for the consensus family configuration.

The Family Sculpture Test can be used in place of family sculpting. It can be very effective with young children who feel uncomfortable positioning (in real life) other family members. Although more information can be gathered through direct observation, young children may be inhibited or intimidated by the presence of other family members. The use of small, inanimate, symbolic figures may reduce such inhibitions, especially if the child is given the opportunity to make family configurations in total privacy (or is observed from behind a one-way mirror).

Kuethe Felt Figure Technique and Related Techniques

The Kuethe Felt Figure Technique was developed by Kuethe during the early 1960s. This technique consists of using a rectangular felt board measuring 2' × 1–½'. Subjects are instructed to place felt figures (7'' to 10'' tall) on the board however they wish. The figures represent a man, woman, child, dog, cat, rectangle, triangle, circle. Once the figures have been placed on the board, the distance between figures is measured.

Kuethe postulated that the placement of figures represents unit-forming principles in social perception. When a person indicates that two figures belong close together, he or she has revealed some internal cognitive schema or plan. Kuethe believes that certain social schemata have high commonality across normal populations in Western culture. Some of these commonly occurring schema are as follows: people belong together; men belong with women; women belong with children; objects should not separate people; neutral stimuli should be organized in a horizontal plane by height.

Kuethe recognized that an individual's placement of figures may not be a valid or reliable configuration and that socially desirable responses may be produced. To circumvent this possibility, he developed a second task, which he called the *replacement technique*. During the free-placement task, individuals are allowed to place figures anywhere, at whatever distance from one another they desire. However, in the replacement task, subjects are asked to look at two stimuli already placed on the felt board (generally 15'' apart).

The figures are then removed, and the subjects are asked to replace them exactly as they had been.

Kuethe (1962) has shown that subjects are able to replace neutral stimuli (e.g., triangles, circles) accurately. On the other hand, when asked to replace pairs of human figures, subjects tend to project their own responses from the free-placement task.

The Use of Photographs

The use of personal photographs to stimulate memories from one's past, to help clients reminisce, to recapture times gone by has been used by clinicians for quite some time (e.g., Akeret, 1973; Coblentz, 1964; Graham, 1967; Kiell, 1965; Miller, 1962; Robbins, 1942). Family therapists have adopted this clinical technique (e.g., Anderson & Malloy, 1973; Bodin & Ferber, 1973; Kaslow & Friedman, 1977) to unearth family members' feelings about past experiences and events. Anderson and Malloy (1976) believe that photographs are akin to dreams, symbolic communications, and slips of the tongue.

Kaslow and Friedman (1977) identified a number of patterns in what they call *photo reconnaissance*. For example:

(1) Families tend to take photographs and films at a particular time and at important developmental stages of the family life cycle.
(2) During periods of family strife and stress, the number of pictures tends to drop drastically.
(3) Firstborns tend to be photographed more frequently than siblings who come later in the family life cycle.
(4) Size and prominence of the display of family pictures and photographs are thought to reflect attitudes about status.

Family photographs provide the therapist with factual and historical data. They can be used to help family members correct distortions (conscious as well as unconscious), to stimulate interaction, to elicit emotional responses, and to expand family members' awareness of their own personalities and identities. They also can be used to identify the specific roles that family members are expected to play in family myths (Bagarozzi & Anderson, 1989).

THE FAMILY FLOOR PLAN

Coopersmith (1980) introduced the family floor plan procedure in order to gain some insights into the recollections and perceptions of one's family of origin. The participant is asked to execute a floor plan of the house he or she lived in as a child, using large sheet of paper and felt-tipped pens or crayons. If the participant lived in more than one house, he or she is asked to select one that particularly stands out in his or her memory.

While the subject draws, the therapist offers some suggestions and asks a variety of questions. These questions and suggestions are designed to help the subject recall important memories that could be seen as representing implicit family rules. Again, structural and process data about the family of origin can be inferred from these productions.

A variation of this procedure can be used to assess the current family. This is especially useful when children are asked to draw a floor plan and parents are asked to observe.

FAMILY MYTHOLOGICAL SYSTEMS

Ferreira (1967) first coined the term *family myth*, which he defined as a series of well-integrated beliefs that are shared by all family members. He postulated that these beliefs prescribe complementary role relationships that all family members must play vis-à-vis other family members. Ferreira (1967) described how these beliefs and roles went unchallenged by family members in spite of the gross reality distortions that were required to keep the myth intact. The family myth is the way the family views itself (insiders' perspective), not how it is viewed by others (outsiders' perspective). Myths offer a rationale for family behavior while concealing the true motive—family homeostasis.

In the early 1980s Bagarozzi and Anderson (1982) and Anderson and Bagarozzi (1983) put forth their views about the nature of family myths. These views differ significantly from those originally presented by Ferreira. These authors postulate that family myths do not remain static and that they evolve over time. They also stress that family myths serve a variety of functions and that their sole purpose is not to maintain family homeostasis. In addition, Bagarozzi and Anderson pointed out that family myths are rarely consciously shared and openly agreed upon by all family members.

Ferreira (1967) believed that there is one focal myth around which the family process revolves. However, Bagarozzi and Anderson found that their clinical research with nondistressed couples and families did not support the notion of one central marital/family myth. Although this may be the case with severely disturbed couples and families, Bagarozzi and Anderson (1982) believe this to be the exception rather than the rule. These authors have offered a wealth of clinical data from their own work as well as from the clinical work of therapists from the United States, Europe, and the Middle East (Anderson & Bagarozzi, 1988). These studies showed that families have a number of intricately interwoven myths that continually change and evolve with time and with the unfolding of the family life cycle. They also demonstrate how myths are hierarchically ordered at different levels of systems functioning.

Bagarozzi and Anderson believe that family myths serve both homeostatic and morphogenetic functions. The functionality of a myth can be determined only by assessing the degree to which it contributes to or curtails the growth and development of each family member and the family system as a whole.

To identify the overarching family myths, one must assess the various levels of the family myth hierarchy. The therapist does this by profiling the personal myths of all family members, the conjugal myths of the spouses, and the family group myths that are shared by all family members. All myths, whether personal, conjugal, or familial, are characterized by a sense of urgency, a sense that life circumstances are beyond the individual's and the family's control.

Once a myth has been established, it is used as an explanation and, often, as a justification for family behavior. The therapist knows when he or she is confronting a myth because it is highly prized and protected, and any perception or any information that conflicts with or disconfirms the myth is defended against by the family system.

Personal Myths Assessment

Bagarozzi and Anderson (1989) have developed detailed outlines that can be used to gain insight into individual, conjugal, and family myths. Personal myths are assessed through a series of structured interviews and projective techniques developed specifically for this purpose.

The Family Relationships History is a structured interview that consists of 41 open-ended questions designed to gather information about the development of the self within the family. In addition to the 41-question interview, each individual is asked to respond to 15 open-ended questions concerning his or her favorite fairy tale, folk tale, nursery rhyme, short story, movie, television series, and so forth.

Bagarozzi and Anderson (1982) believe that, via this projective strategy, emotionally charged and dynamic themes of each family member reveal important unconscious information about unresolved needs, motives, and intrapersonal and interpersonal conflicts.

Conjugal Myths Assessment

To assess a couple's mythology, Bagarozzi and Anderson (1989) attempt to understand how the themes from each spouse's personal mythology dovetail to form a common shared theme in the couple's mythology. This procedure is highly speculative and interpreted and, like most of the projective techniques studied in this section, is limited in terms of reliability and validity.

However, one aspect of a couple's conjugal mythology has been subjected to empirical assessment—the Ideal Spousal Image. In 1986 Anderson, Bagarozzi, and Giddings developed IMAGES, a factor-analyzed questionnaire consisting of 35 Likert-type items asking for conscious comparisons between one's perceived spouse and his or her ideal.

Bagarozzi and Anderson (1989) assume that spouses choose an ideal that they believe will collude with them by playing out complementary roles and scripts. A spouse is chosen because he or she is perceived as one who will allow the mate to relive and correct unresolved personal conflicts. In addition, a spouse is selected because he or she is believed to share certain relationship rules that will require little or no alteration in one's own behavior and self-concept.

After a time together as a couple, both spouses become aware of the discrepancies between their ideal and real mates. When this occurs, each spouse is faced with a conflict that can be resolved in a number of ways. Some resolutions are more functional than others. For example, one can modify one's ideal so that it conforms more to reality, or one can use ego defenses that deny these differences. One can terminate the relationship and begin a new quest for the ideal. Finally, one may set out to change one's spouse, to mold him or her into the desired ideal.

The therapist begins to profile the contents of major themes that constitute conjugal myths by using all the data and information gathered through (1) each spouse's personal Family Relationships History; (2) each spouse's responses to the series of open-ended questions concerning the favorite fairy tale, story, nursery rhyme; (3) IMAGES; (4) the structured interview with the couple; and (5) the therapist's behavioral observations of the couple's characteristic styles of communication, goal setting, problem solving, and conflict negotiation. Behavioral observations are used to highlight major themes, which manifest themselves through redundant conjugal interaction patterns; recurring topics of concern; repeated resurfacing of specific, affect-laden conflicts; and the couple's predominant affective tone.

Family Myth Assessment

A similar procedure is used to profile the themes of family myths. Each family member's Family Relationships History is reviewed, as are each member's responses to the 15 open-ended questions about one's favorite fairy tale, story. In addition to the structured interview with the couple, parents are asked to complete the Ideal Child Profile.

The Ideal Child Profile (Bagarozzi & Anderson, 1989) is another projective instrument used in the assessment of family mythological systems. It is a 26-item questionnaire that parents are asked to complete (without consulting each other) regarding the identified patient and all other children in the family. The Ideal Child Profile is designed to help therapists identify the unique role and script expectations the parents have for their children.

Parental expectations for their children often conflict. This is especially true in regard to the identified patient. Nevertheless each child grows into a particular family role. The themes that develop along with the child's enactment of a particular role and script are complexly related to the roles and scripts of other family members. These make up the central themes in family group myths.

After completion of the Ideal Child Profile by each parent, a structured family interview is then conducted with all family members present. During this interview, all family members share the contents of the Family Relationships History and their responses to the 15 questions dealing with favorite fairy tales, stories.

CONCLUSION

Projective techniques are dependent on the skills of their interpreter. The more imaginative, articulate, and fanciful the interpreter, the greater the possibilities for a variety of interpretations, not all necessarily in agreement with one another. Clearly, some of these techniques are expensive to administer and, often, expensive to score and interpret if the training of the interpreter is included.

Certainly, projective techniques add dimensions and levels of behavior untapped by either observational or direct self-report methods. However, using these techniques, one needs to ask for a rationale for their selective use. Is the amount of information gathered through their use obtainable through any other cheaper method? How expensive are these measures in comparison with other methods of observation and self-report?

The issue here is whether and how the projective level of response is consistent or inconsistent with other, more transparent methods of evaluation. How important and relevant is the information obtained through these techniques? How much can projective techniques add to our understanding of families? Even more pointedly, how can data obtained from these techniques aid in the process of helping couples and families? These are questions that only the proponents of their use can answer.

REFERENCES

Akeret, R. U. (1973). *Photoanalysis*. New York: Wynden.

Alkire, A. A., & Brunse, A. J. (1974). Impact and possible causality from videotape feedback in marital therapy. *Journal of Consulting and Clinical Psychology, 42*, 203–210.

Anastasi, A. (1982). *Psychological testing*. New York: Macmillan

Anderson, C. M., & Malloy, E. S. (1973). Family photographs: In treatment and training. *Family Process, 15*, 259–273.

Anderson, C. M., & Malloy, E. S. (1976). Family photographs. *Family Process, 6*, 313–321.

Anderson, S. A., & Bagarozzi, D. A. (1983). The use of family myths as an aid to strategic therapy. *Journal of Family Therapy, 5*, 145–154.

Anderson, S. A., & Bagarozzi, D. A. (1988), Eds. *Family myths: Psychotherapy implications*. New York: Haworth.

Anderson, S. A., Bagarozzi, D. A., & Giddings, C. W. (1986). IMAGES: Preliminary scale construction. *American Journal of Family Therapy, 14*, 357–363.

Auerswald, E. H. (1968). Interdisciplinary versus ecological approach. *Family Process, 7*, 202–215.

Bagarozzi, D. A. (1981). The symbolic meaning of behavioral exchanges in marital therapy. In A. S. Gurman (Ed.), *Questions and answers in the practice of family therapy* (pp. 173–177). New York: Brunner/Mazel.

Bagarozzi, D. A., & Anderson, S. A. (1982). The evolution of family mythological systems: Considerations for meaning, clinical assessment and treatment. *The Journal of Psychoanalytic Anthropology, 5*, 71–90.

Bagarozzi, D. A., & Anderson, S. A. (1989). *Personal, marital and family myths: Theoretical formulations and clinical strategies*. New York: Norton.

Baughman, E. E. (1951). Rorschach scores as a function of examiner difference. *Journal of Projective Techniques, 55*, 121–147.

Bodin, A., & Ferber, A. (1973). How to go beyond the use of language. In A. Ferber, M. Mendelsohn, & A. Napier (Eds.), *The book of family therapy* (pp. 272–316). Boston: Houghton Mifflin.

Buck, J. N. (1948). The H-T-P technique: A qualitative and quantitative scoring manual. *Journal of Clinical Psychology, 4*, 317–396.

Burns, R. C., & Kaufman, S. H. (1970). *Kinetic Family Drawings (KFD): An introduction to understanding children through kinetic drawings*. New York: Brunner/Mazel.

Coblentz, A. L. (1964). Use of photographs in a family mental health clinic. *American Journal of Psychiatry, 121*, 601–602.

Coopersmith, E. (1980). The Family Floor Plan: A tool for training, assessment and intervention in family therapy. *Journal of Marital and Family Therapy, 6*, 141–145.

Davids, A., & Pildner, H., Jr. (1958). Comparison of direct and projective methods of personality assessment under different conditions of motivation. *Psychological Monographs, 72* (11, Serial No. 464).

Duhl, F. J. (1981). The use of the chronological chart in general systems family therapy. *Journal of Marital and Family Therapy, 7*, 361–373.

Elbert, S., Rosman, B., Minuchin, S., & Guerney, B. (1964). A method for the clinical study of family interaction. *American Journal of Orthopsychiatry, 34*, 885–894.

Ferber, A., & Mendelsohn, M. (1969). Training for family therapy. *Family Process, 8*, 25–32.

Ferreira, A. J. (1967). Psychosis and family myth. *American Journal of Psychotherapy, 21*, 186–197.

Fisher, S., & Mendell, D. (1956). The communication of neurotic patterns over two and three generations. *Psychiatry, 19,* 41–46.

Fournier, D. (1977). *Scoring procedures for the Family Sculpture Test.* Unpublished manuscript, University of Minnesota, Minneapolis.

Friedman, C. J., & Friedman, A. S. (1970). Characteristics of schizogenic families during a joint family story-telling task. *Family Process, 9,* 333–354.

Gallope, R. (1979). *Test profile variables within families and their relationship to family disturbance.* Unpublished doctoral dissertation, Georgia State University, Atlanta.

Golden, R. (1974). *A validation study of the family assessment battery.* Unpublished doctoral dissertation, Georgia State University, Atlanta.

Goldstein, M., Rodnick, E., Judd, L., & Gould, E. (1970). Galvanic skin reactivity among family groups containing disturbed adolescents. *Journal of Abnormal Psychology, 75,* 57–67.

Goodenough, F. L., (1926) *Measurement of intelligence by drawings.* Yonkers, N.Y., World Book.

Graham, J. R. (1967). The use of photographs in psychiatry. *Canadian Psychiatric Association Journal, 12,* 425.

Hamilton, R. G., & Robertson, M. H. (1966). Examiner influence on the Holtzman Inkblot Technique. *Journal of Projective Techniques and Personality Assessment, 30,* 553–558.

Harriss, M., & Landgarten, H. (1973). Art therapy as an innovative approach to conjoint treatment: A case study. *Art Psychotherapy, 1,* 221–228.

Herron, R. W. (1976). A study of couple congruency in religiosity and its relationship to marital satisfaction. *Dissertation Abstracts International, 37*(6-A), 3942-3943.

Hirsch, S. R., & Leff, J. R. (1971). Parental abnormalities in the transmission of schizophrenia. *Psychological Medicine, 1,* 118–127.

Howells, J. G., & Lickorish, J. R. (1973). The family relations indicator. *British Journal of Educational Psychology, 33,* 286–296.

Julius, E. (1978). Family sculpting: A pilot program for a schizophrenic group. *Journal of Marriage and Family Counseling, 4,* 19–24.

Kadushin, P., Waxenberg, S. E., & Sager, C. J. (1971). Family story technique changes in interactions and affects during family therapy. *Journal of Personality Assessment, 35,* 62–71.

Kantor, D., & Lehr, W. (1975). *Inside the family: Toward a theory of family process.* San Francisco: Jossey-Bass.

Kaslow, F. W., & Friedman, J. (1977). Utilization of family photos in family therapy. *Journal of Marriage and Family Counseling, 3,* 19–25.

Katz, L., & Stein, S. (1983). Treating stepfamilies. In B. B. Wolman & G. Stucker (Eds.), *Handbook of family and marital therapy* (pp. 387–420). New York: Plenum.

Kiell, N. (1965). *Psychiatry and psychology in the visual arts and aesthetics: A bibliography.* Madison: University of Wisconsin Press.

Klinger, E. (1966). Fantasy need achievement as a motivational construct. *Psychological Bulletin, 66,* 291–308.

Klopfer, R. R., & Taulbee, E. S. (1976). Projective tests. *Annual Review of Psychology, 27,* 543–568.

Kuethe, J. (1962). Social schemas and the reconstruction of social object displays from memory. *Journal of Abnormal and Social Psychology, 65,* 71–74.

Kuethe, J. (1964). Pervasive influence of social schemata. *Journal of Abnormal and Social Psychology, 68,* 248–254.

Kvebaek, D. J. (1974). *Sculpture Test: A diagnostic aid in family therapy.* Unpublished technical report, Modum Bads Nervesanatorium Vikersund, Norway.

Kwiatkowska, H. Y. (1978). *Family therapy and evaluation through art.* Springfield, IL: Thomas.

L'Abate, L. (1977). *Enrichment: Structured interventions with couples, families, and groups.* Washington, DC: University Press of America.

L'Abate, L. (1983). Intimacy is sharing hurt feelings: A reply to David Mace. In L. L'Abate (Ed.), *Family psychology: Theory, therapy and training* (pp. 101–122). Washington, DC: University Press of America. (Reprinted from *Journal of Marriage and Family Counseling,* 1977, 3, 13–16.)

L'Abate, L., & Wagner, V. (1985). Theory-derived, family-oriented test batteries. In L. L'Abate, (Ed.), *The handbook of family psychology and therapy* (Vol. 2, pp. 1006–1031). Pacific Grove, CA: Brooks/Cole.

L'Abate, L., & Wagner, V. (1988). Testing a theory of developmental competence in the family. *American Journal of Family Therapy, 16,* 23–35.

Landgarten, H. (1975). Group are therapy for mothers and daughters. *American Journal of Art Therapy, 14,* 121–125.

Levy, J., & Epstein, N. B. (1964). An application of the Rorschach test in family investigation. *Family Process, 3,* 344–376.

Loveland, N. (1967). The relation Rorschach: A technique for studying interaction. *Journal of Nervous and Mental Diseases, 145,* 93–105.

Loveland, N. T., Wynne, L. C., & Singer, M. T. (1963). The family Rorschach: A new method for studying family interaction. *Family Process, 2,* 187–215.

MacGregor, R., Ritchie, A. N., Serrano, A. C., & Shuster, F. P. (1964). *Multiple impact therapy with families.* New York: McGraw-Hill.

Machover, K. (1949). *Personality projection in the drawing of the human figure.* Springfield, IL: Thomas.

Manosevitz, M., & Stedman, J. M. (1981). Some thoughts on training the novice family therapist in the art of family assessment. *Family Therapy, 8,* 67–75.

Masling, J. (1960). The influence of situational and interpersonal variables in projective testing. *Psychological Bulletin, 57,* 65–85.

McPhee, J. P., & Wegner, K. W. (1976). Family drawing styles and emotionally disturbed childhood behavior. *Journal of Personality Assessment, 40,* 487–491.

Meyerstein, I. (1979). The family behavioral snapshot: A tool for teaching family assessment. *American Journal of Family Therapy, 7,* 48–56.

Miller, M. F. (1962). Responses of psychiatric patients to their photographed images. *Diseases of the Nervous System, 23,* 296–298.

Moreno, J. (1946). *Psychodrama.* New York: Beacon.

Myers, D. V. (1978). Toward an objective evaluation procedure of the Kinetic Family Drawings (KFD). *Journal of Personality Assessment, 42,* 358–365.

O'Brian, R. P., & Patton, W. F. (1974). Development of an objective scoring method for the Kinetic Family Drawing. *Journal of Personality Assessment, 38,* 156–164.

Olson, D. H., Bell, R., & Portner, J. (1982). *Family Adaptability and Cohesion Evaluation Scales (FACES).* Unpublished manuscript, University of Minnesota, St. Paul.

Oster, G. D., & Gould, P. (1987). *Using drawings in assessment and therapy: A guide for mental health professionals.* New York: Brunner/Mazel.

Papp, P., Silverstein, O., & Carter, E. (1973). Family sculpting in preventive work with "well families." *Family Process, 12,* 197–212.

Prout, C. T., & White, M. A. (1950). A controlled study of personality relationships in mothers of schizophrenic male patients. *American Journal of Psychiatry, 107,* 251–256.

Robbins, L. L. (1942). Photography. *Bulletin of the Menninger Clinic, 6,* 89–91.

Roman, M., & Bauman, G. (1960). Interaction testing: A technique for the psychological evaluation of small groups. In M. Harrower (Ed.), *Creative variations in the projective techniques* (pp. 93–138). Springfield, IL: Thomas.

Rubin, J. A. (1968). Mother and father schemata of achievers and underachievers in primary school arithmetic. *Psychological Reports, 23*, 1215–1221.

Rubin, J. A. (1974). Mother-child art sessions: 1. Treatment in the clinic. *American Journal of Art Therapy, 13*, 165–181.

Rubin, J. A. (1978). *Child art therapy.* New York: Van Nostrand Reinhold.

Rubin, J. A., & Magnussen, M. G. (1974). A family art evaluation. *Family Process, 13*, 185–200.

Rubin, J. A., Ragins, N., Schachter, J., & Wimberly, F. (1979). Drawings by schizophrenic and non-schizophrenic mothers and their children. *Art Psychotherapy, 6*, 163–175.

Russell, C. S. (1979). Circumplex model of family systems: 3. Empirical evaluation with families. *Family Process, 18*, 29–45.

Satir, V. (1972). *Peoplemaking.* Palo Alto, CA: Science and Behavior Books.

Sherr, C., & Hicks, H. (1973). Family drawings as a diagnostic and therapeutic technique. *Family Process, 12*, 439–460.

Simon, R. M. (1972).Sculpturing the family. *Family Process, 11*, 49–57.

Singer, M. T., & Wynne, L. C. (1963). Differentiating characteristics of parents of childhood schizophrenics, childhood neurotics, and young adult schizophrenics. *American Journal of Psychiatry, 120*, 234–243.

Singer, M. T., & Wynne, L. C. (1965a). Thought disorders and family relations of schizophrenics: 3. Methodology using projective techniques. *Archives of General Psychiatry, 12*, 187–200.

Singer, M. T., & Wynne, L. C. (1965b). Thought disorders and family relations of schizophrenics: 4. Results and implications. *Archives of General Psychiatry, 12*, 201–212.

Sohler, D., Holtzberg, J., Fleck, S., Cornelison, A., & Lidz, T. (1957). Diagnosis of family interaction with a battery of projective techniques. *Journal of Projective Techniques, 21*, 199–208.

Sotile, W. A., Julian, A., Henry, S. E., & Sotile, M. O. (1988). *Family Apperception Test manual.* Charlotte, NC: Feedback Services.

Usandivaras, R. J., Grimson, W. R., Hammond, H., & Issaharoff, R. D. (1967). The marbles test. *Archives of General Psychiatry, 13*, 111–118.

Wadeson, H. S. (1972). Conjoint marital art therapy techniques. *Psychiatry, 35*, 89–98.

Wadeson, H. S. (1976). The fluid family in multi-family art therapy. *American Journal of Art Therapy, 15*, 115–118.

Wender, P., Rosenthal, V., Zahn, T., & Kety, S. (1971). The psychiatric adjustment of the adopting parents of schizophrenics. *American Journal of Psychiatry, 127*, 1013–1018.

Willmuth, M., & Boedy, D. L. (1979). The verbal diagnostic and art therapy combined: An extended evaluation procedure with family groups. *Art Psychotherapy, 6*, 11–18.

Winter, W. D., & Ferreira, A. J. (1970). A factor analysis of family interaction measures. *Journal of Projective Techniques and Personality Assessment, 34*, 55–63.

Winter, W. D., Ferreira, A. J., & Olson, J. L. (1965). Story sequence analysis of family TATs. *Journal of Projective Techniques and Personality Assessment, 29*, 392–397.

Winter, W. D., Ferreira, A. J., & Olson, J. L. (1966). Hostility themes in the family TAT. *Journal of Projective Techniques and Personality Assessment, 30*, 270–274.

Zierer, E., Sternberg, D., Finn, R., & Farmer, M. (1966a). Family creative analysis: Its role in treatment. Part 1. *Bulletin of Art Therapy, 5*, 47–63.

Zierer, E., Sternberg, D., Finn, R., & Farmer, M. (1966b). Family creative analysis: Its role in treatment. Part 2. *Bulletin of Art Therapy, 5*, 87–104.

SECTION IV
Conclusion

11

Ethical and Professional Issues in the Evaluation of Couples and Families

The purpose of this final chapter is to review some of the more salient methodological, theoretical, and professional issues that have been touched upon in one way or another throughout this volume. We also take a closer look at some of the practical problems and pragmatic considerations involved in the qualitative practice of marital/family evaluation. Finally, we focus our attention on the importance of developing and selecting evaluation instruments and procedures for work with marital dyads/family systems that can be used both to formulate treatment plans and to provide the clinician with descriptive information about the structure and dynamics of marital and family systems.

To this end, we describe a procedure called Family Psychological Testing (Bagarozzi, 1989) that family psychologists can offer as a service to other mental health professionals, educators, lawyers, officers of the court, social welfare agencies, and so forth. These professionals generally do not have the time nor the expertise to conduct thorough assessments; therefore, they can benefit immensely from the information and recommendations contained in family psychological reports.

METHODOLOGICAL ISSUES

After reading this volume, the reader has probably come to the conclusion that although a plethora of instruments and evaluation procedures exist, those that can be considered reliable and valid are few. If we had excluded all those instruments, questionnaires, tests, procedures, and so forth developed by family sociologists and family studies researchers and if we had included only valid and reliable instruments designed for clinical assessment and/or outcome evaluation, the size of this volume would have been reduced considerably.

As we stated earlier, it is probably time to take stock of what is available to us, to refrain from creating additional measures that only give the field more of the same, and to concentrate efforts on the improvement and refinement of those theoretically derived instruments and procedures that are already in existence. The statistical and methodological technology and know-how required to undertake such projects certainly exist in the social and behavioral sciences. A moratorium on the development of new measures may provide a golden opportunity for therapists to collaborate with psychologists, statisticians, family sociologists, family studies experts, and professionals from allied health professions and related disciplines who are interested in methodological issues, instrumentation, clinical research, and the practical application of computer technology for the betterment of marital/family life.

THEORETICAL CONCERNS

It is our opinion that any instrument or procedure used for diagnostic assessment and outcome evaluation should have its roots in a theory of family process and family development across the life cycle. This theory of family process and development should describe and explain how dysfunctional behavioral/interactional patterns and faulty structures develop in family systems. It also should explicitly state what a well-functioning family system should look like in terms of its structure and functioning. Theoretically based diagnostic and assessment strategies and procedures should specifically target those family structures and processes central to the theory of family behavior under consideration. Such internal consistency is a sine qua non for designing effective treatments that can be independently replicated. Unfortunately, only a handful of instruments and procedures reviewed in this volume come close to meeting these minimal criteria for theory-based assessment and outcome evaluation, and the few that do still do not present impressive data supporting their reliability and validity.

Although we have called for a moratorium on the development of new instruments, we realize that the likelihood of such an occurrence is remote. Therefore, we urge all clinical researchers who feel an uncontrollable urge to invent new instruments to give serious consideration to developing or refining tools that validly and reliably assess those theoretical dimensions agreed upon by family experts to be critical to the successful functioning of marital/family systems.

In addition to developing theory-based treatment, there are at least six additional reasons for engaging in empirically grounded marital/family evaluation: (1) to create a baseline from which to assess progress or the lack thereof, (2) to identify interaction patterns not otherwise available or visible to the therapist, (3) to account in part for outcome effectiveness or deterioration, (4) to assign couples and families to appropriate treatments, (5) to serve as corrective feedback to therapists, and (6) to help locate client families on a functional-dysfunctional continuum.

An important function of evaluation is to create an initial baseline against which treatment changes can be compared. Without a baseline, how can we assess whether improvement or deterioration has taken place? Self-reports may be one way to evaluate change. However, there are serious problems in accepting a self-report as a criterion for evaluating changes in therapy. First, we would be confusing consumer satisfaction with objectively measurable changes. Second, the self-reported satisfaction may be independent or even negatively related to objectively measured changes. Third, self-reports needs to be compared with other measures of change rather than considered by themselves.

Of course, the measurement of change ought to be multidimensional, that is, consisting of a variety of nonoverlapping measures of different dimensions of family functioning and dysfunctioning. In other words, a baseline should consist of many different and distinct measures, that is, a battery of tests (L'Abate, 1993b; Bagarozzi, 1989).

The idea that a professional, no matter how intelligent, astute, and prepared, can distinguish on the basis of one or, at best, two interviews what is relevant to each family is not only grandiose, it is irresponsible. This position makes the therapist the beginning and the end of whatever needs to be understood about a family, without any possibility for correction. No human being should attribute to him or herself such omniscience, even though the practice may be an accepted one in family therapy.

Assessment for its own sake wastes time, money, and energy if there is no reevaluation after treatment. However, this approach seems foreign to current clinical practices in the mental health field, especially in psychotherapy. As a result, we seem satisfied with the therapist's impressionistic perceptions and consumer satisfaction. We do not gather data that would allow us to validate our perceptions. Being human, we are biased at best and faulty at worst. We deny the importance of evidence that is external to and independent of our personal impressions.

As long as we rely strictly on our subjective impressions, how can we distinguish the charlatan from the true healer? How can therapeutic practices improve if we do not validate their effectiveness with valid and reliable measures? Why should our consumers believe us if we do not produce data that justify and support our practice?

As long as we do not evaluate, we may attempt to trust any family that presents itself for therapy. We then assume, fallaciously, of course, that the

same modality of treatment—marital/family therapy—is appropriate for
everyone. This is the same assumption that reduced the credibility of psychoanalysis as a viable treatment for some human problems. If we do not
distinguish among different forms of treatment for different problems, for
different families, for different times in their developmental history, we are
falling prey to the same "uniformity" trap that Kiesler (1966) identified in
individual psychotherapy. Fortunately, if we begin to differentiate treatments
(L'Abate, 1993a & b), it will become easier to establish criteria that will allow
us to determine a much greater specificity of treatment than we do now.

A systematic approach to selecting treatments and therapies is outlined
by Bagarozzi and Anderson (1989). This approach requires an analysis of
the therapeutic matrix, that is, (1) therapist x client match, (2) clinical
method x client system match, (3) therapist x clinical method x client system match, (4) therapist x marital/family life cycle stage match, (5) clinical
method x marital/family life cycle stage match, (6) therapist x clinical method x marital/family life cycle stage match, (7) therapist x clinical method x
marital/family life cycle stage x client system match. Once such analyses
have taken place, data gathered through empirical assessment can be used
most successfully.

External data from objective evaluation should not only guide us in
specifying treatments. It should also be used to corroborate, strengthen,
or weaken any conclusions reached on the basis of subjective clinical impressions.

As long as we have inadequate and unclear criteria to determine
degrees of functionality-dysfunctionality of marital/family systems, we
will be unable to discriminate which families need what types of treatments. L'Abate (1990) has suggested a continuum of interventions based
on 14 criteria for distinguishing primary, secondary, and tertiary prevention.

The challenge for the future consists of developing objective criteria to
discriminate which kinds of families are at risk for which kinds of dysfunctionality, and which treatment offered by which type of therapist is the
most appropriate. Systematic evaluation can take us closer to achieving this
goal.

ETHICAL AND PROFESSIONAL ISSUES

Who Should Evaluate?

One of the reasons that the evaluation of individuals has fallen into public
and institutional disfavor is the power that evaluation has taken upon itself
to deal with, and to dispose of, human life as test scores. Evaluation and

its shortcomings (e.g., ratification of scores, absolute practices, limited range of prediction) have reached a peak of social and professional license. Evaluations have delivered more than they promised and promised more than they could deliver. Hence, issues of evaluation have also become political issues, tied to ethnic and cultural concerns.

The evaluation of families has been plagued by many of the issues associated with individual assessment. Rather than avoid or negate the need for evaluation because of its reputed abuses and misuses, we might more productively address why this state of affairs has come to pass. Part of the answer may lie not with instrumentation, but with technicians who misread and misinterpret findings. Consequently, our concern is with the credentials and qualifications of evaluators and with their conclusions and recommendations.

Reaching agreement about the qualifications of family evaluators is somewhat difficult because, unlike individual evaluations done mostly by psychologists, family evaluation cannot be laid squarely on the shoulders of any one discipline. How can it be argued that psychologists have the primary rights to the evaluation of families? What criteria can be cited? It is difficult, even impossible, to specify which discipline or which representatives of a discipline are best qualified to perform such evaluation.

We are more concerned with the qualifications of evaluators than with the disciplines they represent. Although marital and family evaluation belongs to no single group of professionals, it is essential that whoever takes this responsibility upon himself or herself be well versed in the theory of test construction and measurement, as well as being able to know the limits of the instruments and procedures being used. Knowledge of statistics and research method are essential so that the evaluator can judge whether the instruments are truly valid and reliable.

Which ethical standards should the family evaluator subscribe to? It is not enough to answer, "the highest standards." Each discipline has its standards of practice. Furthermore, there are standards that apply specifically to family work that do not apply to other disciplines. Consequently, even though we assume a knowledge of ethical and professional standards, we want to underscore certain issues germane to family evaluation.

Responsibility

In accepting responsibility for the consequences of their services, family evaluators must ensure that their assessments are used appropriately by consumer families and other professionals. Part and parcel of this responsibility lies in minimizing misleading and slanted interpretations of the findings. The possibility of distortion is minimized by thoroughly knowing the instruments used. Findings should be reported with an awareness of the socioeconomic and cultural context of each family. In institutions or as institutional consultants, evaluators should be sensitive to political and other pressures that may distort the findings or impede their proper professional use. Family evaluators, like all professionals, are accountable to the families they evaluate, to other professionals, and to the institutions with whom they consult. Consequently, they must be prepared to support their conclusions and findings according to responsible practices of evaluation, which go beyond partisan viewpoints and biases.

Competence

Family evaluators should maintain the highest standards of professional competence and should recognize the limitations and boundaries of their expertise. This competence is maintained through degrees of professional certification, licensing, examinations, and peer reviews, as well as through updated knowledge of the literature relevant to the validity and reliability of the instruments used in evaluating families. Continuing education and the upgrading of one's skills in evaluation are important aspects of competence. These can be obtained by attending workshops and specialized professional meetings and by reading professional journals and published findings relevant to the instruments used in family evaluation. In addition, seeking advice and consultation from colleagues and other qualified professionals is an important part of this process. If interpersonal effectiveness is questioned, the evaluator should examine his or her behavior and seek professional assistance if it is thought to be needed.

Moral and Legal Standards

Family evaluators must be cognizant of, and comply with, the accepted norms of moral and legal responsibility as practiced in their respective disciplines. They must be aware of the possible impact of their evaluation on the lives of their clients, other professionals, and the agencies with whom they are involved. Because one's private and public behavior as a citizen can have an impact on professional practice, evaluators should be aware that the two spheres of behavior are inseparable. Under these conditions, they should be able to refuse involvement or participation in practices inconsistent with their own and their profession's legal, moral, and ethical principles.

Family evaluators should also be aware of the legal and civil rights of clients, families, and others who may be affected by their practices. In this regard, evaluators must be conversant with the relevant federal, state, local, and agency regulations that may affect their practice and their relationships with consumers.

Public Statements

Announcements of services and promotional activities help consumers make informed judgments and choices. Family evaluators must accurately represent themselves and their services to the public or to professionals at large. Their professional qualifications, affiliations, and specific functions limiting and qualifying their areas of expertise and competence must also be portrayed accurately. In public statements about family evaluation, they must take full account of the limits and uncertainties of current knowledge concerning these techniques. Family evaluators should avoid sensationalism, commercialism, and any form of publicity that could mislead the public concerning their skills and functions.

Confidentiality

The primary obligation of family evaluators is to safeguard information obtained through testing about the family and its members. Such information should not be communicated to another party without written authorization from all adults and guardians of the children who took part in the evaluation procedures.

Research Activities

Evaluation is sometimes considered one form of research; as such, it should be done with respect for the families being evaluated and with concern for their dignity and welfare. Written consent, contracts, or agreements should be prepared to ensure knowledgeable action on the part of consumers.

Use of Assessment Techniques

Family evaluators should be aware that families have the right to be informed of results, with an explanation of grounds for interpretations and conclusions, and, where appropriate, the bases upon which ultimate recommendations have been made. Evaluators should provide requested information to explain decisions that may have effects viewed as adverse by the family members. However, one should avoid distributing unnecessary or irrelevant information that could compromise the security of the evaluative techniques used.

Evaluators are responsible for explaining tests and test results in language that clients can understand. Evaluation should be based on tests of proven scientific and professional usefulness. If a new technique of questionable validity and/or reliability is used, conclusions based on that technique should be given tentatively, but clearly. In other words, reservations about an instrument's range of validity should be included to temper any conclusion.

Test reports are the final outcome of any evaluator's work and, as such, should avoid unusual technical jargon and complicated ad hoc interpretations not related to data available in the report. When writing a report, one should consider whether it could stand cross-examination in a court of law and whether it can be read by the evaluated family. Assets as well as liabilities should be considered; emphasis on liabilities and the possible absence of assets should be explained. The report should not be so long or so technical that it could not be understood by the family as well as by other agencies and professionals involved with that family. An example of such a report can be found in Bagarozzi (1989).

Economy in Measurement

Green and Kolevzon (1983), in what is a very crucial and methodologically important work, evaluated 78 families by using a plethora of individual measures of emotional maturity, anxiety, self-esteem, and locus of control; dyadic measures of marital quality and parent-child relationships; and triadic measures of the families' hierarchical alignments. They found that the dyadic measures were much more powerful predictors of functionality-dysfunctionality than were individual or triadic measures.

> The perception of family health was most clearly a function of the family's dyadic characteristics. . . . Since moderate correlations were also observed between the individual and dyadic characteristics, it may be that individual characteristics of family members influence family health indirectly through their influence on the quality of these dyadic relationships. In turn, these dyadic relationships may directly influence the quality of family life. Thus, higher levels of individual functioning may promote higher levels of dyadic functioning which, in turn, promote more healthy patterns of family interaction. (p. 83)

If we interpret these results correctly, they imply that so-called systemic thinking, based on holistic, antireductionistic, and antiempirical biases (L'Abate & Colondier, 1987; Peterson & Cromwell, 1983), has no valid premise. A return to individual and dyadic characteristics (Fisher, 1982) may furnish the basis for linking family therapy to the rest of psychological knowledge rather than considering psychological knowledge irrelevant and in some cases trivial for family therapy (Keeney, 1983; Keeney & Cromwell, 1977).

Conclusion and Pessimistic Note

In spite of many exhortations about the need for a reunion and a joining of research and practice (Gurman, 1983; Wynne, 1983), we are very pessimistic that this marriage will ever take place. The first barrier is the therapist's tendency toward immediate action rather than delay. Delay is more likely to be the researcher's tendency. Clinicians and researchers also have different weltanschauungs. Most researchers may also be clinicians, but few clinicians are researchers. Their value systems are also different. Most therapists operate out of a context of discovery; most researchers operate out of a context of justification (L'Abate, 1986). The best evidence is the record of most mental health disciplines: psychiatry, clinical psychology, social work, counseling, and guidance—none has incorporated objective evaluation into its therapeutic practices and codes of ethics.

The worst offender has been clinical psychology, which came into being as the evaluator for psychiatry. But as it grew larger and more independent, it abandoned the evaluator role for the greater seductiveness (and income!) of psychotherapy. Although claiming to follow the scientific model, psychotherapy has, in practice, followed a practitioner's model, eventually abandoning even the pretense of evaluation. Evaluation, as practiced now, in a large-scale, institutionalized fashion, especially with school children, focuses strictly on the child, accepting unquestioningly the family's and the teachers' definition of the child as the source of the family's problems.

Ignoring evaluation has resulted in most mental health disciplines and movements becoming static in their ideologies and practices. The inadequacies of evaluation have doomed these movements to become passing fads, as has been true of psychoanalysis, systems thinking, behavior therapy, and humanism. Each of these movements began by promising a new, all-powerful, all-curing approach. After a peak at 5 to 10 years, each of them has, after just about a generation (15 years), abandoned its original claims and status, becoming just one of the many other approaches available.

Although this variety has allowed a great range of differentiation, the public may find the range confusing, even maddening. By the same token, family therapy is now riding a boom. However, its minimal standards of training (master's level), the antiempirical stance that usually results from limited training, and the ultimate rejection of evaluation from its practices are ominous. Family therapy may become just another of the many approaches available, no more and no less powerful or relevant than others.

As long as family therapy is controlled, influenced, and governed by systems thinking, objective or semiobjective evaluations are not likely to be standard operating procedure in clinical practice. In spite of the overwhelming growth of works dedicated to family evaluation and diagnosis in the past few years (Bailey & Simeonsson, 1988; Corcoran & Fischer, 1987; Fredman & Sherman, 1987; Grotevant & Carlson, 1989; Howells & Brown, 1986; Jacob, 1987; Jacob & Tennebaum, 1988; O'Leary, 1987), evaluation remains neglected by the majority of practitioners. Everybody wants to help; very few want to evaluate. Systems thinking, with its clearly antiempirical bias (Keeney, 1983), is probably one of the main stumbling blocks to objective evaluation, even though one must admit that objective evaluation in general has always been shunned by most systems theorists and therapists (Falzer, 1986; L'Abate & Colondier, 1987; L'Abate & Jurkovic, 1987; Lilienfeld, 1988; Shields, 1986).

Evaluation will become standard operating procedure only when consumers and third party providers require it. L'Abate (1990) maintains that when one uses the criteria of objective fruitfulness and the generativity of programs in primary and secondary preventions, the humanistic and behavioral programs remain in front while psychoanalysis and systems thinking fade. The problem then becomes one of integrating humanistic and behavioral theories into a new theoretical framework that is consistent with psychology as a science and as a profession. Such an integration is based, in part, on Foa and Foa's (1974) resource exchange theory, which allows theories and primary, secondary, and tertiary prevention approaches (L'Abate, 1993a; L'Abate & Hewitt, 1988) to be put into one integrative framework.

REFERENCES

Bagarozzi, D. A. (1989). Family diagnostic testing: A neglected area of expertise for the family psychologist. *American Journal of Family Therapy, 17,* 257–272.

Bagarozzi, D. A., & Anderson, S. A. (1989). *Personal, marital and family myths: Theoretical formulations and clinical strategies.* New York: Norton.

Bailey, D. B., Jr., & Simeonsson, R. J. (1988). *Family assessment in early intervention.* Columbus, OH: Merrill.

Corcoran, K., & Fisher, J. (1987). *Measures for clinical practice: A sourcebook.* New York: Macmillan.

Draper, T. W., & Marcos, A. C. (Eds.). (1990). *Family variables: Conceptualization, measurement, and use.* Newbury Park, CA: Sage.

Falzer, P. R. (1986). The cybernetic metaphor: A critical examination of ecosystemic epistemology as a foundation of family therapy. *Family Process, 25,* 353–363.

Fisher, L. (1982). Transactional theories but individual assessment: A frequent discrepancy in family research. *Family Process, 21,* 313–320.

Foa, U. G., & Foa, E. B. (1974). *Societal structures of the mind.* Springfield, IL: Thomas.

Fredman, N., & Sherman, R. (1987). *Handbook of measurements for marriage and family therapy.* New York: Brunner/Mazel.

Green, R. G., & Kolevzon, M. F. (1983). The correlates of healthy family functioning: The role of consensus and conflict in the practice of family therapy. *Journal of Marital and Family Therapy, 12,* 75–84.

Grotevant, H. D., & Carlson, C. I. (1989). *Family assessment: A guide to methods and measures.* New York: Guilford.

Grunebaum, H. (1988). The relationship of family theory to family therapy. *Journal of Marital and Family Therapy, 14,* 1–14.

Gurman, A. S. (1983). Family therapy research and the new "epistemology." *Journal of Marital and Family Therapy, 9,* 227–234.

Howells, J. G., & Brown, H. W. M. (1986). *Family diagnosis.* Madison, CT: International Universities Press.

Hurt, S. W., Reznikoff, M., & Clarkin, J. F. (1991). *Psychological assessment, psychiatric diagnosis, & treatment planning.* New York: Brunner/Mazel.

Jacob, T. (Ed.). (1987). *Family interaction and psychopathology: Theories, methods, and findings.* New York: Plenum.

Jacob, T., & Tennebaum, D. L. (1988). *Family assessment: Rationale, methods, and future directions.* New York: Plenum.

Karpel, M. A., & Strauss, E. S. (1983). *Family evaluation.* New York: Gardner.

Keeney, B. P. (Ed.). (1983). *Diagnosis and assessment in family therapy.* Rockville, MD: Aspen.

Keeney, B. P., & Cromwell, R. E. (1977). Toward systematic diagnosis. *Family Therapy, 4,* 226–236.

Kerr, M. E., & Bowen, M. (1988). *Family evaluation: An approach based on Bowen theory.* New York: Norton.

Kiesler, D. J. (1966). Some myths of psychotherapy research and the search for a paradigm. *Psychological Bulletin, 65,* 110–136.

L'Abate, L. (1986). *Systematic family therapy.* New York: Brunner/Mazel.

L'Abate, L. (1990). *Building family competence: Primary and secondary prevention strategies.* Newbury Park, CA: Sage.

L'Abate, L., (1992). *Programmed writing: A self-administered approach for interventions with individuals, couples, and families.* Pacific Grove CA: Brooks/Cole.

L'Abate, L. (1993a). *A theory of personality development.* (Submitted for publication).

L'Abate, L. (1993b). *Family evaluation: A psychological interpretation.* Newbury Park, CA: Sage.

L'Abate, L., and Colondier, G. (1987). The emperor has no clothes! Long live the emperor! A critique of family systems thinking and a reductionistic proposal. *American Journal of Family Therapy, 15,* 19–33. (Reprinted in L. L'Abate [Ed.] [1987], *Family psychology II: Theory, therapy, enrichment, and training* [pp. 3–17]. Lanham, MD: University Press of America.)

L'Abate, L., & Hewitt, D. (1988). Toward a classification of sex and sexual behavior. *Journal of Sex and Marital Therapy, 14,* 29–39.

L'Abate, L., & Jurkovic, G. (1987). Family systems theory as a cult: Boom or bankruptcy? In L. L'Abate (Ed.), *Family Psychology II: Theory, therapy, enrichment, and training* (pp. 19–27). Washington, DC: University Press of America.

Lilienfeld, R. (1988). *The rise of systems theory: An ideological analysis.* Malabar, FL: Krieger.

O'Leary, K. D. (1987). *Assessment of marital discord: An integration for research and clinical practice.* Hillsdale, NJ: LEA.

Perry, S., Frances, A., & Clarkin, J. (1985). *A DSM-III casebook of differential therapeutics: A clinical guide to treatment selection.* New York: Brunner/Mazel.

Peterson, G. W., & Cromwell, R. E. (1983). A clarification of multisystem-multimethod assessment: Reductionism versus wholism. *Family Process, 22,* 173–177.

Seligman, L. (1990). *Selecting effective treatment.* San Francisco, CA: Jossey-Bass.

Shields, C. G. (1986). Critiquing the new epistemologies: Toward minimum requirements for a scientific theory of family therapy. *Journal of Marital and Family Therapy, 12,* 359–372.

Touliatos, J., Perlmutter, B. F., & Strauss, M. A. (Eds.). (1990). *Handbook of family measurement techniques.* Newbury Park, CA: Sage.

Wynne, L. C. (1983). Family research and family therapy: A reunion. *Journal of Marital and Family Therapy, 9,* 113–117.

Wynne, L. C. (Ed.). (1988). *The state of the art in family therapy research: Controversies and recommendations.* New York: Family Process Press.

NAME INDEX

SUBJECT INDEX